Printed in Utopia

The Renaissance's Radicalism

Printed in Utopia

The Renaissance's Radicalism

Ed Simon

Winchester, UK
Washington, USA

JOHN HUNT PUBLISHING

First published by Zero Books, 2020
Zero Books is an imprint of John Hunt Publishing Ltd., No. 3 East St., Alresford,
Hampshire SO24 9EE, UK
office@jhpbooks.com
www.johnhuntpublishing.com
www.zero-books.net

For distributor details and how to order please visit the 'Ordering' section on our website.

ISBN: 978 1 78904 383 9
978 1 78904 384 6 (ebook)
Library of Congress Control Number: 2019943767

A CIP catalogue record for this book is available from the British Library.

Design: Stuart Davies

UK: Printed and bound by CPI Group (UK) Ltd, Croydon, CR0 4YY
US: Printed and bound by Thomson-Shore, 7300 West Joy Road, Dexter, MI 48130

We operate a distinctive and ethical publishing philosophy in
all areas of our business, from our global network of authors to
production and worldwide distribution.

Contents

Preface

Though the essays in this volume are often substantially altered from their original appearance, several of these pieces did see place of first publication at a variety of different sites. "Martin Luther on the Toilet," "Here I Stand; I Can Do No Other," and "Of Canons and Marginal Poets" all appeared in *Queen Mob's Teahouse,* and "Et in America Ego" appeared in *Berfrois,* where I am an editor. Both sites are edited by the incomparable Russell Bennetts, who has created two of the best British cultural sites today, which posterity will one day remember as an important literary movement.

Thanks to Nadja Spiegleman and Dan Piepenbring at *The Paris Review* for place of first publication for "A Rude Railing Rhymer" and "One Devil Too Many Amongst Them." Thank you to Kathryn Brownell of *The Washington Post,* which ran a much shorter version of "Last of the Insurgents." Thank you to Jeremy Lybarger of *Poetry* for his editorial work on "Among Tyrants." "A Time to Mourn, and a Time to Dance: The Last Carnival" first appeared in *Religion Dispatches,* thanks to Evan Derkacz for his work on that piece. "A New Reformation" was part of *Commonweal's* coverage of the five-hundredth anniversary of that event, thanks to Matthew Sitman for that opportunity. Thanks to Adam Green of *The Public Domain Review* for running "Robert Greene, first of the Bohemians."

"But a Walking Shadow, or: The Metaphysics of Shakespeare" was published in *LitHub* as part of their observance of the four-hundredth anniversary of Shakespeare's death, thanks to Emily Firetog. Both "The Unfortunate Invention of White People" and "Cycle and Epicycle, Orb in Orb" first appeared in *Aeon,* thanks to Sam Dresser. Both "The Dark Lady Inscribed in the Book of Life" and "*Monarch of Letters:* 'Rabbi' John Selden and the Restoration of the Jews" were first published in *Tablet,* thanks to

Matthew Fishbane. "Preachers from the Palace of Wisdom, or: Ranterism in the UK" was first published in *The Revealer*, thanks to Kali Handelman, and "Praying for the Awful Grace of God" was published by *McSweeney's*, thanks to Daniel Levin Becker. A version of "The Thinking Reed Tries God's Luck" was published in *Nautilus* by Brian Gallagher. "Fuckadillia's Man at Court" first appeared in *JSTOR Daily*, thanks to Benjamin Winterhalter. Both "The Science Fiction Before Science" and "John Milton, One of the Roughs, An American" were published in *The Atlantic*, thanks to Lenika Cruz.

Several of these pieces were first published at *The Millions*, where I'm a staff writer. These include "The Other Folio," "East of El Dorado," and "God in the Trash Fire: The Inflammable Thomas Traherne." I have such gratitude to the opportunities that the editors I've worked with there, Lydia Kiesling and Adam Bortez, have given me. I must also mention *The Millions'* founder C. Max Magee, who was instrumental in making *The Millions* one of the best American literary sites of the new millennium. Being able to contribute to that mission has been an incredible honor.

Finally, I must acknowledge the unwavering support and love of my family over the course of writing these essays, including my late father Matt, my mother Janet, my brother Jacob, and particularly my wife Meg.

Prologue: Writing the Renaissance Imaginary

As you read through the chapters in this book, you may notice that there's a particular narrative conceit that I'm fond of. A tendency to begin each piece with a representative historical anecdote, normally presented *in media res,* with possibly some sensory detail borrowed from the tool-kit of the fiction writer, which is then used to demonstrate some theoretical argument that I'm making about the time period. Some people like this method, others resolutely do not; such as the brave, anonymous gentleman of the internet who complained that when I described a seventeenth-century Oxford library in the autumn as being "cold," that I couldn't have possibly known this (I still maintain that it was a decent guess).

For some, this particular rhetorical trope by which I begin many of my essays may seem fundamentally suspect, so ingrained is that division between history and fiction, logic and poetry, which goes back to the ancient Greeks. Yet for me personally, such a stylistic gambit derives from my own particular philosophy of composition. I feel rather strongly about it, and in explaining my reasons, in giving a bit of an *ars poetica* for the genre defined by *starting-a-piece-with-a-pithy-story-that-may-or-may-not-ultimately-have-much-to-do-with-the-essay's-subject*, I think that something can be said about not just how I write about the Renaissance, but how we've collectively imagined the Renaissance.

Too often we divide style from subject, but I empathically declare that rhetoric is content. Rhetoric is ideology, too. There is no easy linguistic separation between how we tell a story, and what the argument of that story is; no simple division between narrative and theme. In proffering a defense for my writerly philosophy, the most honest *mea culpa* is simply that I write the way that I do because I enjoy the way that I write. Maybe it sounds self-indulgent – perhaps we all train to be that master of authorial asceticism who slashes at their darlings with the deleter's scythe, who with the plucky enthusiasm of a marketing major writes for the broadest possible audience, and I'd be lying if I said that I too didn't aspire for readership. Ultimately, however, I've always taken my prime audience to be myself, and should that sound egotistical, I don't care. I enjoy the process, and I suspect any writer who says that they don't. If you didn't, why do it? There are plenty of other talented writers.

Why I enjoy that particular narrative trope could perhaps be explained by the reality that I'm not a historical scholar, but at heart still an English major. This is not an incidental autobiographical fact; it's instrumental to understanding my justification for this style. Like most people drawn to the study of literature, whether they care to admit it in the post-Theory world or not, what attracted me to the discipline was nothing so complicated as *stories*. If all of reality is composed by the atoms of language, then narrative is the very medium in which meaning operates. As such, while I'd not embrace any particularly subjective epistemology, nor does my metaphysics veer towards the relativistic, I do think that plot and story suffuse everything, that even the driest of accounts evidences narrative sources, and thus that ultimately literary criticism is the Queen of the Humanities. "Objective history" may be a discipline written in archives, composed of demographic and census data, but what I'm doing is (clearly) something different.

My ownership over the Renaissance, if one can have such a thing, comes from the discipline of literary study. When studying the distant past a literary scholar must rely on the work done by historians, it's unavoidable. Gratitude must be offered to those who spend that time more soberly writing so that people like me can drunkenly conjecture. At the risk of sounding pat or cliched, what I'm trying to do is tell a story. All of the historical information in the book is derived from scholars more qualified than I am to say what happened when to whom. Nor are any of the events, texts, or figures discussed within *Printed in Utopia* novel, they're all filched by me – not from the specialized archive, but rather from the regular old library. That's not to say that I haven't done archival research – I have. It's reflected in scholarly work and peer-reviewed writing which I have done, and such experiences were central to what I aimed to do in this volume. But what I'm doing in this volume is something different.

If anything is novel it's precisely in how I've chosen to tell this particular story of what the Renaissance should mean. It's a theoretical work, an analytical work, a critical work. Which is to say that at its core, I've intended it to be a *creative work*. Insomuch as history is empirical, that old dichotomy between it and poetry has some merit. History is arguably closer to science in that manner, but what I've hoped to do is rearrange the raw materials of the sixteenth and seventeenth centuries to interpret what those twenty decades could possibly mean to us a half millennium later. What's new isn't the notes, but the scoring; not the materials, but the pattern that I've put them in. That, I would venture, is always the job of the theorist and the critic, and as theory and criticism are what I'm trained in, I feel no need to be bashful about that fact.

While some literary critics, of the dry, arid, quasi-scientific schools, have been queasy about that reality, the tradition in which I was trained was steadfastly not. Propriety of course compels me to admit that my favorite narrative conceit – the introduction of an arresting detail written in imitation of the novel and then following through on the more technical matters – is written throughout literary scholarship. It's particularly identified with a group of scholars who gained preeminence in the 1980s who are known as the New Historicists. Associated with critics whose names you will see referenced throughout the book, this movement includes figures like Stephen Greenblatt, Roland Greene, Jeffrey Knapp, James Shapiro, and Stephen

Orgel, and arguably emerged in reaction to the staid formalism of the Yale New Critics, while being incubated in the temperate climes of Berkeley, California.

That all of these scholars are early modernists is important, for they write history as those in the Renaissance also did – not as technical brief, but as story. In terms of their theoretical orientation, the New Historicists regarded literature as embedded in the material conditions of history, and saw literature as historical evidence to be analyzed, but while also arguing that the cultural context of a text's creation is central to the proper interpretation of that text. Trained either by New Historicists, or by people who were trained by them (or went to school with them), their mark can't help but be seen in my approach.

More importantly than just their ideological orientation, for my purposes, was their way of writing the Renaissance. For a critic like Greenblatt, who even though he often (though necessarily) engages complicated technical terminology, history is first and foremost presented as a story that can be told. A mistake to think that this is because of anything as mundane as "popularization" (though in Greenblatt's case he's found that to be pretty lucrative), but rather because the New Historicists, whether literally stated or not, understand history to be a literary text like any other that is open to interpretation at the hands of the adept critic, and so their scholarship reflects that same literary flair. The reading public today knows Greenblatt for his bestsellers like *Will in the World* or the (from my position, historically compromised) *The Swerve,* but read his earlier books like *Renaissance Self-Fashioning* as well. It holds with the best of Greenblatt's writing, a theoretical work which poses complex scholarly questions, but which also presents a drama about people where the stakes are high. My point is that *the man can turn a phrase.*

If the New Historicists inherited that approach, they arguably got it from European theorists and cultural materialists, from the

Birmingham School for Social Research of Raymond Williams and Stuart Hall, and particularly from the post-structuralist historiography of Michel Foucault. Those European antecedents tended to reflect a Marxist political gloss that their American counterparts have, in true American fashion, eliminated in favor of a more general discussion of race, class, and gender. Even Foucault, for all of his reputation of disparaging "meta-narratives," has more of a Marxian pose than do his American students. Nevertheless, what the Americans didn't take in politics, they did in rhetoric. Drawing from the example of Foucault, the New Historicists embraced "Theory" that is engaging to read. So complete has the denigration of Foucault been at the hands of conservative critics who've never read him, so total is his reputation for writing turgid, obfuscating, complex prose, that many first-time students who encounter him in *Discipline and Punish* or *History of Madness* uncover a delightful fact – *that man could really turn a phrase.*

Consider Foucault in *Discipline and Punish,* and tell me that this man couldn't write:

The condemned man found himself transformed into a hero by the sheer extend of his widely advertised crimes, and sometimes the affirmation of his belated repentance. Against the law, against the rich, the powerful, the magistrates, the constabulary or the watch, against taxes and their collectors, he appeared to have waged a struggle with which one all too easily identified. The proclamation of these crimes blew up to epic proportions the tiny struggle that passed unperceived in everyday life. If the condemned man was shown to be repentant, accepting the verdict, asking both God and man for forgiveness for his crimes, it was as if he had come through some process of purification: he died, in his own way, like a saint.

I would put the writing of Michel Foucault up against any of the English or American novelists of the 1960s and '70s. That passage reads like Dickens or Austen to me. Foucault has a sense of narrative, a sense of phrasing. And none of that is incidental to what he's doing, it's not simply to make his writing more enjoyable to read, for it does do that, but often enough Foucault is complicated when he needs to be so that it's clear "popularization" is not simply his goal. Again, rhetoric is content. In making history into a narrative, there is an implicit argument about the ways in which we interpret and reinterpret the past, the ways in which we create time periods out of the raw materials of dates, facts, and events. Alongside "micro-historians" like Carlo Ginzburg and Robert Darnton, a historian like Foucault was instrumental in writing history as poetry.

Foucault arguably got his own narrative affectations from early schools of French historiography, particularly the Annales School of historians like Lucien Febvre and Marc Bloch. As with Foucault, and the later New Historicists, these were scholars who crafted history as story. That both Febvre and Bloch tended to be resistant to Marxist interpretation, at least the most vulgar materialist permutations thereof, speaks to how the question of rhetoric can in some cases be divorced from ideological concerns. But in a more subtle, more ghostly way, I think that their essays evidence a certain continuity, a certain understanding of how our interpretive glosses must always begin and end in narrative, understanding that history and literature can't be understood as if they were physics. If we wish to trace such an approach to the essay back to its origin, we could move from the Annales School to the very genesis of the genre's form, the great Renaissance essayist Michel de Montaigne.

For the sixteenth-century writer, the essay was a brief prose experiment into some sort of realm of experience. Like the New Historicists, Montaigne would mingle together disparate references, events, and evidence, mixing classical aphorism, scriptural quotation, accounts of cannibals, and observations of his own cat, to produce works that could begin in the simple, arresting narrative detail, but then move outward to consideration of everything from Christian charity to colonialism. Such an approach was the prose equivalent of *Wunderkammers*, the "Wonder Cabinets," then proliferating in the collections of moneyed gentlemen, shelves filled with an assortment of artfully arranged shells and feathers, fossils and artifacts, with their very organization posing some kind of implied argument for each individual display. As the master himself wrote, the affairs of humans are "marvelously vain, diverse, and undulating...It is hard to found any constant and uniform judgement." And so, in arrangement and rearrangement of the objects on our shelves, we pose new interpretations, new analyses, new readings, new regenerations. New creations.

That may speak to why I chose to write the way that I did, why I enjoy it, and why I think it's important, but what exactly are the interpretations that I'm proffering? How am I imagining the Renaissance? Such requires a few brief words, for my positions on the study of that time period both reflect much of the mainstream of academic scholarship for the past two generations, but which I think perhaps tie all of my pieces together into a comprehensive whole that is slightly different as well. Strange to think of it, though it's also true for all other defined epochs, but the Renaissance hasn't always been with us. Obvious of course that there wasn't a Renaissance before the time period itself, but I'm speaking to an issue of later, scholarly imagination. While the humanists of the sixteenth century (and certainly earlier in Italy) spoke of themselves as brokering something new in the intellectual world, of perhaps rupturing their connection to a medieval past, the word "Renaissance" as a scholarly designation didn't emerge until well into the nineteenth century, and there were reasons for and implications to that.

Two scholars were primarily responsible for the model of the Renaissance which is still taught, that the age heralded a rebirth of lost classical knowledge and moved Europe away from the barbarism of the Middle Ages. Those scholars were the Swiss historian Jacob Burckhardt and his French contemporary Jules Michelet. Teacher of Fredrich Nietzsche, Burckhardt's 1860 *The Civilization of the Renaissance in Italy* may no longer be current as a work of scholarship, but its influence on the way we speak of those centuries has endured. Burckhardt was as responsible for inventing the Renaissance as Petrarch was. This was a depiction of that era as being one where "both sides of human consciousness – the side turned to the world that turned inward – lay, as it were, beneath a common veil, dreaming or half awake." Burckhardt continues by claiming that:

The veil was woven of faith, childlike prejudices, and illusion; seen through it, world and history appeared in strange hues; man recognized himself only as a member of a race, a nation, a party, a corporation, a family, or in some other general category. It was in Italy that this veil first melted into thin air, and awakened an objective perception and treatment of the state and all things of this world in general; but by its side, and with full power, there also arose the subjective; man becomes a self-aware individual and recognizes himself as such.

Burckhardt's prose remains arresting, even as his conceptual framework is suspect. Today, only someone like Harold Bloom would argue that the Renaissance actually invented what it means to be human. Not for nothing, in graduate school we were still expected to read all of *The Civilization of the Renaissance in Italy,* for though Burckhardt's claim that the Renaissance was a grand rupture from a dark and dismal past into a more enlightened future seems hopelessly chauvinist and patrician to us, it's still the view which dominates popular conceptions. And of course, *Burckhardt knew how to turn a phrase as well.*

Michelet was arguably even more responsible for the invention of the Renaissance than Burckhardt, as he was the first to popularize the term with all of its connotations of rebirth and intellectual rejuvenation. Burckhardt was a staunch republican, and in the Renaissance city-states of Italy he saw political justification for his own politics. Similarly, Michelet was a steadfast Huguenot, who disdained the Catholic Middle Ages as backwards and superstitious, and so in the Renaissance he saw a decisive and beneficial break with that dark past. His *History of France* promulgates an understanding of the period which sees it as throwing off the shackles of primitive archaism, of medieval tyranny, and of marching forward to a grander, more beautiful future.

Michelet's perspective has perhaps fared worse than Burckhardt's, though it too still reigns triumphant whenever a pundit uses the word "medieval" as a slur. His reductionisms tend to flatten the distinction between the medieval period and the Renaissance, a difference which people living at the time wouldn't have seen. He gives no credit to the Middle Ages, a period which saw the technical proficiency of being able to construct architectural marvels such as the great gothic cathedrals, which produced equivalent works of literature and philosophy, and which arguably had more just and equitable social arrangements than the exploitive nascent capitalism of the Renaissance. Historians and philosophers of science like Pierre Duhem, George Sarton, and James Franklin have argued for a "continuity thesis," claiming that there was no major rupture between the medieval and the Renaissance, and in their most radical permutations that the later period didn't even really exist.

Such work is arguably instrumental in the transition to speaking of the sixteenth and seventeenth centuries not as the

"Renaissance," but as the "Early Modern Period." Much to recommend in this recategorization; "Renaissance" is a loaded word, for all of the reasons listed above; there can be something simplistic in grouping disparate movements and groups together under one humanistic banner, and "Early Modern" makes more sense in grouping the Renaissance together with the other great movement of the era, the Reformation. No doubt Michelet may have seen the Reformation and the Renaissance as inseparable, and some strains of both certainly were, but an equivalent argument could be made that Luther and Calvin signified a sort of "Counter-Renaissance," the better to avoid theoretical debate when we're describing what time period we study by simply calling it the early modern.

Yet this book is entitled *Printed in Utopia: The Renaissance's Radicalism*. I didn't just pick the more popular word out of some cagey and misguided hope at having a larger general audience; I picked it because I think that the idea of the Renaissance still has some oomph. No doubt there are plenty of books on the time period written with a mind towards "popularization," and while I think that as a strategy such an approach has some pedagogical justifications for it, I also wanted to avoid the cheapness of writing about the people of the Renaissance as if they were just like you, except with more dirt on them. If that's what you go in for there are thousands of books written under the imprimatur of the Shakespeare Industrial Complex. Sometimes, it's true, I'll connect subjects to later cultural phenomenon, but such genealogies are never done in bad faith, and I try to the best of my ability to avoid committing that presentist fallacy which reads all of the past as mere prologue to the present.

Rather, I use the word "Renaissance" because I think there is a radicalism in the idea. Perhaps not in how it happened, perhaps not in how it's remembered, but a latent subversiveness that goes back to the humanists themselves. I can affirm the continuity thesis while also acknowledging that by the sixteenth century something clearly different was happening. Calling the period the "early modern" actually does more to affirm that reality, for the sixteenth and seventeenth centuries strike me as unassailably the cradle of modernity. Intellectually, the Christendom of the Middle Ages remains more of a foreign country than the sectarianism of the Renaissance. For better, and often for worse, we are children of that time period. Capitalism, colonialism, positivism, puritanism, and globalization can all be traced back to the Renaissance. And far from being an enthused cheerleader for all developments from that era (while still hypocritically enjoying all of the fruits of the scientific revolution), I would argue that much which has fractured, broken, and disenchanted our world emerged then as well. New means of exploitation were developed then; the body count became much higher.

Yet one of the motivating beliefs of my writing is that if the Renaissance saw the emergence of modernity in all of its malignancy, it also provided some of the most potent, beautiful, sublime, and sacred means of resisting that very same malignancy, for the Renaissance was large – it contained multitudes. The Renaissance saw the exploitation of the New World, but it also developed the vocabulary of utopianism, liberated from the myths of Eden. The Reformation saw the disenchantments of Luther, but it allowed for the antinomian mysticism of radical religious non-conformists. The Renaissance heralded globalization, but it also increased the multitude of individual subjectivities, the possibility of empathy across radically different cultures. If the Renaissance didn't invent the individual, we can be forgiven for thinking that it did.

My approach then shares much with the past two generations of scholars who rightly wished to return contemporary marginalized voices to the center of what we talk about when we talk about the Renaissance. Such is evidenced in essays about figures who you've probably never heard of, like the poets John Taylor and Richard Barnfield. *Printed in Utopia* isn't meant to be an exploration of merely the eccentric and marginal, but hopefully a rearrangement of the illuminating as well, a desire for new focus. You'll find Shakespeare and John Milton engaged with repeatedly in these pages as well, and you scarcely get older, whiter, and deader than those two (though based on the Chandos portrait I've got some questions about how white Shakespeare was, but that's for a different book).

There is a bevy of scholarly writing that this book is built upon. As ambivalent as my own attitude is to academic writing, I'd be remiss not to acknowledge how much of this project has to be constructed upon the laborious work of other scholars, for whom I owe my gratitude. This isn't a scholarly book, at least not in the traditional sense. That doesn't mean that it's always an easy book. I've tried to write in a manner that's engaging to an educated general audience; where at most you might be expected to look up that with which you're not familiar. I've wanted to avoid the generalities of popularization, however; not just to introduce readers to that which they're unfamiliar with (as admirable a goal as that is), but to pose an argument about what the Renaissance means, about why it is an important concept.

Rather than merely mining the archive for ephemera, my desire is to produce a *Wunderkammer* from texts both obscure and canonical, as well as figures both forgotten and enshrined, so as to make an argument about how the Renaissance has an emancipatory potential that can free us from the worst legacies of modernity. If it's true that the interpretive humanities are always a creative act, then I wish to write in a mode that I call the "Renaissance Imaginary." This is an understanding of the period which sees it not simply as rupture from the past, or as continuation from the medieval era, but which understands it as something new in its own right, albeit mysterious. Furthermore, the Renaissance Imaginary is a mode which revels in the very contradictions and paradoxes of that era, which celebrates those creative tensions as being the ground for utopian possibility. Because ultimately, my claim is that whether the Renaissance actually happened or not, it remains a pretty good idea.

Introduction: Pilgrim in Münster

On January 5, 1535 a baker named Jan Matthys from Haarlem in the Low Countries declared that the Westphalian city of Münster was the New Jerusalem. Matthys' was the very banner of heaven, and in declaring this earthly city to be a reflection of that eternal, perfect order he was joined with a number of revolutionary compatriots, a vanguard composed of the rising members of the mercantile bourgeoisie who wished to fashion a divine New Order here in Münster. One contemporary observer writes about how the city became a symbol of radicalism, so that the "Dutch and the Frisians and scoundrels from all parts, who had never settled anywhere: they flocked to Münster and collected there." In that city, the radical Anabaptists, a broad Protestant sect that understood the Reformation to have so far been anemic and milquetoast, were to establish a divine society on earth, where all property would be owned in common for the service of God – a sort of communist theocracy.

For the Anabaptists, Münster represented an Apocalyptic second-chance, the possibility of rectifying the failures of the German Peasant's War of a decade earlier. Led in part by the charismatic theologian Thomas Müntzer (whose very name reminds us of that later New Jerusalem), Anabaptists across the Holy Roman Empire fought a crusade against land-owners and noblemen so as to institute an order whose central law would be "Omnia sunt communia." With echoes of a later German thinker, Müntzer's formulation is best translated as being that "all things are to be held in common and distribution should be each according to his need." In a sermon about the prophetic book of Daniel, Müntzer declared in a pique of castigation that was both millennial and anarchic, that the "priests and all the evil clerics are the snakes...and the secular lords and rulers are the eels."

The German Peasant's War of 1524-1525 was immediately influenced by the example of Martin Luther's *Ninety-five Theses*, but the ostensible father of Protestantism was always, at heart, a conservative. He dismissed Müntzer as a "rebellious spirit" and a "bloodthirsty Satan." For his part, Müntzer called Luther "Brother Fatted Pig." Historians have debated how much of Luther's condemnation of the rebellion led to its eventual defeat. No doubt the former Augustinian priest was by that point a man of tremendous power with mighty friends, his rhetoric having torn Christendom asunder in less than a decade. Leaders of the Peasant's Rebellion made their appeals to Luther, whose support could have theoretically bolstered their cause, but the man who enshrined a priesthood of all believers couldn't countenance the idea of *masterless* men. As Frederick Engels writes in his 1850 *The Peasant War in Germany,* Luther had "dropped the popular elements of the movement, and joined the train of the middle-class, the nobility and the princes." Such developments indicated fault lines in the Reformation itself, as medieval millenarianism mutated into new and potentially dangerous forms, creeds which Luther had helped to instigate, but which he now denounced.

Luther's feelings were made clear in his pamphlet *Against the Murderous, Thieving Hordes of Peasants,* wherein he wrote that the rebels were the "worst blasphemers of God and slanderers of his holy name," the former monk whose patron was Frederick III, Elector of Saxony, argued that to kill a rebelling peasant was a blessed act. Contemporary artist and Lutheran propagandist Albrecht Dürer designed an unbuilt triumphal column in commemoration of the war. A surreal obelisk featuring a representation of milk jugs, butter kegs, and "hoes, pitchforks, flails" all piled one on top of each other, which as Dürer described is ultimately capped with an "afflicted peasant with a sword stuck into his back." Scholars have debated the ambiguity of that image since the sixteenth century. Dürer's monument was never built; Müntzer waited five centuries to appear on an East

German bank note. By the end of the war, over 100,000 people were dead. One of them was Müntzer, who before his execution was tortured and forced to recant his heresies.

A decade later Münster became a means of resurrecting Müntzer. The intellectual genealogy of the Anabaptists, initially defined by their commitment to adult baptism, runs back towards figures like Müntzer, and forward to utopian groups that emerged after the tragedy of Münster, like the Amish and the Mennonites, with arguably the English-speaking Baptists also drawing inspiration from the continental movement. In Münster, more than just adult baptism was at issue, but a radical reorganization of society that harkened back to the Apostles, and forward to the Jacobins and the Bolsheviks. As one of the revolutionaries, Jan Bockelson, would put it, "all things were to be in common, there was to be no private property and nobody was to do any more work, but simply trust in God."

Led in part by a Lutheran minister Bernhard Rothmann, who would come to embrace the Anabaptists, men who'd previously been tailors and bakers suddenly declared that all private property was as theft, and instituted the most radical economic and social experiment of the Renaissance. Historian Norman Cohn in his classic study of medieval and Renaissance apocalyptic radicalism *The Pursuit of Millennium* writes that in Münster "The abolition of private ownership of money, the restriction of private ownership of food and shelter were seen as first steps towards a state in which…everything would belong to everybody and the distinction between Mine and Thine would disappear." From early in 1534, until the summer of 1535, a combined force of both Catholic and Lutheran soldiers besieged the walls of Münster to arrest, try, and execute the commune's leaders. Matthys didn't make it that long, it was Easter of 1534 when he approached the encampment of Franz von Waldeck, Münster's expelled bishop who was then embroiled in the struggle to retake the city. In an exhibition of Christian charity, von Waldeck had Matthys decapitated, his head put on a pole that was visible over the city walls, and his severed penis nailed to the gate of Münster. Matthys' comrades would last a few months longer, but would come to similarly gruesome ends. Bockelson, who was a 25-year-old baker, would declare himself to be "John of Leiden," the messianic "King" of Münster, this New Zion, and he would reign in an increasingly brutal fashion, instituting polygamy and unleashing a violent campaign of iconoclasm in Münster's churches and cathedrals. After the city was taken, he was executed in the central marketplace alongside the radical mayor Bernhard Knipperdolling and another leader named Bernhard Kreching. Their corpses were placed in ugly, wrought-iron cages and hung from the steeples of St. Lambert's Church. For five decades they were allowed to hang there, decomposing and stripped clean as carrion by the hungry fowl of Münster. The cages themselves, though empty now, still hang from that gothic steeple.

The narrative of Münster was one of trauma which reverberated through a radical Europe that was undergoing violent convulsions of change. For both Catholic and Magisterial Protestants (such as the Lutherans, the Calvinists, and the nascent Church of England) there was a warning about what happens when Reformation goes too far. Matthys, Bockelson, and Knipperdolling were condemned for their theology certainly, but for their ideology as well. As with the Peasants Rebellion, the theocrats of Münster were seen as instituting an unbiblical order in violation of Paul's injunction from Ephesians 6:5: "Servants, be obedient to them that are your masters according to the flesh, with fear and trembling, in singleness of your heart." Cohn, no political radical himself, draws a direct line between the millenarianism of groups such as the Anabaptists of Münster and the utopian promises of contemporary Marxism (and fascism for that matter).

For contemporaries and those living in the immediate

aftermath of the siege of Münster, the moral was as clear as those wrought-iron cages hanging from St. Lambert's. The Reformation had no shortage of horrors, from the martyrdoms recorded in John Foxe's 1563 *Acts and Monuments* to the 1572 St. Bartholomew's Day Massacre. Münster terrified Protestants and Catholics alike in an even more primal way, an illustration of where the logical conclusion of the Reformation should ultimately end. Such was the exploitive gloss of the "wonderful spectacle of bloodshed" as enumerated by writer Thomas Nash in his brilliant 1594 picaresque and forerunner to the modern novel *The Unfortunate Traveler; or, the Life of Jack Wilton*. Nash's titular character traverses a Europe that is being immolated in religious fervor, and in his perambulations, he is witness to the siege in that doomed city, where in "their Anabaptistical error they might all be new christened in their own blood."

Adhering to a fundamentally traditionalist view of hierarchy, Nash mockingly presents the Anabaptists as a pathetic rabble, Bockelson depicted as wearing "a cross on his breast like a thread bottom, a round twilted tailor's cushion buckled like a tankard-bearer's device on his shoulders for a target, the pike whereof was a pack-needle...and on his head, for a helmet, a huge high shoe with the bottom turned upwards." Their punishment is as just as their appearance is threadbare, with Nash, that defender of the High Church, writing "How John Leyden died, is that it? He died like dog; he was hanged & the halter paid for. For his companions, do they trouble you? I can tell you they troubled some men before, for they were all killed, & none escaped." The Anabaptists of Münster were slaughtered, the survivors embraced a pacifism evident in their pacific descendants of the Mennonites and Amish. A potent warning to the radicals in Nash's own England, for "Hear what it is to be Anabaptists, to be Puritans, to be villains; you may be counted illuminate botchers for a while, but your end will be, *Good people, pray for us*."

How you read Münster depends in large part on what your

politics are. In the aftermath of Münster, the pacifist Amish and Mennonites developed in reaction to the violent overthrow of Münster, and currents of Anabaptist thought similarly influenced both Baptists and the Society of Friends in England. More obscure groups, like the sixteenth-century mystical-minded Familia Caritas, rejected Münster's anti-intellectualism but embraced its otherworldly concerns. For all of those groups there was a potent message born from the blood and fire of Münster; that to reform society by the dictates of God will only ever end in corruption, that violence is no strategy and that only in quarantine from the fallen and corrupt world could any divine order be instituted. And so, the utopia of reformed civil society would be replaced with the circumscribed "intentional communities" of the eighteenth, nineteenth, and twentieth centuries.

Similarly, for secular readers, such as conservatives like Nash, or a half millennium later Cohn, the lesson is clear – *to rewrite the world is to court horror*. For left-wing historians, with a fair bit of revision that often deletes the religious nature of Münster, the city demonstrates a different example. Czech philosopher and renegade Marxist Karl Kautsky wrote in his 1897 *Communism in Central Europe at the Time of the Reformation* that the commune was composed of an "originally quiet and peaceable people" who were "systematically stigmatized as a hand of bloodthirsty and lascivious villains, simply because on one occasion, under the oppression of constant maltreatment and danger, they did not passively submit to destruction, but rose in energetic resistance."

In his revisionism of the event, Kautsky defends the actions of Münster's citizens, and in their defeat, he mourns that "Christian communism came to an end in the sixteenth century." For Kautsky, the scurrilous rumors about mass executions and forced polygamy were status quo propaganda, and the example of Münster rather indicated an anarchic possibility for radical egalitarianism in what was a profoundly unequal age. He writes that that "century saw the birth of an new system of production, the modern State and the modern proletariat; and it saw also the birth of modern socialism." In the philosopher's eyes, Leiden, Matthys, and all the rest were precursors and inspirations for the future emancipation of mankind.

The reality, as is often the case, is more complicated of course. While Kautsky's point about potential libel is well taken, some of the most disturbing accounts of what occurred in Münster, from both critics and supporters, confirm the position of the city's detractors. Bockelson as an individual became increasingly unhinged, as much a Reverend Jim Jones as he was a Che Guevara. To bracket out the literalism and fervor of the Anabaptists is to delete the experience of those forced into plural marriages against their will; it's to obscure the executions that happened in the shadow of St. Lambert's and culminated in the revolution's termination itself. Kautsky is correct that a genealogy can be credibly claimed between Münster and, say, the European revolutions of 1848 or the Paris Commune of 1871 (or we might add the strikes of 1968), but there's arguably a similarity to the Islamic State as well. If the Zapatistas have a precursor at Münster, then so does the People's Temple. The difficulty with such paradoxes – that Münster signifies both the millennial hope for a newer, more just, fairer, more equitable world must be combined with the terror that her revolutionaries unleashed – is unfortunate for radical historiography.

Such ambiguities lend themselves to a certain anti-idealism, to what the philosopher Russell Jacoby notes in his encomium *Picture Imperfect: Utopian thought for an Anti-Utopian Age* as being a situation where "most observers judge utopians or their sympathizers as fool-hardy dreamers at best and murderous totalitarians at worst." Such is the self-serving, "pragmatic" *realpolitik* of the entrenched, for whom any discussion of equality must inevitably lead to the gulag. Thus, do we derive at our current predicament, where an un-dreaming and un-feeling neoliberalism forces us to pretend that this is the best of all possible worlds, where we are limited by the strictures of what critic Mark Fisher called "capitalist realism." We need neither spurn nor embrace Münster to acknowledge that latent utopianism has something to recommend in it; Jacoby's argument that "practical reforms depend on utopian dreaming." That is of course a liberal argument, and the rare one to embrace utopianism, but on the left, there is either a blanching at the accusation of utopianism, or an embrace, but rarely a sense that the concept is only useful for practical reforms. Rather the left can dream grander, embracing what Slavoj Žižek in his appropriately entitled *In Defense of Lost Causes* describes as being "unashamedly committed to the 'Messianic' standpoint of the struggle for universal emancipation."

Cohn makes clear that as dramatic as Münster was, it's certainly not an anomaly in Abrahamic religious tradition. Such messianism, such millennialism, goes back to the book of Daniel, runs through the apocalyptic tradition of the Apostles, bursts forth with potent fervency among medieval Catholic groups with exotic names like the Beguines, the Beghards, and the Joachimites (and less exotic ones like the Franciscans), which ultimately transitioned into the dissenting groups of the radical Reformation. Such a golden thread connects not just the Anabaptists, but the non-conformists of the English Revolution, radicals of the seventeenth and eighteenth centuries with names like the Ranters, Seekers, Levellers, Muggletonians, and so on. Kautsky reclaimed the Anabaptists for a secular revolutionary moment, but their origin from the rich soil of theology has to be acknowledged. If there were biblical defenses of what was happening in Münster – regardless of how a Luther or a Nash might interpret it – then there was also a new vocabulary independent of scripture that could be used to explain their aims. Münster may have dreamt of millennium, but they tried to enact utopia.

Kautsky makes the point that Thomas More's *Utopia*, written in 1516 less than two decades before those bloody events, was popular throughout Holland, Germany, the Swiss canons, the Holy Roman Empire. Indeed, German was the first language after English that More's Latin text was translated into, and it's impossible to imagine that a major city like Münster would have been devoid of such a seminal humanist book. More's classic, a romance presenting an imagined New World society that has attained moral, ethical, and political perfection, has long been defined by its contradictions. The attorney who imagined a country without lawyers, the wealthy politician whose book eschewed wealth and inequity, the increasingly zealous Catholic who made overtures to religious freedom, the future saint honored by a memorial in the Kremlin. So rife are the contradictions in *Utopia* that all political theory has been dogged by its example since More conceived of it, regardless of whether his book is a blueprint or a joke.

Not much about Utopia and Münster necessarily look that similar, and yet More's imagined country is defined by a similar critique, a belief that "wherever you have private property and all men measure all things by cash values, there it is scarcely possible for a commonwealth to have justice or prosperity – unless you think justice exists where all the best things flow into the hands of the worst citizens or prosperity prevails where all is divided among the very few." Questions of narrative genre define *Utopia* – whither prescription or satire? – but in allowing for the imagined possibility of a restructuring of society that did not rely on prophetic, apocalyptic, or supernatural intercession, More did provide an incredibly potent new word. Rebellions had happened before Münster, and they would happen again, but the events in that Westphalian hamlet are the first that any observer, for better or for worse, would have been able to call "utopian."

Certainly, More was aware of what had happened in Münster. By one of those fortuitous coincidences, the city itself would fall in June of 1535, and only a month later the former Lord Chancellor would find his head on the block in the Tower of London. If there was any confluence between More's utopian enthusiasms almost twenty years before and the dictates of the Münster revolutionaries, they had certainly dissipated by that summer. While firmly the liberal humanist who penned Utopia, confidant of Erasmus and advocate for progressive reforms, More had also become draconian as regards the Lutheran question.

An increasing defender of Catholic orthodoxy, for which he would ultimately give his life, More correctly followed through on the dangerous potential in Luther's maxim of the priesthood of all believers, where there would be "almost as many sects as men." Liberty of conscience would necessarily lead to a breakdown in social hierarchy, and More's task later in life wasn't simply steadfastly conservative, it was resolutely anti-utopian. More rejected any pretense to the religious freedom or economic egalitarianism which he had seemingly once defended, especially during his tenure as Lord Chancellor when the kingdom was still Catholic, and it was his job to ferret out, interrogate, and order the execution of heretical schismatics. Several of those men were personally tortured by More, in the basement of his house.

In More's understanding, such religious liberty couldn't help but lead itself to the fractured anarchy of a Münster, and decades after Utopia he abjured those earlier views. His 1531 Confutation of Tyndale's Answer, his longest book at half-a-million words, polemically responded to the Lutheran sympathies of the New Testament translator William Tyndale, and make More's feelings towards Utopia clear. More writes that in this era of interpretive anarchism, when biblical interpretation is given over to any man, and where the subsequent social cost is in conflagrations like the Peasant's Rebellion and the commune at Münster, then the saint

25

argues that should books like *Utopia* find themselves translated into English, "I would not only my darling's books but mine own also, help to burn them both with mine own hands."

More remains a helpful signifier for the Renaissance's ambiguities, its paradoxes, its contradictions. His simultaneous utopianism and anti-utopianism, his status as the first citizen of that land and its first dissident as well. It neither obscures nor invalidates. As metonymy, such a status is allegorical for the strange disjuncts of that age which historians for the past two generations of scholarship have appropriately enough called the "early modern period." Appropriate, I say, for the sixteenth and seventeenth centuries are frequently configured as marking the emergence of a new type of being, of modernity. Such a critique can seem painfully triumphalist to medievalists who embrace a "continuity hypothesis" that emphasizes the complexity of earlier eras; it can seem reactionary to radicals who identify the Enlightenment of the eighteenth century as the locus for modernity's genesis. By contrast, New Historicist critic Stephen Greenblatt in *Renaissance Self-Fashioning: From More to Shakespeare* argues that this was a period categorized by a "Change in the intellectual, social, psychological, and aesthetic structures that govern the generation of identities."

After all, the Renaissance – to use a more old-fashioned term – as well as the Reformation, were periods that saw the origins of mercantile capitalism and the very beginnings of the industrial revolution, the development of positivism as a philosophy of science, the ascendancy of colonialism and the institution of the slave trade, and the exchange, both forceful and voluntary, that define globalization. If we're to think of the Renaissance as populated by "early moderns" that's because in very many ways they resemble us, they are our antecedents in modernity. By the late seventeenth century, the end of any period which could be credibly thought of as the early modern period, the inhabitants of London would have read newspapers covering parliamentary arguments in their favorite coffeeshops, as clearly as anyone in a Fleet Street Starbucks can read about Brexit on their smartphone today.

They're our antecedents in a certain cruelty that marked the time as well, for in the imposition of things like slavery and sectarian violence, the Europe of the Renaissance marked itself as particularly horrific for the lives of everyday people. Sing of light and rebirth all that you want, the fact is that the quality of life for people in the early modern world, from exploitive conditions in urban centers to the elimination of common grazing ground, was far worse than it would have been a few centuries before, even as Michelangelo was able to paint some pretty pictures. So often is the designation "medieval" used as a slur to denote backwardness that it obscures the reality that the most violent wars in European history, until our contemporary era, awaited the sixteenth and seventeenth centuries. The Hundred Years War of the fourteenth century pales in comparison to the death count of the seventeenth century's Thirty Years War.

We are children of that moment, and children of the secular triumphalism that celebrates the Renaissance, and of the Protestant triumphalism which valorizes the Reformation. We often forget what the wages of modernity actually are. If we're to identify any moment at which our current epoch of the Anthropocene might be dated, we could do worse than the early modern period, when the ecological transformations of the Columbian exchange altered the world irrevocably, when the Reformation heralded a certain disenchantment, when odious ideologies of pseudo-scientific racism began to hold sway. If all of those conservative historiographies of the period, with their great men and their great books, and all of those dead, white males, hoisted the Renaissance upward as the pinnacle of human expression, then this is clearly a chauvinism of which I'm not guilty. But that's of course not the entire story of the Renaissance, as *Utopia* makes clear.

The Renaissance is its own diagnosis and its own prescription; it is the disease and the cure. The paradox is that if the worst of modernity was born from those years – the capitalism, the slavery, the positivism – then the best of our utopianism also emerged then as well. The Renaissance and Reformation are neither wholly one thing nor the other, and as More's example makes clear, such utopianism and anti-utopianism could exist in tandem, even in the heart of one man. If we're children of that age, then it behooves us to interrogate that era as it contains our inheritance, for both good and bad. A standard view of the Renaissance can limit its radical possibility, but in examining the borderlands, the margins, the crawl-spaces of history we can exhume and resuscitate the Münsters of that era. This is to take part in a tradition of progressive scholarship that goes back to the 1970s, which recognizes the complexity of representation and restores marginalized voices, but what I wish to speak of is something slightly different, though it certainly encompasses those earlier methodologies. It is to examine the latent radicalism of the Renaissance, its implicit subversiveness. To resuscitate what is revolutionary about it, not in spite of its contradictions, but because of them.

And so, a parable. In the decade before both of their executions, More and Tyndale were engaged as interlocutors in a war of pamphlets, which was often the early modern precursor to actual wars. Tyndale was a convert to the Lutheran cause, particularly in the injunction of *sola Scriptura* which called for vernacular bible translations which would be the ultimate arbiter of theological truth. Tyndale's New Testament was the first contemporary English translation in its entirety, and so sublime are his turns of phrase that the far better known and celebrated translators of the King James Version of eight decades later cribbed the majority of Tyndale's original. For More, such translation was inherently dangerous for the same reason he wanted lay people not to read *Utopia*.

There was a bottled electricity in books such as these, a type of fire that could threaten to engulf the world if those books weren't consumed first – as indeed had happened at Münster. Tyndale was forced to print his English New Testament on the continent, in the Low Countries as fate would have it, not far from where Münster would have its last stand. Smuggled back into England with the assistance of Lollards, a medieval proto-Protestant sect who dominated the wool trade, Tyndale's bibles were distributed throughout London, and it was Lord Chancellor More's job to track them down and have them burnt. On the first page, Tyndale included a little cheeky act of defiance which he knew More would see. Where the place of printing would normally be displayed, Tyndale couldn't possibly indicate the real location. Instead, his bible read – "Printed in Utopia."

Martin Luther on the Toilet

"Love has pitched his mansion in/The place of excrement"
W.B. Yeats

"The anus produces life, waste is fecund, from death new landscapes emerge."
Leo Bersani

"Devil, I have just shit in my trousers. Have you smelled it?"
Martin Luther

Martin Luther was often constipated. While this is certainly not the most important fact about the father of the Reformation, it shouldn't be excused as merely incidental either. Much in history has hinged on less than a proper and satisfying bowel movement. Generations of Protestant triumphalist historiography have subconsciously described the Reformation in language that does nothing so much as evoke a satisfying, too-long-in-coming, defecation. Or, at the very least, the Reformation is configured as an act of simplification, of cleaning up, of tidying, of freshening; while by contrast medieval Catholicism is impugned with the rhetoric of filth. Historian Owen Chadwick, mostly passed over now by revisionist scholars though his introduction remains excellent, wrote in 1964 that medieval Christianity "had been like a church where the furniture is cluttered, the altar obscured, and the corners undusted." And in the years before Luther at Wittenberg, "everyone that mattered in the Western Church was crying out for reformation" like a traveler in search of a bathroom. The period before reform is sometimes described in language that evokes the straining, tense, uncomfortable holding onto matter better dispelled. And when evacuation finally arrives there can be a fresh, new, purified, cleansing renewal. Don't take my word for it, it was Luther himself who apparently said, "I'm like a ripe stool and the world is like a gigantic anus."

There will be many considerations of Luther as we recognize the five-hundredth anniversary of his nailing of the Ninety-Five Theses to the door of the Wittenberg Cathedral Church. Essays which consider his historical significance, his influence on Christianity and modernity, his conflicted legacy, and his contradictory biography. Articles which do justice to the founder of Protestantism. I've written a few of those myself. This will not be one of those pieces. As my motivating task, rather, I hope to provide some thoughts regarding the psychologist David B. Meyer's pertinent question concerning Luther: "What is one to do when a religious leader refers so persistently to the anus?" Folklorist Malcolm Jones claims that as concerns scatology, "Academically, as far as this particular topic is concerned, we are still toddlers, merely dabbling with it," but dabble in it we must. To that end, what I want to do is give Luther credit for something often obscured with our awkward laugher, but which I suspect is not without theological import.

Luther produced thousands of pages of vibrant, visceral, vernacular German prose which explored faith, grace, and ritual, but he also developed a profound rhetoric of shit. In an era where metropolitan eras exploded in sheer human numbers, and where human waste became very much an aspect of everyday life (and a public health concern), Luther would, as others did, have a preoccupation with feces. And from that rich manure would come good trees, and as the reformer reminds us, good trees bare good fruit. And with no snark or irony I attest to the freshness of Luther's shit theology. Please, do not read the second to last word in the previous sentence as an adjective, but as a noun. In that I mean to say that Luther took waste seriously, used it to great rhetorical effect, and took part in intellectual disputations which utilized sublime examples of what literary critic Susan S. Morrison calls "fecopoetics"; that is Luther was engaged with adversaries from Ulrich Zwingli and Thomas More in what could best be described as shit-fests. Psychoanalyst Erik Erikson writes that revelation is always associated with "a cleansing, a kicking away; and it would be entirely in accord with Luther's great freedom in such matters if he were to experience and to report this repudiation in frankly physical terms." Morrison explains that this language of "Fecopoetics explains how the excremental is used as a vital element in poetic and cultural enterprises," and as such Luther is no exception. In fact, he is a representative example.

Don't misinterpret my intent as to slur Luther, rather I am acknowledging the scatological genius of his bawdy prose, the German peasant boy who couldn't help but have some familiarity with crap during his lifetime. His rhetoric paradoxically reached the height of excremental apologetics, a veritable Ninety-Five Feces. If such discussion about the great man seems unbecoming on this exalted anniversary, recall that in his 1545 pamphlet Against the Roman Papacy an Institution of the Devil he makes reference to "pope fart-ass" and refers to Christ's vicar on Earth who sits on Peter's throne as the "assgod in Rome." In that same work Luther writes of the Catholic condemnations of his movement that "such a great horrid fart did the papal ass let go here! He certainly pressed with great might to let out such a thunderous fart – it is a wonder that it did not tear his hole and belly apart!"

If flatulence is a bit too PG for you, what about the many references to shit and anuses from his Table Talk, the posthumous collection of notable conversations with Luther compiled posthumously, from which the quote that I ended the first paragraph finds its origin? Or when he claims that the papacy's rituals figuratively stink "worse than the devil's excrement?" Or when during a contemplative dinner he marveled "that man hasn't long since defecated the whole world full, up to the sky?" And lest you think that I've cherry-picked these selections, I refer you to an analysis of his close to four hundred letters, almost 40 percent of which had some sort of reference to either butts, shitting, shit, and anuses, in that order of descending popularity. Scholars Joseph Schmidt and Mary Simon (no relation) write that Luther "provided the scatological with a fervor never read nor heard before" and historian Danielle Meade Skjelver concurs that "clearly Luther's scatology went beyond the rules of decorum even for his own era" while drily noting that "it seemed to work for him." Luther, who believed he could chase away both pope and the Devil with but a fart, had a little bit of a preoccupation it would seem.

An important preoccupation, for it was precisely while on the shitter that Luther supposedly had his epiphany that it was faith alone which merited salvation, having written that this realization occurred to him while he was contemplating Romans 1:17 "in the sewer," that is while he was pooping. He writes that the foundational cornerstone of the Reformation, of sola Fide, was "given to me by the Holy Spirit on this Cloaca in the tower," with "cloaca" a Latin euphemism for toilet. He writes that following that successful evacuation of his bowels along with the remnants of his Romish superstition that he "felt totally newborn, and through open gates I entered paradise." There has been some debate as to whether we should read Luther's account of his bathroom revelation as literal or merely figurative, but as Heiko Overman (who did more than any scholar to connect Luther back to the Rabelaisian world of late medieval theology) helpfully explains, it might not matter, because "behind Luther's statement there is a firm medieval tradition in which concepts like cloaca, latrina, faeces or stercus were used simultaneously in the physical and in the metaphysical way." As helpful as that analysis is, tracing as it does Luther's reliance on an allegorical scatology which was popular in the late medieval world which was the reformer's intellectual birthright, it can't help but be disappointing to those who wish to see the actual toilet.

That desire smacks a bit of the very obsession with material faith which Luther and his descendants so deplored, for the Reformation of course impugned the superstitious trade in relics and the venturing of pilgrims, but for those for whom a bit of the old faith still clings like a pungent odor in the atmosphere – fear not. A relic of Luther's intestinal theophany was apparently discovered by archeologists in 2004, to which a BBC article breathlessly informs us that "Luther's lavatory thrills experts." At Wittenberg's Lutherhaus Museum researchers found in an annex what was presumably Luther's toilet, the very one on which one of his pivotal five solas was first conceived. Director of the Luther Memorial Foundation, Stefan Rhein, matter-of-factly said of the 30cm stone seat with a hole in the center that, "This is where the birth of the Reformation took place." Before anyone accuses me of irreverence or libel against Luther, I ask them to defer to Mead Skjelver, who writes that though the reformer's central insight "hit him in the latrine," this was an event which should serve to remind us that "God would go anywhere to reach His children," to which I agree.

All of that straining, spiritual and otherwise, marked Luther in the eyes of some critics and subsequent historians as an aberrant personality. A pathological head-case obsessed with shitting. That fellow founder of a new Teutonic inflected faith, Sigmund Freud, described the anal stage as the second in five stages of psychosexual development into which one might get "stuck." He explains that there are "few neurotics who have not their special scatologic customs," and when we consider the young obsessively scrupulous Augustinian monk who had his life-long fixation with feces, it's hard not to think that there may be some merit in Herr Doktor Freud's theory as concerns Herr Doktor Reverend Luther. Freud helpfully writes that, "In later neurotic diseases they exert a definite influence on the symptomatic expression of the neurosis, placing at its disposal the whole sum of intestinal disturbances...one should not laugh at the hemorrhoidal influence to which the old medical literature attached so much weight in the explanation of neurotic states." In Freud's theory concerning psychosexual development, a personality which becomes psychosexually "stuck" in the anal stage will become fixated on the anus as a site of both pleasure and punishment, with the anal expulsive type being one who is not only filth obsessed and who derives pleasure from the act of defecation, but is also prone to willfully obstinate rebellion. Sound familiar?

Psychoanalyst Erik Erikson certainly thought so in his contested 1958 classic Young Man Luther: A Study in Psychoanalysis and History, in which he mines the rich fecopoetic aesthetic threaded throughout the reformer's writings, so as to derive a theory concerning the anal expressiveness inherent in the founder of Protestantism's rhetoric. Erikson, most famous as the originator of the concept of the "identity crisis," finds in Luther a convenient confirmation of his theory. Luther, the nervous boy terrified by a thunder-clap in 1505 who turned his soul over to the protection of St. Anne, and as a result of her assistance turned his life over to ordination? Luther, who so resented the exacting ritualized dictates of Rome, which manifested in his obsessive scrupulosity, that he confided to his confessor Johann von Staupitz that he feared he secretly hated God (and Freud tells us that, "God is nothing more than an exalted father"). Luther, for whom even when his soul was calmed upon his discovery of the means to salvation couldn't help but project his rancor onto that other father, il papa, the pontiff, the pope, that "assgod."

For the armchair Freudian who wishes to parse the biography of Luther, there is more than just the reformer's anal fixation, there is also his latent oedipal complex: the son of an economically upwardly mobile copper miner who refused his father's admonishing to practice law, rather preferring to become an Augustinian monk. Erikson writes that the young anal expulsive Luther rebelled "first against his father, to join

35

the monastery; then against the Church, to found his own church – at which point he succumbed to many of his father's original values." For Erikson, Luther's "anal defiance" was born of his "neurotic suffering," the result of "active remnants of childhood repressions," specifically related to his father's profession which he refused to enter. Hans Luder made a comfortable living from the hazardous labor of copper mining, yet according to Erikson it was his journey into the subterranean, intestinal "fickle and dangerous bowels" of the earth which so traumatized young man Luther that he couldn't help but develop the anal fixation which so defined his vulgar rhetoric.

Freudian interpretations are less vogue now, with the good doctor's reputation slowly chipped away by Popperian philosophy, feminist criticism, and the empirical dictates of neuropsychology which has no place for the quasi-mystical ghost in the machine that is the Id, Ego, and Superego. Oberman, neither a Popperian philosopher, a feminist critic, or a neuropsychologist, used simple historiography to refute Erikson's arguments, generously writing that his biography is "both a brilliant analysis and a garbled distortion – because it is unhistorical." Freudianism, like any totalizing theory, is in some ways equally satisfying and simultaneously deficient – satisfying because it seems to cross all the t's and dot all the I's in explaining every conceivable situation, behavior, personality, and event; deficient because all of the fascinating nuance and subtly becomes the collateral damage enacted by the universalizing violence of the theory itself. Oberman's point about the medieval tradition of vulgar critique, of archetypal scatological tricksters, or the rhetoric of filth as an aesthetic mode in its own right and not just something that results from hemorrhoids, is a point well taken. Freudian analysis, as helpful as it may be in some contexts, can have the effect of reducing the sublimity of fecopoetics, by making it a mere symptom of a neurotic condition. Better to consult Mikhail Bakhtin's analysis in his groundbreaking work on the carnivalesque as a subversive medieval mode, part of which hinges on the parodic possibilities of the abstracted grotesque body.

In Rabelais and His World, Bakhtin writes that to "degrade also means to concern oneself with the lower stratum of the body" and that it "therefore relates to acts of defecation." He continues by explaining that the subversive art of vulgar medieval polemic is one where "Degradation digs a bodily grave for a new birth; it has not only a destructive, negative aspect, but also a regenerating one…Grotesque realism knows no other level; it is the fruitful earth and the womb. It is always conceiving" (think of Luther's comparison of himself to a turd about to be expunged, a type of fecal birth in its imagery). Suddenly Erikson's interpretations of Luther's theology as only being the result of childhood trauma seems incredibly limiting, the better to embrace a Bakhtinian approach which considers shit in all of its multifaceted, mythic, splendid possibilities. An analysis of Luther's pathological coprophilia which reduces the phenomenon to only his individual peccadillos is also lacking, because unlike Oberman and Bakhtin's survey of the period and its continuities to the ribald, bawdy, earthy medieval past, it brackets out just how common Luther's rhetoric was in the wider realm of religious disputation. Luther happened to be a particularly adept enthusiast of the fecopoetic arts, but he was simply a master surrounded by the middling. His language was hardly unique in early modern Europe, as a Freudian analysis might imply, rather he was part of an ongoing tradition, for this was an era awash in shit.

The rhetoric of Reformation wasn't just one that had a centrally focused fecopoetic, the visual culture embraced a similar aesthetic. Protestant aesthetics is often conceptualized entirely in terms of iconoclasm – the white-washed walls of the chapel, the smashed statuary, stripped altars, and relics consigned to the bonfire, replaced in the households that once featured them with the secular masterworks of the Northern Renaissance. But Reformation aesthetics also borrowed heavily from a certain medieval earthiness, content to muck around in the profane and fallen world of human waste so as to score points in the volleys that went back and forth in the argumentative war of pamphlets that marked the early sixteenth century and that prefigured the shortly coming actual wars of religion. No artist was as pivotal in the paramount development of a new Protestant visual code that needed to fill the void left from the coming iconoclastic fury (though note that Luther himself was not particularly averse to religious images) than Lucas Cranach the Elder. If Luther was the great mass-media juggernaut of his day, taking full advantage of the printing press's power to disseminate information quickly and widely, than Cranach was his partner in fusing word with image, creating a visual idiom that called to mind nothing so much as comics, and which often had at its core a scurrilous, hilarious, scatological base.

For example, his illustration which accompanied Luther's 1545 pamphlet Depiction of the Papacy, which illustrates the Pope holding a literally flaming anti-Protestant encyclical, whose fires are being tamed by the winds of farting German peasants, whose asses are directed at the throne of St. Peter and its current occupant. A stoically faced attendant (a cardinal perhaps) stands next to Paul III. In that same pamphlet, Cranach plays even bluer, when he presents an image of Landsknecht mercenaries electing to challenge the Pope with a "weapon other than the sword," in the coy words of Mead Skjelver, or indeed with a weapon other than a printing press as well. Rather one determined fellow is poised crouching over a positively massive papal tiara, taking a dump into its cavernous, bee-hive like interior. Both of these illustrations depict flatulence, shitting, and all of their attendant physical phenomenon as an instrument of justice against a corrupt Church, a means of leveling the falsely prideful and inflated institution of man with the very detritus of that which man produces. A profane reminder that all men are born between piss and shit, the Pope included.

But if excrement is a potent means of resistance against injustice and corruption, then it was also useful to Cranach and other Protestant propagandists as a convenient slur to mark their enemies as themselves being a type of waste. In Depiction of the Papacy Cranach conceptualizes feces as not just a way to diminish, mock, and blaspheme the Church, but indeed he sees the Church and her princes as excremental in their own right. Consider the image which presents the Pope's birth, emerging not from the vaginal canal of a human woman, but rather from the quivering, prolapsed rectum of a hideous she-devil, the papacy reduced to a fecal still-birth passed through the ulcerated sphincter of a sulfurous demon.

Not an anomalous image, for Cranach and those who worked in the tradition he inaugurated produced a preponderance of images which associated the Pope, and his very existence and origin, with the expulsion of excrement. In the tradition which conceptualizes of the Pope in the language of the turd, Luther, Cranach, and indeed all speakers of Germanic languages had a fortuitous coincidence in the false cognate between the words "Pope" and "poop." No etymological relation between the words, of course – the first was from the Vulgar Latin "papa" for "father," and the latter either from Middle English "poupen" or the Low German "pupen," both meaning, well, what they mean.

But for Cranach and Luther, that "Pope" and "poop" were but one mispronounced phoneme away from each other perhaps couldn't help but to be evidence of German's special genius at being able to strip reality bare to the basic truth, a scatological version of the poet George Herbert's contention that English was specially blessed because "sun" and "Son" were homophones (albeit a baser typological philology). Incidentally, waste wasn't only a rhetorical trope, sometimes it was a literal weapon as well. Jones writes of a "1528 pamphlet [that] told how Luther had been sent a copy of a work attacking [him]...in scurrilous terms which was taken off to the privy by several of Luther's supporters in Wittenberg, used as toilet paper, and then sent back to its authors in Leipzig." When considering both the image and actions of Cranach and others, as well as the general iconoclastic fecal-aesthetics of the Reformation, it helps to remember that though the chapel walls may have been white-washed, they sometimes were also figuratively coated in a thick crust of human excrement as well.

Protestants weren't the only ones willing to smear their rhetorical dung upon the pamphlets of their enemies. It speaks to the limitations of any interpretation which reduces Luther's scatological theology to merely personal neurosis that this sort of language was so common during the era, but not just common among advocates for Reform, indeed the very princes of the Church had no compunctions about flinging a little bit of caca back at their detractors. Anti-Lutheran invective could be just as rich in fecopoetic imagery as was that by Luther himself, with many instances of Catholic polemicists turning over the figurative outhouse just as zestfully as Protestants did. Such ribaldry had its origins in the working-class humor of medieval Europe, as indeed Luther's language did, and which of course was also part of the cultural inheritance of the Catholic Church itself. We need not view late medieval and early modern peasantry as exclusively being the earthy and stinky denizens of a Brueghel painting proffering smoked hams and quaffing weak ale as they dance on a feast day to some hurdy-gurdy player, and yet such a tableau has some veracity to recommend in itself.

Jones reminds us that "the Reformation era was not the first time such scatological imagery was employed to satirize the clergy," and indeed it's important to remember that both Luther and Church were the inheritors of that Chaucerian and Rabelaisian aesthetic of base things profoundly wrought and profound things profanely depicted. That was the exact attitude engaged by a popular song in Poland (which we often forget was once a site of major sectarian difference) disseminated some seven years after that fateful first Reformation Day: "Since Luther considers everyone shit compared with him,/And in his filthy mouth has nothing but shit,/I ask you, wouldn't you say that he's a shitty prophet?/Such as a man's words are, so is the man himself." Admittedly lacking a bit of poetry in translation, the broadsheet reverses Luther's own transgressive pose and projects it back onto him, evidencing that Jones' contention that "Scatology is an important weapon in the armory of trickster figures" is appropriately enough a tricky one – since who is performing the prank and who the prank is being performed on can be ambiguous. When we're covered in shit it can be hard to properly identify anyone, which, it might seem, is one of the possible readings of the song.

But the Counter-Fecopoetics of the Magisterium wasn't just limited to Boschian peasants with their Polish drinking song. More exulted personages than that prolific author Anonymous also took a bit of the piss out of Luther. One particular unlikely master of the shit-drenched insult quip was none other than the great Utopian himself, Saint Thomas More, who was more than willing to utilize all of the most appropriate words in his Anglo-Saxon vocabulary. The future martyr described Luther as a "buffoon" and compared the mouth which uttered such schismatic heresies to "cesspools, sewers, latrines, shit and dung." If that seems a bit tame in comparison to some of Luther's saucier statements, More rises to the level of master insult comic playing the dozens when he describes his German adversary, in admirable Anglo-Saxon alliteration and with a sense of biblical parallelism, as "A mad friarlet and privy-minded rascal with his raging and raving, with his filth and dung, shitting and beshitting. Luther has written that he has the right to besmatter and besmirch the royal crown with shit...to lick the posterior of a pissing she-mule." If Protestants could accuse the Pope of being the turd of Satan, then Catholics could accuse Luther of being an enthusiast of bestial anilingus.

If we're to believe More in some of his other writings, part of what troubled him so as concerns Luther wasn't just that he had conceived of "the very worst and most harmful heresy that ever was thought up; and, on top of that, the most insane," but also that such theological error forced him into the latrine with Luther himself. More would have us believe that it pained him to be lowered to Luther's level, to have to engage with the sick rhetoric of fecopoetics. Rather, the Utopian would have us think of him riding on horseback with Erasmus discussing Latin declensions in the Vulgate or tutoring his young daughters in the finer subtleties of Greek conjugation. But something about More's shit-talking comes a little too naturally and seems a bit too much fun for me to totally trust More when he claims that he wasn't enjoying his own language on some level. No neophyte would be able to easily pen of Luther that he should "throw back into your paternity's shitty mouth, truly the shit-pool of all shit, all the much and shit which your dammnable rottenness has vomited up, and to empty out all the sewers and privies onto your crown."

If Freud remains an inadequate explanation for the anal expulsions of an entire epoch, then what accounts for the veritable coprophilia of that age? When both More and Luther could dwell in the sewers, peasants could sing of the reformer's shit-filled mouth, and wealthy German burghers could wipe their ass with papal polemic? Freud and his student Erikson built one totalizing theory, but yet another Teutonic prophet might provide another. I'm speaking of Marx, of course, or at least a variety of Marxian materialist consideration. For it's all good and easy to talk about feces as a transcendent abstraction, but excrement is not just a symbol. Shit is very much real. The material considerations of shit as waste – its color, its odor, its texture, and the process by which it is produced – are precisely what make it such a potent object in both Reformation and Counter-Reformation rhetoric. Shit by any other name would smell just as foul. But when we talk about early modern Europe as being awash in shit, it's helpful to remember that this refers not just to its representations, but its reality as well.

Furthermore, when hypothesizing as to why there is such scatomania during the era, one might consider that the reality is precisely what led to the rhetoric. Economic, technological, and medical concerns are prime in understanding the manner in which an increasingly urbanized culture had to grapple with waste, both yours and others, in an unprecedented way. Hygiene (and its inadequacy) as well as plumbing (and its inadequacy as well) must have impacted the perseveration on excrement which is smeared across the historical record. After all, this was a century in which the English poet Ben Jonson, writing his mock heroic "On the Famous Voyage," could sarcastically ponder that great urban thoroughfare of the Thames as a type of modern Styx and which the urban population explosion in London had turned into a massive toilet, a place of "filth, stench, and noise" where "Arses were heard to croak, instead of frogs" and where the floating, monstrous turds required "the unused valor of a nose." Representations of waste as mediated through culture are one thing, but as the reality on the ground reminds us, actual shit very much happens.

So that then may explain some of Luther's language of the latrine, that the whole world was his and everybody else's toilet. Social historian Emily Cockayne explains that rather than being able to use the convenience of naturally running water, many early modern urban toilets had to often be "located above cesspits that needed to be emptied periodically," making excrement something that people had to physically deal with rather than enjoy the convenience of simply flushing, for these "Cesspits were not watertight, enabling liquid waste to leak away." With a lot more people in that world, Europe proverbially had gone to the shitter. Partially this was a direct result of the massive boom in population in the sixteenth and seventeenth centuries, as Europe rebounded from both plague and famine, and the development of nascent capitalism encouraged the massive transfer of people from the commons of the countryside into the chaotic world of the city. London, for example, had a population of only about 25,000 people in 1350 (making it a little under half the current size of booming Bethlehem, Pennsylvania). By 1546, the year Luther died, London had around 120,000 souls (and thus was closer in size to Allentown, Pennsylvania).

By the end of the sixteenth century, London's population had risen to 200,000, and by the years of civil war she had half-a-million inhabitants. Wittenberg never reached such heights of population, today only 50,000 people call her home, and she had a reputation for a certain sleepiness even when Luther made that veritable backwater his base of operations. And yet even for the relative small size of such communities when compared to the megacities of today, their growth represented a veritable population explosion which was unprecedented, the biggest gathering of human bodies in European cities since the fall of the Roman Empire. But where there are people there are asses, and where there are asses there must be crap. And what to do with this crap becomes an issue of sanitation, hygiene, medicine, and plumbing, and where there are deficiencies in those endeavors it will by necessity be reflected in the language of the era, where shitty base must beget shitty superstructure.

There are so many theories we can formulate as to the origin of Luther's strange obsession, with explanatory overtures to the psychoanalytical, the carnivalesque, and the materialist. But one perhaps obvious explanatory system has so far gone unremarked upon – the theological. After all, with his head in the heavens but with his ass on the toilet, how could the possibly theological disposition to his fecal obsession not be conjectured toward? When Luther's scatological interests are mentioned – and I am but a single singer in a massive choir of those who've remarked upon it – it's normally in the spirit of a type of jocular, bemused, perhaps slightly embarrassed commentary on the peccadillos of the great man. Luther's bawdy prose is the stuff of the internet "Lutheran Insult Generator," or of saucy memes shared by that one evangelical friend you have who likes craft-beer a little too much. Language that is taken as a given coming from a grosser, stinkier, more viscerally earthy time than our own. Rarely is Luther's rhetoric of scatomania taken seriously on its own terms; to my knowledge never taken theologically seriously beyond the discourse analysis of its rhetorical efficacy in popularizing the Reformation among a bawdy peasantry.

But what is the theological significance of shit? It's a question that Luther himself might not have quite thought to phrase, even if it pulses throughout his letters and pamphlets. Such a question might seem intemperate or lacking in seriousness, but though I don't ask it without a bit of the spirit of toilet humor, I also ask it genuinely and honestly. After all, the scandal of Christianity has always been that Christ was incarnated as man, and died the indignant death of man. In between nativity and crucifixion, He inevitably must have shit as well. To be offended by that reality is to be offended by Christianity, but to acknowledge that the living God is one who has to have shat is to embrace the living God. Christianity, in its Nicene form (and thus including both Catholicism and Protestantism), is a faith which grapples with the paradoxically ineffable corporeality of God, which must include acknowledgment of the basest of all things, a religion of "the least of these." Peter Stallybrass and Allon White in their classic The Politics and Poetics of Transgression explain that "cultural categories of high and low, social and aesthetic...are never entirely separate." And certainly cultural studies makes that abundantly clear, the entire tradition of the carnivalesque as vulgar pressure valve releasing social tensions and ensuring a type of order says as much. But cultural studies must always be the poor handmaiden to theology, for one could say that Christianity by its very incarnational logic ensures that the "high and low...are never entirely separate."

Writing about fecopoetics, critic Eileen Joy argues that "the excremental body is the body each one of us possesses," which I would unironically argue must also be an observation of Christian universalism as well. Joy continues by claiming that "Part of our civilizing process is to recognize the value of that which we deem uncivilized and to see ourselves in that threatening, filthy alterity." Conservative critics may scoff, but the critical work of fecopoetics has allowed for that "civilizing process" in the reading of literary texts, but where does theology ever do anything equivalent? Where is the corollary to fecopoetics, where is corpotheology? To pass over Luther's fecal utterances in embarrassed laughter is to abandon one part of his inheritance, his gestures to an emerging but never quite delivered corpotheology. An early modern English saying had it that "he who wrestles with a turd is sure to be beshit," an apt description of Luther's career, but also not one that is intended to be an insult. Shitting, it should go without saying, is a rather central aspect of the human condition. If theology is that which simultaneously deals with the most profound of questions as they intersect with the human condition, to ignore shitting is gross negligence. A squeamishness Luther did not have, for salvation which doesn't grapple with shit is no salvation at all. The rest of us it seems have found that where we are too embarrassed to speak, we have rather decided to pass over with a silent fart.

A Rude Railing Rhymer

"What could be dafter/Than John Skelton's laughter?"
Robert Graves

Sometime early in the sixteenth century, a frequently hungover, perennially in trouble, and womanizing priest named John Skelton took the lectern at his church, faced his angry congregation, and tried to explain the bastard child born to his mistress. Despite his Cambridge education, his humanist credentials, the fact that he'd once been tutor to Prince Henry, and the immaculate poetry he'd penned, the good Christians of Diss, Norfolk, had complained to their bishop about the priest's behavior. Skelton may have claimed that he'd imparted "drink of the sugared well/Of Helicon's waters crystalline," but his congregation was less than impressed. The priest penned inspired lyrics like "Speake, Parrot," "Phillip Sparrow," and that which we celebrate the five hundredth anniversary of this year, the immaculate doggerel "The Tunning of Elynour Rummyng," across which he developed an innovative rhythm known appropriately enough as "Skeltonics." But that was of no accounting to the bishop. Laity and clergy alike cared not for the literary pretensions of this self-styled "British Catullus." Perhaps it was clear that ordination was not Skelton's calling, for what could the parishioners expect, sacraments administered by a man who once wrote that: "To live under law it is captivity:/ Where dread leadeth the dance there is no joy nor pride."

A failure of imagination, for Skelton was no mere parish priest who scribbled "trifles of honest mirth"; rather he was, in the words of critic Michael Schmidt, a bard in Calliope-green who "stands like Janus at the threshold of the English Renaissance." A poet of a gloaming period, gesturing back to the verse of Chaucer and forward to that of Shakespeare. Skelton, who nostalgically pined for Merry Old England, while anticipating a coming Golden Age, while singing in the bawdy prosody of the ale-house and the vulgar profanity of the bed-chamber. Sublime Skelton, who has long troubled literary historians, even as Schmidt argues that he was "the first modern English" poet, read "without recourse to a glossary." There can be difficulty categorizing a man included as Poet Laurette alongside Dryden, Wordsworth, Tennyson, and Hughes, but who was also a consummate master of "flyting"; a type of improvised verse competition reminiscent of a rap battle. The Scottish poet Alexander Barclay described Skelton as a "rascolde poet," two centuries later and John Milton accused him of being "one of the worst of men," while Alexander Pope simply called him "beastly Skelton." A satirist of anti-clericalism at the verge of Reformation, but also an embodiment of said abuse. Skelton was a maker in the sublime poetry of hypocrisy, but whatever his moral lapses may have been, he was either the last medieval poet, or the first poet of the Renaissance, whose bawdy, alliterative, hurdy-gurdy verse, in the words of scholar Gerald Hammond, "rivals anything the Elizabethan lyricists" achieved.

Skelton was known to keep a "fair wench in his house," and the bishop informed him that the woman must be "expelled through the door." Interpreting orders with an opportunistic literalness, he did as instructed, only to let his mistress back in through the window. The bishop had long grown wary of these antics, writing that the priest was "guilty of *certain crimes* AS MOST POETS ARE." With his son, there was now permanent evidence of his indiscretions, for which the bishop required him to answer. There are no contemporary depictions of Skelton, no accurate engravings or Holbein paintings. But I like to envision the canny old poet as tall and thin and just handsome enough, a consummate performer, so confident that his palms weren't even damp when he appeared before his flock with both mistress and bastard. Holding his infant aloft, Skelton asked if he was not perfectly formed, perfect evidence of God's glory? Then who were these vipers, these clucking townspeople, chastising *God*? The congregation was cowed. Skelton kept his job. Until he got a better one, when Prince Arthur died and Skelton's former tutelage Henry VIII, assured of his kingship, invited the priest to Court.

Conversant with both Erasmus (who wrote approvingly of him) and Luther, Skelton was less than impressed with the latter, explaining in denunciatory anaphora and hypnotic end rhyme: "Against these frentics,/Against these lunatics,/Against these schismatics,/Against these heretics." But if Skelton was not willing to go Lutheran, his anti-clerical doggerel proved useful to English reformers a generation later, for in his rough, alliterative, and very Anglo-Saxon Skeltonics, Protestant propagandists saw a vehicle for delivering invective against the Church. After all, Skelton knew well of clerical abuse, and pointed his barbs at appropriate targets; having been imprisoned for slandering Cardinal Wolseley.

In 1517, the same year Luther affixed his own anti-clerical "poem" to a church door in Germany, Skelton penned his forgotten masterpiece "The Tunning of Elynour Rummyng," written in profane imitation of the Catholic liturgy. Anthologized alongside lyrics like "Phillip Sparrow" (with its erotic evocations of loss), or "Speake, Parrot," which charmingly begins with "My name is Parrot, a bird of paradise." The latter counts as the first mention of that species in European literature, with Skelton using the creature as a metaphor for the caged court poet himself. By contrast, Schmidt writes that "Elynour Rummyng…is certainly not charming." Skelton at his bawdy, wanton, disgusting, chauvinistic best (worst?). An account of the titular bar wench, supposedly based on an actual tavern owner, who "dwelt in Surrey,/In a certain stead/Beside Leatherhead." Elynour's surname is a pun on alcohol itself (notice the first syllable), and "tunning" is an archaism for bottling. She is described as "Droopy and drowsy,/Scurvy and lousy;/Her face all boozy,/Comely crinkled,/Wondrously wrinkled,/Like a roast pig's ear." Skelton describes how the ale woman sometimes "blends/The dung of her hens/And the ale together...The ale shall be thicker." Despite his misogynistic description of drunk housewives, who "come unbraced,/With their naked paps/ That flips and flaps...Like tawny saffron bags...All scurvy with scabs," Elynour remains a character with admirable agency.

Also a striking poem about "liquid oblivion" as Hammond describes it. While being careful not to project modern concern onto the distant past, Skelton's poem conjures the desperation of the junky, especially with the customers willing to pawn their possessions for a dram of Elynour's swill. An egalitarian affliction, for it effects "travelers, to tinkers,/To sweaters, to sinkers,/And all good ale drinkers." Trained in scholastic philosophy, he was adept in the allegorizing, but like Chaucer he was capable of endowing his creations with a rich interiority. "Elynour Rummyng," for all of its intentional ugliness is a description of those who have lost everything. He simply writes: "Her lips are so dry/Without drink she must die." Vulgar verse of rough but exquisite beauty.

That's his genius, taking the wool of common speech and spinning a resplendent banner of poetry from it. The poet Henry Wotton complained that Skelton deployed "the most familiar phraseology of the common people." On the verge of Renaissance, Skelton's idiom would wait for its appreciators. One of those more recent fans, W.H. Auden, explained that Skelton exhibits "the natural ease of speech rhythm." As the bard of the barroom and the poet of the pub, Skelton has more in common with de Quincey than Wordsworth or Bukowski than Frost. Rough-hewn verse, a poet whom the Elizabethan rhetorician George Puttenham, in imitation of his Anglo-Saxon alliteration, disparaged as merely a "rude, railing, rhymer."

Yet both Auden and Robert Graves drew inspiration from

Skeltonics, the sing-song, alliterative trimeter which thrums like an electric undercurrent beneath the staid Latinisms of canonical poetry. Scholar Ruth Kaplan explains that for Skelton, "Rhyme, rather than meaning, seems to drive the poems forward," which he acknowledged himself: "For though my ryme be ragged,/ Tattered and jagged,/Rudely rayne-beaten,/Rusty and mothe-eaten,/Yf ye take well therewith,/It hath in it some pyth." Kaplan explains that the logic of Skeltonics are such that the poem will continue "as long as the resources of the language hold out," according to the indomitable wisdom of what rappers call "flow." Forgive my anachronism, a pose normally deployed to convince undergraduates to enjoy antique poetry, and often failing. Yet there is a thread connecting Skelton to all who hear poetry in rough speech, or overhear at the bar, or on the subway, or street. A rough voice all the more powerful for it; the artful artistry of appearing without art. Skelton awaits his audience – yet his voice is all around us.

Last of the Insurgents

In 1497, the navigator Giovanni Caboto, whom posterity would Anglicize as John Cabot, placed upon the cold, rocky shoals of what is today the Canadian province of Newfoundland an English flag in honor of his patron Henry VII and the standard of his native Venice, which both framed a painted, carved, life-size crucifix. Historian Daniel K. Richter in *Facing East from Indian Country: A Native History of America* explains that "there is no record of what happened to Cabot's crucifix and flags." We've no idea as to if any of the indigenous Beothuk people came upon this tableau left by Cabot.

Imagine those barren shores punctuated with the red-cross of St. George, the intricate gold-threaded banner of Venice with its winged lion of St. Mark standing resplendent with a paw holding the gospel, and the life-like carving of the Christian God, dead on the cross, with eyes closed and wounds red. What are we to conjecture any wandering Beothuk might have made of these artifacts, constructed with technology they did not have, and defined by symbolism they were not yet fluent in?

For a human not conversant in the semiotics of European symbols, what could the fantastic beast of a lion whom you'd never seen before possibly mean? What would the abstraction of the red-X in the English flag signify? Unlikely that you'd understand them as implying legal ownership of your land as claimed by a monarch from a country you've never heard of, governed under a system you've no idea about. And most disturbingly of all, how would you properly interpret the meaning of a crucifix, not privy to a millennia-and-a-half of scripture and theology? Doubtful that you'd independently arrive at the concept of the incarnation and atonement soteriology, though perhaps the implications of a violently bloodied corpse are as close to a universal system of symbols that can exist, and thus arguably the most prescient of the relics left by Cabot.

This is the unanswered narrative thread of all such accounts of "first contact" – their side of the story. Colonists and conquestadors, missionaries and explorers, thrust upon natives demands in a language and faith that was completely foreign to them, with all of the tragic consequences such an interaction will ultimately avail. Tales of first contact often have certain commonalities; the configuration of natives as being a sort of "Noble Savage," the lists of trinkets given to the credulous aborigines, and a profound condescension that assumes a profoundly foreign people will be conversant with the intricacies of the invading culture that sees itself as primary.

We see it in 325 BCE when the Greek cartographer Pytheas of Massalia recounted his discovery of Britain, a travelogue which survives only in quotation and where the explorer describes the natives as being "of simple manners." It's evidenced in 1312 when the Genoan Lancelotto Malocello tried to instate himself as ruler among the native Guanches of the Canary Islands, which itself prefigured another Genoan sailor, employed by the Spanish Crown. Who in 1492 would write about the Carib and Arawak Indians that "the people are ingenious, and would be good servants."

And such themes are born eternal when Alabama-native John Allen Chua bribed fishermen to take him to the protected Andaman archipelago in the Indian Ocean, where he wished to "establish the kingdom of Jesus on the island," but was instead killed by the Sentinelese tribesmen, among the last uncontacted pre-Neolithic tribes on Earth. In a particularly American spin on the first contact narrative, the trifle for the natives which Chua brought with him was a football.

Chua's strange mission, a tragedy in which a disturbed 27-year old wasn't dissuaded of a dangerous adventure in which he threatened to introduce germs to which the Sentinelese have no natural resistance, has understandably engendered a fascination.

The death of the young American reminds us of narratives that seem from a distant past, it embodies the threatening wonder that there are still people who live in such radically different ways from us on this planet, and in that way it suggests to us that alternatives to modernity are not yet precluded for everyone – though it seems that rapidly they will be.

Chua's "martyrdom" harkens to tales from centuries ago. He evokes Ferdinand Magellan who in 1521 died in an almost identical manner, when Filipino natives "rushed upon him with iron and bamboo spears and with their cutlasses" as a witness wrote. Chua's "gift" of football and fishing hook parallels Christopher Columbus presenting to the Arawak "red caps... strings of beads to wear upon the neck, and many other trifles of small value," or of the "plate of brasse" which Francis Drake left behind in "Nova Albion," somewhere north of San Francisco Bay in 1579, where like Chua he hoped to establish a millennial Protestant kingdom, the plaque affixed as "a monument to our being there."

Literary critic Stephen Greenblatt in *Marvelous Possessions: The Wonder of the New World* analyzes early modern first contacts, where a "blank refusal of logical connectives" characterizes early travel writing. Colonizers' belief in the native desire to barter erroneously leads to the "conclusion that they would be easy to convert." Christ as imparted through trifle (and with the economic benefits of far more worthwhile trinkets given in exchange). Reality was often very different, tragically so for the native victims of colonialism. Chua's death demonstrates a similar refusal of "logical connectives," when in his notes he writes of the Sentinelese that "I have been so nice to them, why are they so angry and so aggressive?"

Chua believed his charge to be benevolent, but like many other historical missionaries he betrayed an incredible narcissism and an inability to empathize with the profoundly foreign worldviews of uncontacted peoples. Richter might as well be speaking of the football offered to the Sentinelese when he asks, "what might these particular oddly wrought symbols have meant to them?" The historian's study imagines what anthropological first contact may have looked like from the perspective of those who were "discovered," but the tragedy of colonialism is that any attempt at a work like this is by its nature haunted by absence and incompleteness.

"First contact" is the most enduring trope of the discovery narrative, the account of explorers (or colonizers) and their initial interactions with the indigenous people who are always configured as being part of the environment more than human agents in their own right. The most famous example happened in the autumn five years before Cabot's sojourns in the north Atlantic, when Columbus arrived among the Caribbean Arawak. In his *Journal of the First Voyage* Columbus (with his own interest in mind) writes that the Arawak were "very friendly to us" and he "perceived that they could be...easily converted to our holy faith." The Genoan claims that the natives were "much delighted, and became wonderfully attached to us." With a certainty as to the native's intent and feelings that we can't help but be cynical about, Columbus "translates" the Arawak language, but what's actually conveyed is the cultural context and language of Columbus' own medieval Catholic imagination. We've no clue as to how the Arawak themselves actually saw the Spanish, but we do know that the mythopoeic tongue through which Columbus described them has more to do with Eden than it does with the reality of America.

Our fascination with first contact betrays a similar profound narcissism – we're always so interested in what the natives could think of us; what did they feel when they saw Captain Cook's ships off the coast of Australia, what do the Sentinelese think when they see airliners soaring above the Indian Ocean, when they witnessed the helicopter which crashed on their Andaman island in 2014, when they riddled Chua's body full of arrows?

These are the "hundred-odd individuals [who] survive on tiny North Sentinel Island," as Madhusree Mukerjee writes in *The Land of Naked People: Encounters with Stone Age Islanders*, noting, "They may be the most isolated people on Earth."

What is the worldview of the Sentinelese, their incredibly alien cognitive universe, their perspective and understanding of reality that is completely Other from anything we're familiar with? How can we imagine the symbolic matrix through which they conceive of existence, for theirs is a way of being not only totally foreign to us but also (to the Sentinelese' credit) totally unavailable to us, even as missionaries thirst to preach the gospel to them? Though the existence of the Sentinelese has been known since Dutch sailors saw them on Andamanese shores in the seventeenth century, our actual knowledge of them is so scant that we don't know their language – we're unsure as to if they're able to make fire. So resistant are they to outside incursion that their narrative is of the most successful colonial resistance tales in five centuries.

Anthropologist Elizabeth Marshall Thomas in *The Old Way: A Story of the First People* says of her travels among the !Kung people of the Kalahari Desert (made famous in the problematic 1980 South African film *The Gods Must be Crazy*) that she felt as if she had "voyaged into the deep past through a time machine." Here among the Namibian hunter-gatherers she felt that she "saw the Old Way, the way of life that shaped us, a way of life that now is gone." It's this sense of loss, and of our culture's role in that loss, that shapes our fascination with uncontacted peoples, and it explains some of the guilty *Schadenfreude* that accompanied Chua's death. In the ever-dwindling numbers of people who've had no contact with modernity we in part mourn the loss of the "Old Way" that Thomas writes about, but we also mourn a more complex loss – the sense of wonder that once accompanied the mystery of other people, the knowledge that there were entire continents of humans whom you knew nothing about.

The last uncontacted aboriginal Australians were discovered as recently as 1984. There are several tribes of which anthropologists know nothing about who dwell in Papua New Guinea. Ishi, a Yahi Indian, was the last uncontacted indigenous North American, when he discovered America by walking into Oroville, California in 1911. Ishi's last days were spent living in a San Francisco Museum, not far from where Drake may have once affixed his brass plaque, and his discovery drew to a close that era which began with Columbus' disastrous contact of the Arawak people. Today there are several dozen groups of uncontacted people living in South America, the majority in Brazil, whose existence is threatened by the president-elect Jair Bolsonaro's horrific Amazon policies. Soon all peoples will have been contacted, and in that whole universes will have been lost.

Charles C. Mann in *1493: Uncovering the World Columbus Made* writes that since the initial colonial moment the "world has been in the grip of convulsive transculturation," where for "five centuries now the crash and chaos of constant connection has been our home condition," it would seem, save for the Andaman Islands. Part of us realizes that unchecked modernity will complete that process initiated by Columbus, that soon there will be no uncontacted peoples left, and lost will be the enormity of their worlds which we are not privy to, nor were meant to be welcomed into. Gone will be the wisdom that there are realities which are not always ours to acquire, people that we shall not always impose our faiths onto.

Chua's death is certainly a personal tragedy, the account of a disturbed man who potentially threatened the continued existence of these people. But the greater tragedy of Sentinelese extinction has been avoided for at least a few more years, where in a deluge of arrows we witnessed a counterfactual version of colonial history. In this telling, Columbus and Cabot were repelled by the natives. Because of that temporary fantasy we know that the Andamanese inhabitants are safe, at least for a few more years.

Among Tyrants

The 190th sonnet of Petrarch's *Canzoniere* presents the "sweetly austere" image of a "doe of purest white upon green grass." Petrarch, a fourteenth-century Italian poet, contemplates the mystical deer with devotion; it is, after all, a stand-in for his beloved, Laura. Around the deer's throat is a necklace studded with diamonds and topaz, symbols of steadfastness and chastity respectively – an appropriate bit of mineralogical allegory for a poet so identified with idealized love. It's telling that when the English poet Sir Thomas Wyatt reimagined Petrarch's sonnet some two centuries later, he deleted the detail about the topaz. Petrarch wrote about chastity; Wyatt wrote about anxiety.

Wyatt was the first English poet to write sonnets, and he was indebted to Petrarch, as were almost all other Renaissance poets. Yet even a cursory consideration of Wyatt's "translation" reveals how the poet subverted his predecessor. Petrarch's language is ethereal, characterized by words such as *purest, sweetly, treasure,* and *pleasure.* Wyatt prefers a vocabulary of nervous menace. He writes of "vain travail" and of his "wearied mind" and of a deer's collar that warns she is "wild for to hold, though I seem tame." Wyatt even invents an entirely different first line, rendering Petrarch's "A pure white hind appeared to me" as "Whoso list to hunt, I know where is an hind." Moreover, he replaces the virginal gloss of Petrarch's poem with a sexually predatory pursuit. The Italian version comes off as luminous and transcendent; Wyatt's English iteration connotes worry and paranoia. These differences are perhaps attributable to the woman with whom Wyatt supposedly had an affair: Queen Anne Boleyn.

Historians are uncertain whether Wyatt actually had a relationship with King Henry VIII's doomed wife, famously beheaded in 1536. The possibility, though, speaks to Wyatt's proximity to power as a courtier among the Tudors. Indeed, his sonnet is about power. "Whoso List to Hunt" takes as its subject the experience of living under the control of an all-powerful state. This is arguably the theme of all Wyatt's verse and a theme prevalent in much poetry of the period. One need only read Stephen Greenblatt's recent book *Tyrant: Shakespeare on Politics* (2018), which investigates the ways in which the Bard explores questions of political absolutism, for examples of such concerns in the literature of the age. Wyatt's closeness to the centers of power, however, and his implication in their crimes, gives his voice unique personal authority. He is the first great poetic explicator of totalitarianism, and his writing records the conscience of one individual grappling with radically dangerous politics. Placing him fully in his own era allows him to speak to the anxieties of our own.

In his poems, Wyatt explores everything from lost love and the male ego ("They Flee From Me") to political cynicism ("Mine own John Poynz") to aspirations of national greatness ("Tagus, Farewell"), but regardless of subject, his chief literary moods are anxiety and ambivalence. True to these emotions, Wyatt was both a victim and a collaborator in a new kind of political system: the totalitarian state. The sixteenth century may have been the golden age of English literature, but it also fostered an increasingly draconian monarchy. During Wyatt's career, the Tudor dynasty had ruled over England for only a generation, and the family's ascendancy was built on shaky claims, born from Henry VII's famed defeat of the final Plantagenet king, Richard III, in 1485. The second Tudor king's reign was primarily marked by Henry's separation from the Roman Catholic Church and the establishment of an independent, national Protestant church. Parliamentary legislation and royal decrees between 1532 and 1534 contributed to rapid changes across almost every aspect of life, from demographics to religious reform. Overseeing it all was an increasingly centralized government that both employed and punished Wyatt. As his most recent biographer, Nicola Shulman, notes in *Graven with Diamonds: The Many Lives of Thomas Wyatt: Poet, Lover, Statesman and Spy in the Court of Henry VIII* (2011), "Wyatt, like Mandelstam or Akhmatova, was a poet writing under tyranny, who might yield insights into life under the Tudor Stalin." Wyatt's great theme is the very modern subject of the individual's moral ambiguity when implicated under an oppressive power.

Wyatt was the product of an age that Greenblatt describes in *Renaissance Self-Fashioning* (1980) as "dominated by a ruthless despot and pervaded by intrigue and envy." Indeed, Wyatt's age was marked by secrecy, paranoia, treachery, and the delicate dance between subversion and complicity. In the twentieth century, the German philosopher Walter Benjamin observed that "there is no document of culture which is not at the same time a document of barbarism." This is especially true (albeit retroactively) in Wyatt's lyrics. Consider a Wyatt poem that, like all the verse written in his lifetime, was preserved only in manuscript (in this case included in a collection known as the *Devonshire Manuscript*).

To counterfeit a merry mood
In mourning mind I think it best,
But once in rain I wore a hood
Well were they wet that barehead stood.
But since that cloaks are good for doubt
The beggar's proverb find I good:
Better a path than a hall out.

These lyrics concern the guile that's sometimes necessary to survive – the guile of counterfeiting "a merry mood" in which pantomime, deception (of self and others), and obsequiousness may help one avoid the axe. (It's all the more important to counterfeit such emotions in "mourning mind," with a pun on the adjective because morning was the traditional time for executions, and a merry mood the only possible insult against the executioner.) Wyatt was a sometimes-trusted adviser to Henry VIII and was part of a failed 1527 mission to Rome to convince the pope of the king's right to annul his marriage to his first wife, Catherine of Aragon, and marry Boleyn. The poet's commitment to the Tudor monarchy also implicated him in a later unsuccessful plot to assassinate Reginald Pole, an English cardinal who almost became pope himself. But Wyatt could be Henry's victim too, imprisoned twice on murky charges and always at risk of punishment. (Fellow poet Henry Howard was the last man executed before Henry died in 1547). How history should judge Wyatt is debatable. Even the poet himself writes that "cloaks are good for doubt," and when in rain he "wore a hood," making it difficult to determine whether he means the costume of the executioner or the executed.

In *Writing Under Tyranny: English Literature and the Henrician Reformation*, Greg Walker notes that writers were "forced back upon their own intellectual resources in wholly new and more urgent ways." But was the Tudor regime totalitarian in the modern sense? Political philosopher Eric Voegelin, a refugee from Nazi Germany, thought so. In the fifth volume of his *History of Political Ideas*, he describes Henry's regime as the "first totalitarian state." Henry consolidated and bureaucratized power while also eliminating rival claimants, such as an independent church. With the separation from Rome, an important check on Henry's power was eliminated, as all ecclesiastical authority was vested in the monarch. That's not to claim that previous monarchs were paragons of fair play – far from it.

Rather, Henry had absolute authority through a centralized legal system in which regional authorities were subsumed under Henry's increasingly absolutist rule, leading to the monopolization of its subjects' livelihoods and attention. This was an era, as Greenblatt writes, when punishment "becomes so much more protractedly and agonizingly brutal" in comparison to the "fairly straightforward executions...of the Middle Ages." Henry introduced a veritable theater of cruelty, in which the execution of men, including former advisers Thomas More and Thomas Cromwell, and of his wives Boleyn and Catherine Howard "become virtuoso performances of torture, as if the physical torment of the traitor had to correspond fully to the incorporation of power," as Greenblatt writes. Far from being a throwback, Henry was the first of a type: the totalitarian dictator.

Parliament passed legislation instrumental to the construction of this state, including the *Acts of Supremacy* and the *Treason Act of 1534*, which established Henry as being above criticism. These laws elevated the king to a position of supreme control, whereby "all honours, dignities, preeminences, jurisdictions, privileges, authorities, immunities, profits, and commodities to the said dignity" were owed to Henry. Heresy and treason were folded into each other so that anyone who would "maliciously wish, will or desire by words or writing, or by craft imagine, invent, practice, or attempt any bodily harm to be done or committed to the king's most royal person...or slanderously and maliciously publish and pronounce, by express writing or words" any opposition to the sovereign would now be labeled as "heretic, schismatic, tyrant, infidel or usurper of the crown." This was the first such law of its kind, designed, at least in part, to punish those who sang scurrilous songs about the king in taverns. No system of government demands more of those it ostensibly governs than totalitarianism. The individual has no recourse, and every subject is implicated in its oppressive machinery – "my King, my Country, alone for whom I live," as Wyatt writes in "Tagus, Farewell." After all, Wyatt had to *actually talk to the dictator*, and as Greenblatt quips, "conversation with the king himself must have been like small talk with Stalin."

Small talk had its benefits, though. In 1540, Henry "gifted" the monastery at Boxley to Wyatt in recognition of the latter's service. Still, Henry was a vain, intemperate, narcissistic ruler, prone to outbursts and retaliation and governed by a fickle nature that celebrated one day and punished the next. Wyatt was imprisoned on charges of having an affair with the queen, only to be later granted rare clemency from death. Despite being a victim of the king's mercurial nature, Wyatt apparently had no compunctions about celebrating the aspirational greatness of the Tudor regime. In "Tagus, Farewell" he writes:

> [...] that westward, with thy streams,
> Turns up the grains of gold already tried,
> With spur and sail for I go seek the Thames,
> Gainward the sun that show'th her wealthy pride,
> And to the town which Brutus sought by dreams,
> Like bended moon doth lend her lusty side.
> My King, my Country, alone for whom I live,
> Of mighty love the wings for this me give.

Recalling the diplomatic work he did in Spain on Henry's behalf (the Tagus is a river in that country), Wyatt evokes the mighty Spanish Empire's colonial magnificence, storehouses of Aztec and Incan "grains of gold" lining the coffers of King Charles V. Regardless of Spain's grandeur, Wyatt sees the future as belonging to Britain, for he can turn his back on the Tagus and "seek the Thames," which "Gainward the sun that show'th her wealthy pride,/And to the town which Brutus sought by dreams." Wyatt invokes as his muse the mystical Brutus, the Trojan founder of Britain who was appropriated from legend to sing of future English greatness. Crucially, the myth of Brutus was central in justifying Britain's ecclesiastical independence, and he was enlisted in legal opinions claiming Britain's separate religious founding from Rome. Wyatt may be on a government mission to Toledo in the poem, but the Spanish capital's magnificence doesn't impress him, for the

Tagus flows westward, the direction of dusk and death, and the Thames flows eastward toward youth and promise. Wyatt's protestation that his European travels are for "my King, my Country, alone for whom I live" places an extreme emphasis on loyalty, so much so that "anxiety sweats from every line," as Shulman writes. And with good reason.

"Tagus, Farewell" was composed in the context of Wyatt's nefarious intelligence work for the king, such as the aforementioned conspiracy to assassinate Cardinal Pole, a Catholic exile from England who had a legitimate claim to the throne and who was an anti-Protestant leader. But Wyatt knew how erratic Henry could be. Only three years earlier, the poet had been imprisoned on charges of infidelity and cuckoldry (with Boleyn). If "Tagus, Farewell" was circulated among other members of the court to exalt Henry, then more private poems indicate Wyatt's deeper ambivalence. During his lifetime, a close-knit group of courtiers traded the handwritten manuscripts of Wyatt's poems, reading them as part of courtly practice rather than as art for art's sake. Wyatt wrote verse to demonstrate his skill and erudition in the shifting world of political intrigue. In that context, the purpose of "Tagus, Farewell" is clear. Even more interesting, however, are the lyrics that weren't widely distributed or included in the miscellany of Wyatt's work, published fifteen years after his death. Many of these lyrics are found in the *Devonshire Manuscript*, mostly compiled by three women who were attendants to Boleyn, which is the most significant anthology of Wyatt's uncollected poems. Among the most remarkable is one titled "Who list his wealth and ease retain." Reflecting on his time in the Tower, with Boleyn and condemned men in nearby cells, Wyatt writes:

The bell tower showed me such sight
That in my head sticks day and night.

There did I learn out of a grate,
For all favour, glory, or might,
That yet *circa Regna tonat*.

The Latin epistrophe – *"circa regna tonat"* – can be loosely translated as "thunder rolls about the kingdom," an invocation of a nation in disarray. That's a far cry from Wyatt's reference to "the town which Brutus sought by dreams." In blunt and chilling language, Wyatt describes his own experience of "bloody days" that have "broken my heart." No couplet is as horrifying in what it *doesn't* say as when the poet observes that the "bell tower showed me such sight/That in my head sticks day and night." Wyatt alludes to his trauma but lets readers guess what it might be. It calls to mind Matthew Zapruder's argument in *Why Poetry* (2017) that "in a poem, we feel what is there, but also what is not." Critics have argued that Wyatt witnessed the execution of the other condemned men in the courtyard of the Tower or perhaps Boleyn's decapitation. Whatever the case, Wyatt doesn't name what he witnessed nor is he at liberty to describe it, either because of his own trauma or because of expedient self-censorship.

Other lyrics in the *Devonshire Manuscript* indicate the survival lessons the poet learned while imprisoned. Mystery surrounds Wyatt's release, although most historians point to the close relationship between the poet's family and Thomas Cromwell, the king's chief minister who was ultimately executed. If Cromwell intervened, then part of the poet's role in this exoneration may be indicated by another uncirculated lyric in the *Devonshire Manuscript*. Wyatt writes that "never was file half so well filed,/To file a file for every smith's intent,/But I was made a filing instrument,/To frame other, while I was beguiled." The poem plays with ambiguities around the word *file*, which connotes both the industrial filing of metal and the modern sense of systematized paperwork. The word also prefigures the twentieth-century philosopher Hannah Arendt, who observed that administrative paperwork is at the core of totalitarianism's "banality of evil." Wyatt ultimately exonerated himself by being "made a filing instrument,/To frame others." In short, Wyatt's salvation was because he named names.

That's the moral complexity of collaborators, whether they're enthusiastic partisans or merely trying to save their own lives (Wyatt was both). Wyatt was no different from those who through compromise or cooperation find themselves both victim and perpetrator. He understood the negotiations and personal treasons that one must countenance when confronted with fickle absolute power, as displayed in another uncirculated poem, this one from the Egerton collection, another cache of Wyatt's documents. He writes of "Whom thou didst rule now ruleth thee and me./Tyrant it is to rule thy subjects so/By forced law and mutability." Perhaps with parliamentary legislation such as the *Acts of Supremacy* or *Proclamation of the Crown Act of 1539* in mind, Wyatt condemns the tyrannical disposition of "forced law, and mutability." But Wyatt's poetry is also an example of the ways in which any critic must amend, deflect, or deny his unequivocal condemnations of the "tyrant." Consider "Song 135," in which Wyatt walks back proclamations made perhaps too rashly, writing that "what I sung or spake;/Men did my songs mistake," as if accusations of Henry's tyranny were just honest misunderstandings. Poetry written in a free society can be about any subject, and even poetry written under chaotic or oppressive governments still has some latitude, but verse written in a truly totalitarian state is indelibly curtailed by the state. Wyatt's genius, a trait shared by any great poet writing under such conditions, is to convey subliminal messages.

That returns us to Petrarch's 190th sonnet. Chalking up the differences in tone between the two versions as differences in the poets' sensibilities would be easy, but the most salient distinction is that as politically tumultuous as Petrarch's era was (and an era with rival popes couldn't help but be tumultuous), Wyatt lived during the establishment of a truly modern totalitarian state. At the *volta* of both sonnets, it's revealed that the jewels "in letters plain...her fair neck round about" spell out on the hind's collar the traditional mark that branded all imperial deer owned by the Roman emperor. But the hind's declaration of her servitude to an authority far greater than that of the narrator does something more radical than merely commemorate Wyatt's rejection: it expresses a fundamental truth about authoritarianism. In the original, Petrarch writes in the vernacular: "*Nessun mi tocchi,*" which roughly translates to "Let no one touch me," but Wyatt skirts blasphemy by translating that clause into the Vulgate Latin, writing in his sonnet's penultimate line that the collar was inscribed "*Noli me tangere,* for Caesar's I am."

Wyatt quotes John 20:17, in which Jesus tells Magdalene not to touch him. Here, those words are imparted unto the king's property. Conventionally dated to either 1526 or 1527, Shulman argues the composition should be dated to 1532, given that the comment is likely a reference to Henry's new religious authority. More important, Wyatt makes a disturbing theological point, for if the hind has been bound and constrained by Caesar – if Christ has been circumscribed by Henry – then all authority has been collapsed into one man, one power. No longer do you render unto Caesar and render unto God, but rather you render all unto Henry, for the authority of both church and state are now singularly invested in him. His state is totalizing, he is the object of faith, and as in any totalitarian state, his will cannot be ignored. Henry's was a rewriting of divine authority, a transition so complete that by 1559, when his daughter Elizabeth I ruled, a Protestant polemicist could confidently write that "God is English."

The darkest implication of the language is that Christ belongs to Caesar, and by proxy, all of Caesar's subjects do too. They all should have "Caesar's I am" tattooed around their necks.

Thus the absolutist logic of the Fascist, for whom all subjects are property. Indeed, it'd be fair for Wyatt to have about his neck a constraint reading "Henry's I am." That's the despairing lesson of all poetry produced with collars around their creators' throats. All of Wyatt belonged to Caesar: his complicity and subversion, his collaboration and victimization, his career and punishments, his triumphs and abjection, the very poetry he wrote.

Here I Stand; I Can Do No Other

There is no time more appropriate than the 500th anniversary of Martin Luther (which passed last month) nailing his complaint to the Wittenberg Cathedral door to admit that this Catholic is a bit of a Protestant. Or "Protestant," rather. You see, I'm surprised to have acquired this self-designation because I was not raised in any Protestant denomination. Not to mention that when it comes to the theological postulates of the Reformation, such as salvation through faith alone or a reliance on scripture over tradition, I am entirely emotionally unmoved.

This piece will not be a conversion narrative; I have no road to Damascus moment, no account of being "born again" while holding hands aloft at some revival. I don't subscribe to any of the multitude of Protestant theologies, from Calvinism to Arminianism, and I'm not an adherent of any of those confessions named after places like Augsburg and Westminster. By no standard definition could I be considered a literal Protestant (save for perhaps according to some of the most liberal flavors). So, in what sense can a guy who was nominally raised as a Catholic, and who now considers himself to be culturally Catholic, or Post-Christian (or whatever), claim to also be *Protestant?*

Well, it's easy. Because I'm a "Protestant," you're a Protestant, Barack Obama and Donald Trump are Protestants, and maybe even Pope Francis is a "Protestant." Some traditionalist Catholics might enthusiastically assent to my last example, but don't misconstrue my snark. I'm not condemning, merely observing. Because in 2017 everyone, regardless of denomination, or even whether or not they consider themselves to be a Christian (or a theist for that matter) is now a "Protestant" of a sort. There are Catholic Protestants, Jewish Protestants, Muslim Protestants, atheist Protestants, sometimes even Protestant Protestants – Protestants all.

Luther's redefinition of religion was so complete and total, that we're all basically working from his template. In privileging faith over ritual and practice, Luther made creeds paramount, and in the process, religion inadvertently became something separate from the rest of culture. For better and for worse, modernity is in large part the result of the Reformation, and as children of modernity, divergent though we may be in theology and perspective, we can't help but also be children of Luther. This is not a position that I arrive at lightly, and I should confess that as an uneasy child of modernity I wear this mantle of counterfeit Protestantism uncomfortably as well. Growing up in Pittsburgh, one of the most Catholic cities in the United States, it certainly didn't feel like I was Protestant, particularly because until I was an adolescent, I'm not even entirely sure if I knew what one was. The vast majority of my friends were Catholic or Jewish, the smattering of Protestants tended towards High Church affectations and thus the difference didn't register.

But although I didn't become a Protestant, during my academic training I still caught the Reformation-bug as it were, and since then I have become a particularly unlikely specialist in Puritanism. Telling people who sit next to you on a plane that you spend your time reading and writing about the hell-fire sermons of Cotton Mather and Jonathan Edwards has proven to be an effective way to enjoy a quiet flight. But in addition to discovering a handy way of silencing chatty seat-mates, I also developed my contention that Luther, John Calvin, and the other reformers so indelibly altered how we think about religion that they initiated a veritable revolution in belief, and that as the result of that aftermath we can't help but all be Protestantism's heirs.

We often approach texts in light of Luther's rallying cry of "Scripture alone" and we celebrate a cult of individualism derived from his "Priesthood of all Believers." Especially in the United States, we prioritize belief as the most important element in religion – echoing his call for "Faith alone" – while minimizing the significance of tradition, ritual, and even ethics. In everyday life, people may be religious or not, but the definition of religion that they're working from is often Luther's. The questions of reformers settled at Augsburg, Speyer, and Dort, or by their opponents at Trent, matter much less now than they did in an era where people were willing to go to war over how to interpret the Eucharist. That we mostly no longer kill each other over questions concerning salvation is unequivocally good. And though few men were as certain of their theological positions as was Luther, it was arguably the radical potential at the core of a "Priesthood of all Believers" which ultimately made strict enforcement of religious conformity impossible.

If Luther made "faith alone," *sola Fide,* the center of his theology, then in some ways we've moved beyond faith to prioritizing how religion makes us feel. Ours is the era of "feeling alone," of a *sola Affectus.* Arriving at this point has been part of a long process, inadvertently initiated by Luther. On this 500th anniversary he would be loath to see what the Reformation inadvertently wrought, after all one of the criticisms of Luther during the Counter-Reformation was that his theology would lead to a type of spiritual anarchism, with every person a religion unto themselves. But, they were correct in that, if wrong about the disastrous repercussions. In separating religion from culture, Luther made the former a matter of private conscience, so in truth everyone can be the prophet of their own religion, author of their own gospel, priest of their own church. A spiritual anarchism I zestfully embrace; for though I remain unmoved by virtually all of the details of his theology, it is by being a priest in Luther's church of all believers that it is possible for me to reject the rest of him, as I see fit. And so on this 500th Reformation Day I give thanks to Luther, as a faithful "Protestant."

A Time to Mourn, and a Time to Dance: The Last Carnival

"Whiche voyde of wysdome as men out of theyr mynde
Them selfe delyte to daunce to lepe and skyp
In compase rennynge lyke to the worlde wyde
In vnkynde labour, suche folys pleasour fynde."
Sebastian Brant, Ship of Fools (1494)

"Calling out around the world
Are you ready for a brand-new beat
Summer's here and the time is right
For dancing in the street."
Martha and the Vandellas, "Dancing in the Street" (1964)

On July 14, 1518, Frau Troffea began to dance in Strasbourg's central marketplace. This otherwise unremarkable Alsatian woman began to kick up her legs and flail her arms rhythmically to some unheard music. She did so for six days, stopping only to briefly sleep, before her frenzied dancing would resume. By the end of the week she would be joined by three dozen fellow dancers. By the end of the month the crowd had swelled to 400 women and men.

A strange, eerie, and disturbing carousing, whereby sufferers were seemingly compelled to hold a never-ending carnival. The surreal horror of the uncontrollable, entranced, ring dances was succinctly described in plain detail by a contemporaneous, anonymous poet as quoted by medical historian John Waller in his indispensable *The Dancing Plague*: "There was a very strange obsession at/that time/Among the people/Many people started out of nonsense/To dance/By day and by night/Without stopping/Until they fainted/And many died."

Strenuousness in the endeavor meant that dancers were

continually expiring – from exhaustion, from injury, from heart attacks. An average of fifteen a day died from the rapidly spreading "plague." Whether hysteria, delusion, mass psychosis, trance, or something else, dancing plagues had reoccurred throughout Europe from the twelfth-century through the decades after the outbreak of 1518. That cracked festival, whose 500th anniversary we mark this summer, was the second largest incident on record, and the largest after the invention of the printing press. Guttenberg's device spread the news of said marathon throughout Alsace, the Rhineland, and the Low Countries (which all saw their own outbreaks), in turn inspiring new flares of this psychic contagion.

In 1526, the physician Theophrastus von Hohenheim, whom posterity remembers as Paracelsus, scoured the city archives for data to be used in his pragmatically titled *Diseases That Rob Men of Their Senses*. It was in that volume where he categorized the dance mania as *"chorea lasciva,"* and its sufferers as "choreomaniacs." The affliction, Paracelsus noted, was marked by dance that was "free, lewd, impertinent, full of lasciviousness without fear or respite." Strasbourg had been stricken with the "voluptuous urge to dance."

Consider a smaller outbreak of chorea lasciva, decades later in 1564 at Molenbeek in Flanders, as depicted by the Netherlandish painter Pieter Brueghel. A disquieting scene – at the edges of the painting are two peasant women in bonnet, skirt, and apron, held upright by men on either side of them preventing their collapse; mouths agape, faces contorted, clogged feat kicking in a jig. Between the pair are two musicians, nervously looking over their shoulders as they play the bagpipes. The infernal circle, with perhaps dozens more unseen, rotate about a thicket of brambles or thistles, with the yellowing grass of autumn giving an infernal, golden glow.

Bagpipers are not without precedent, for as Waller explains, physicians during the earlier outbreak in Strasbourg had moved the dancers to guildhalls and paid professional musicians to play droning music on "tambourines, drums, fiddles, fifes, pipes, and horns," with the logic that they'd be able to exhaust the dancers. A serious mistake, for as Waller notes in an article for the British medical journal *The Lancet,* "nothing could have been better calculated to turn the dance into a full-scale epidemic than making its victims perform their dances in the most public of spaces. The authorities turned a crisis into a nightmare scenario worthy of a canvas by Hieronymus Bosch."

Breughel's painting can scarcely impart the full nightmare of Strasbourg's dance plague, when what was typically joyful was transformed into something hellish. The gaping mouths and spinning eyes, arms and legs akimbo, leather shoes in bloody tatters and broken bones, the stench of evacuated bowels, piss, and puke upon the straw floor as dancers refused relief and harried musicians marched out tunes in 6/8 tarantella time. Brueghel may have painted the plague, but there is something more generally of the *danse macabre* about the epidemic; that medieval conceit which depicted grinning, grimacing, laughing skeletons in a strained embrace, circling about, and about, and about in a frenzied and eternal dance.

Before summer's end it would subside. Frau Troffea, who as the first patient was what epidemiologists call an "index case," would be ultimately sent by her horrified husband to a shrine dedicated to St. Vitus, the patron saint of dancers. Similar ecclesiastical solutions ultimately soothed the souls and soles of revelers, many of whom believed that the ancient martyr had cursed Strasbourg. Contemporary physicians like Paracelsus had their own diagnoses, often with recourse to the classical authority Gallen's humoral theory, hypothesizing that an infusion of "hot blood" was responsible for the affliction. Our present etiologies can be similarly lacking. Historians of medicine have conjectured that the mania was due to some kind of collective epilepsy, or mass poisoning by the hallucinogenic fungus ergot.

Most experts find these theories to be unconvincing; the arrhythmic, nervous twitching of ergotism is unlike the coordinated *dancing* of the choreomaniacs, with Waller emphasizing that "No chemical or biological agent known to sixteenth-century Europe could have impelled Frau Troffea... to dance for several grueling days." Connections are made between northern European dance manias and southern Italian tarantism, the practice of frenzied dancing to nullify the venom of spider bites. Regarding such comparisons, Barbara Ehrenreich in *Dancing in the Street: A History of Collective Joy* reasons that "rye does not grow in Italy, nor do tarantulas menace Germans," concluding that nothing ingested has been "found to induce anything resembling dancing mania." Witnessing the Strasbourg pandemonium, and without better explanation, the German humanist Otto Brunfuls compared it to a variant of ancient Dionysian cults that would drunkenly rampage, remarking "What else is it but Korybantism...when, transported into delirium, they were led to dance in union without cease?"

Waller observes in *The Lancet* that the "victims of the dancing epidemics...[experienced] altered states of consciousness...[as] indicated by their extraordinary levels of endurance. In a trance state, they would have been far less conscious of their physical exhaustion" and pain. By that score, Brunfuls' hypothesis has surprising merit, for the participants in their trances appear as like the Maenads whom the humanist invoked. Epidemiologists have proffered many a materialist hypotheses, perhaps it's time to put the ghost back into the machine as it were, and consider that both God and the devil have their role in such hellish festivities?

Anxieties of an uncertain era naturally led to mass hysteria. Alsace had been illuminated with strange portents in the sky and terrorized by the genital sores of the new disease syphilis, which seemed to judge sexual improprieties. Strasbourgeois were buffeted by famine and peasant rebellion, by accounts of the twisted bodies of monstrous progeny and of the Ottomans pushing on the eastern edge of Europe. The Holy Roman Empire was inundated with apocalyptic pamphlets, which included apocryphal accounts of mass armies of the Purgatorial dead rampaging across Germany, some holding their severed limbs, some holding their severed heads. Christendom itself was on the verge of mutilation, as Martin Luther had initiated his Reformation only nine months earlier, the very world turned upside down. Society itself seemed to mimic the chaos of the medieval Shrovetide which saw the ordination of an Abbot of Unreason or the coronation of a Lord of Misrule. Should it be any wonder then, this state of eternal carnival? For the subjects of Strasbourg, the Abbot of Unreason found a home within their very minds, the Lord of Misrule residing in their souls.

Scottish journalist Charles Mackay contends in his 1841 classic *Extraordinary Popular Delusions and the Madness of Crowds* that during times of social disarray we "find that whole communities...become simultaneously impressed with one delusion, and run after it," or rather dance after it. With such uncertainty, Europeans experienced the simultaneous birth and death pangs of two different eras, where Waller claims choromania as a "hysterical reaction...one that could only have occurred in a culture steeped in a particular kind of supernaturalism," but which "also makes sense in the context of our irrational fears and beliefs."

Collective delusions can be triggered by collective anxieties, but what unnerves is that the Strasbourgeois should in particular dance. Could one not envision a mass psychosis of group crying, or praying, or laughing – as indeed the latter occurred at a boarding school in 1963 Tanzania? What is it about dancing, about Brunful's "Korybantism," that in particular drew hundreds to rotate in ring and *reigen*, kept in tempo by the beat of *jongleurs*? Dance, like all things universal, has something exceedingly odd about it. That is the great contribution of Strasbourg's condemned; they have defamiliarized a practice so intimate and shared and made it strange to us, and terrifying too. Waller claims that chorea lascivia conveys "an important truth: that the dancing manias could not have happened had it not been for the potential strangeness inherent in all of us." There is a cracked value in that.

Virtually any activity, especially one as widespread as dance, can be made novel if viewed from the proper perspective, and there can be something eerie in the rhythmic, ritualized, choreographed, social movements of humans. Ehrenreich observes that uncanny attribute of being "so aroused by watching others dance that we have a hard time keeping ourselves from jumping in." Something is unique in dance, leading the occult writer Aldous Huxley to note that "Ritual dances provide a religious experience that seems more satisfying and convincing than any other...It is with their muscles that humans most easily obtain knowledge of the divine," while remembering that the transcendent has origins in directions both above and below.

Strasbourg appears as a fairy tale, there is the whiff of allegory about their revels, but the dance plague is neither fairy tale nor allegory – it actually happened. If we're to derive any symbolic significance from the few hundred peasants who literally danced themselves to death, it's in seeing their cruel, self-inflicted pantomime of joy as the last carnival, that subversive holiday that scholars Peter Stallybrass and Allon White celebrate in The Politics and Poetics of Transgression as that which "attacks the authority of the ego...and flaunts the material body as a pleasurable grotesquerie – protuberant, fat, disproportionate, open at its orifices."

On the brink of modernity, with its attendant children of Protestantism and positivism, capitalism and colonialism, these old modes of the ecstatic divine were going extinct. Ehrenreich notes that people had to be "transformed into a disciplined, factory-ready, working class…[for there] was money to be made from reliable, well-regulated, human labor," and in this world the "old recreations and pastimes represented the waste of a valuable resource." No longer would revels fit into a system designed for efficiency; no longer would feasts be allowed to turn the world upside down. Now joy must be commodified and turned into another product, another aspect of the vast, parsimonious machine that was then being constructed.

What was called for, and delivered, was such an enigmatic "celebration" to mark this transition, by engaging in a grotesque imitation. That is the context for those contorted bodies and tortured faces. Ultimately, the dance plague of Strasbourg was the wake for that old world. In their agony, they performed a paradoxical mimicry of *Fastnacht*; from their movements there is an inscrutable and terrible wisdom, whereby the ecstasies of collective joy would be purged in one last carnival, though horrible and twisted, before the long Lent of modernity.

A New Reformation

October 31 marks the quincentenary of a certain Augustinian monk nailing his ninety-five theses to a church door in Wittenberg, Germany – a perfect moment to consider having a repeat. Pundits often claim that Islam needs its own Reformation. But maybe all of us – Christian and non-Christian, believer and non-believer – would benefit from a New Reformation, one that changes our sense of what the word "religion" means. Present conditions indicate that we might be on the verge of another Reformation anyhow.

In some ways, Martin Luther's world was not so different from ours. In 1517, old certainties were failing, and politics was in turmoil. New discoveries transformed understanding, and poisonous nationalisms emerged. Media technology altered how people received information. And most crucially, a crisis of faith marked his world. We suffer from a similar malady, one that, ironically, was in part precipitated by that brave monk himself.

Depending on whom you ask, Luther is either to thank for liberal modernity, or to blame for the doctrinaire, literalist form much of Christianity now takes. Scholars debate the details of the Reformation, concerning both timeline and implications, but maybe it's still too early to know what Luther's full influence will be. In any case, the romance remains half a millennium later, the image of the man who bravely declared, "Here I stand; I can do no other."

Despite Luther's popular image, since the early twentieth century there has been the creeping suspicion among some thinkers that he helped set in motion the disenchantment of the West. Terry Eagleton claims that "the Protestant self moves fearfully in a darkened world of random forces, haunted by a hidden God." Eagleton argues that the Reformation altered the relationship of the sacred and the profane. We're all Protestants now, in the sense that we adhere, mostly unconsciously, to the parameters that marked out Luther's understanding of religion. His emphasis on religion as defined through faith alone made creeds, confessions, and denominations more significant than they should be. A New Reformation could reinvigorate practice, ritual, and culture over mere propositional belief, and in the process allow for a more expansive definition of religion.

Luther's call for "Scripture alone" ultimately privileged literalist reading, which led to fundamentalism. Literalism isn't the relic of a barbaric medieval past but the consummate product of modernity. Literary scholar James Simpson describes the method of reading advocated by the early Protestants as "immensely demanding and punishing...marked by literalist impersonality." Medieval thinkers were at home with allegory, but that way of reading is now minimized, and instead an idol is made out of "original intent," whether in the Bible or elsewhere.

Finally, with his insistence on the interior disposition of the individual soul and its unmediated relation to God, Luther inadvertently weakened the connection between meaning and the world. Philosophers Hubert Dreyfus and Sean Dorrance Kelly explain that "Reform Christianity had the effect of emphasizing the individual as defined by his inner thoughts and desires at the expense of...worldly meanings outside the individual," with the result that Luther accidentally "prepared the way for the active nihilism associated with the death of God."

For all that was valuable about Luther's rebellion – and even most Catholics would now admit that he had good reasons for his dissatisfaction with Rome – let's also acknowledge that the Reformation introduced ways of thinking about faith that make it narrower and more rigid than it should be. I am not arguing that we must return to primitive Christianity, as Luther claimed he had. Nor am I arguing for a return to some faux-medieval tableaux of relics, pilgrimages, and liturgical celebrations. The bare ruined choirs will remain empty. There is no going back;

there is no undoing or escaping modernity.

And yet, as a growing crisis of meaning seems ever more apparent, it's fair to ask what can possibly come next? The literary historian Andrew Delbanco says that in contemporary society "the ache for meaning goes unrelieved" and an "unslaked craving for transcendence" seems almost universal. Where there are aches, there are eventually analgesics; where there is craving, there must eventually be sustenance. The issue, then, isn't whether there should be a New Reformation, but rather what kind of Reformation it will be. Will it be a retreat to the pleasures of certainty, a doubling-down on literalism? Or will it offer new possibilities for sacred meaning, and even perhaps re-enchantment? Could it challenge the idols of our age, including the Market? The truth is I don't know. I have no theses to nail to any church doors. But that a shift in religious consciousness is necessary to address the maladies that confront us, from ecological collapse to authoritarianism, I heartily affirm – for I can do no other.

Robert Greene, the First Bohemian

The only known image of the dramatist, poet, pamphleteer, and initially unrepentant libertine Robert Greene is a woodcut from John Dickenson's *Greene in Conceipt*, printed in 1598, six years after its subject had died an early death at the age of thirty-four. Dickenson's book pretends to be a posthumous publication of the still infamous raconteur, bawd, and wit; the frontispiece depicts Greene as bundled up in his death shroud, a cloth topknot twisted off at the peak of his head. He sits in an ornate chair, hunched over a book in which he is scribbling desperately. Greene seemingly needs to write as much as possible before his untimely expiration; it is an image of the debauched bohemian penning some sort of confession for his wanton, drunken, scurrilous ways. His bearded face pokes through the death shroud like a woman peeking out through a babushka, and he has a look of dour concern, as if he is aware that his gossipy printed accusations against colleagues, his addiction to sack, his whoring, his mistreatment of his family, and his prolific writing for money has led to the sick dissolution he finds himself in. He perhaps is worried about a worse punishment in the hereafter. Yet the woodcut is amateurish in a way that makes it inadvertently hilarious: the viewer is able to see under the table-clothed desk that Greene writes upon, yet his legs are not visible, making one wonder if he is without them, or if they are simply very stubby. His arms are thin and awkward-looking, and the bundled death shroud gathered about his figure acts less like the *memento mori* the artist no doubt intended it to, but instead makes Greene appear to be nothing so much as a particularly erudite, sentient onion.

Greene has recently had a resurgence in scholarly interest, in part because he was no slouch of a writer. His 1589 *Friar Bacon and Friar Bungay* is a rarely performed gem of the early English theater, engaging themes of magic, power, and vanity, and if it is not the equal of Marlowe's *Doctor Faustus*, it is at least a worthy companion piece to it. In the play, Greene fictionalizes the career of the infamous medieval Franciscan (and precursor to a modern scientist) Roger Bacon and his attempts to build a massive, divinatory, conscious bronze head. The piece is thematically fascinating from our contemporary standpoint and deserves more critical attention than it has received, not least because the bronze head is evocative of a digital artificial intelligence, while the friar's attempts to encircle Britain in a massive brass wall remind one of current security state paranoia.

In addition to his dramatic career, during his short life Greene produced twenty-five prose works, in which he established himself as a London literary character whose personality was as commodified as his actual writing, and whose seemingly outrageous and sinful lifestyle was a promotional measure for his pamphlets. Professional writing was a completely new concept in late Elizabethan England, and though playwrights and poets like Jonson certainly had a knack for self-advertising, they still craved the respectability of aristocratic patronage, and sometimes displayed a wariness about the so-called "stigma of print." Greene didn't exhibit the same uneasiness: he pumped out books at an astonishingly prolific rate. Dr Johnson famously said that only an idiot would write for a reason other than money; if this is the case, then Robert Greene was a very smart man, even if his lifestyle was sometimes more threadbare than he would have liked.

As with any writer whose oeuvre is as wide and diverse as his, Greene's output can be of spotty quality. He developed a reputation for desiring notoriety more than fidelity to artistic vision, and yet in this he prefigures the professional writers of subsequent generations, and also the bohemians with whom his name is so often associated. It's true that bohemianism is a nineteenth-century affectation, drawing its name from the

1851 novel *La Vie de Bohème* by Henri Murger and celebrated by Giacomo Puccini's 1896 opera *La boheme*. It could be argued that the sort of marginal, transgressive, romantic lifestyle attached to art itself requires the deprivations and degradations of a capitalist economy to really develop, something that was nascent in Greene's day. And in a more practical sense, one could think that Greene's own crass devotion to making money from cheap print was a rejection of the utopian aestheticism embraced by true bohemians. This, however, would be a mistake: if anything, Greene's grubby, opportunistic attitude towards literary work, coupled with his public persona as an outcast, makes it hard not to see him as a consummate bohemian. This is not in spite of, but precisely because of, his higher education. A recipient of an MA from Cambridge, Greene was labeled alongside other dramatists such as Christopher Marlowe, Thomas Kyd, and John Lyly as a "University Wit," something that he could be overwhelmingly elitist about.

If anything, bohemianism from the French symbolists to the Lost Generation to the Beats didn't just accept a certain elitism, but thrived on it. The bohemian is after all separate from the stultifying strictures of bourgeois or square society. Central to this vision – whether you're Rimbaud in the steep, crooked lanes of Montmartre, or Allen Ginsberg in the alleyways of Greenwich Village – is a sense of slumming it. Greene was a good Cambridge man, getting drunk in taverns and whorehouses, denouncing fellow writers in print, and greedily pawing the returns from his work. This doesn't contradict his classification as a bohemian; it confirms it.

With the incantatory and psychedelic style of *Friar Bacon and Friar Bungay*, the university training, and the rows of smudged pamphlets bringing bank into Greene's pockets (which ensured another hungover morning) he resembles a sort of early modern William S. Burroughs. Like Greene, Burroughs was also slumming it and his avant-garde novels with lurid covers and names like *Junky* and *Queer* could be found lining the magazine stalls of mid-century Grand Central and Penn Station. These twentieth-century cheap paperbacks with their primary colored illustrations of leggy dames and muscular young men are the equivalent of Greene's "coney-catching" pamphlets, which provided the respectable with the secrets of rakish and criminal life much as Burroughs told the middle-class tales of *anomie* among the marginalized addicts and perverts of New York.

Greene titillates readers with stories about "coney-catching" (a euphemistic metaphor for theft; a "coney" was an early modern term for a rabbit), and cut-pursing, which involved literally cutting open someone's bag without them noticing. In his accounts Greene reports the exploits of seedy, dissolute Londoners for his respectable audiences in a glassy and journalistic tone, supposedly narrating in a repentant voice, but with a sense that a bit of the amoral still clings to its supposedly reformed author.

Greene's most famous work is *A Groatsworth of Wit Bought with a Million of Repentance*. It is in a manner a conversion narrative. Yet unlike John Bunyan or John Wesley, Robert Greene has one eye open while he is in penitential prayer. Reformation audiences were like modern evangelicals, they loved a good sinner's tale, and Greene knew how to lay it on thick. *A Groatsworth of Wit* combines several modes together: fable, poetry, and memoir are exhibited in the relatively short text, reflecting the promiscuous relationship between fiction and non-fiction that was so popular in Renaissance romance.

The pamphlet purports to be the story of two brothers, Roberto and Lucanio, and their time spent with a courtesan named Lamilia. Her name is evocative of the succubus Lamia, a beautiful daemon and muse of classical mythology (enshrined in John Keats' poem of 1820). Upon the death of their father, industrious Lucanio is left the entirety of the inheritance, and Roberto, who is a lay-about, loafing, forever speculating scholar, gets only a groat. After a night of storytelling, songs, and sexual innuendo supplied by Lamilia, Roberto attempts to conspire with the courtesan to fleece his own brother. She betrays Roberto's confidences and he is cast out. He eventually meets an actor who convinces him of the financial possibilities of the theater. Soon Roberto becomes a successful playwright, while Lucanio spends all of his money on Lamilia and ends up working as a pimp.

Ultimately, Roberto's bohemian excess leaves him sick, dying, and broke. While waiting to die, he writes about several playwrights he has known, and warns anyone who may be interested in working in theaters about the perils in encountering these figures, judged to be every bit as nefarious as the courtesans and pimps of Lamilia's den of iniquity. He writes of a famous dramatist guilty of atheism who many assume to be Marlowe, of a modern Juvenal who it is hypothesized is Thomas Nash, and of a third acquaintance driven to "extreme shifts" to survive, and which it has been conjectured may refer to George Peele.

Eventually Greene, rather predictably, reveals that the story which has been told is actually his own. He bemoans how being a Southwark dramatist has doomed his morals and health. Greene unconvincingly asks for repentance, and writes in feigned fear of his impending death. As is the narrative convention of the conversion tale, the reader is treated to some juicy details of not just "Roberto" Greene's life, but indeed of his interactions with the increasingly famous members of bohemian London. In this way, Greene basically invented the gossipy celebrity tell-all, just as trashy as a tabloid account about the predilections and peccadillos of the inhabitants of Sunset Boulevard. Greene's pamphlet may have contained a plea for salvation, but he wasn't going to go to hell before settling some scores.

Greene, Marlowe, Nash, and Peele were all college-educated and represented an upwardly mobile intelligentsia that was reshaping English society by finding success through intellectual acumen and not just aristocratic connection. For though they were men denied their "groatsworth," that is, not aristocrats, they were still classically educated, firm in their Greek and Latin, and conversant with traditional culture. Greene reveled in the exploits of the degenerate in his coney-catching pamphlets, but he was resentful of those he viewed as outside his class having the hubris to see themselves as capable producers of culture (even though his own academic record at Cambridge was less than impressive).

Greene's chief target was "an upstart Crow," who "supposes he is as well able to bombast out a blank verse as the best of you." Readers would have understood the "upstart Crow" to be an actor – crows being mere mimics of actual voices and having no language of their own. As an "upstart" he would be one whose young age betrays his ambition as arrogant and naïve. That this actor-turned-playwright "supposes" he is able to "bombast out a blank verse" (the alliteration of the line being slightly ridiculous and also mimicking the explosive "bombast" and arrogance of this writer), belies the fact that this upstart crow is simply a "Johannes factotum," that is a "Johnny Do-It-All," or a Jack-Of-All-Trades (and master of none).

This Johnny-Do-It-All has beautified his verse "with our feathers." He has appropriated the "mighty-line" of Marlowe's unrhymed iambic pentameter with blustery confidence (though he is a mere technician). He has a "tiger's heart, wrapped in a player's hyde," unable to fully escape the stigma of first playing on the stage before he would write for it. This line makes more sense when placed in some context – it's a parody London audiences would recognize – "Oh, tiger's heart wrapped in a woman's hide" – from a play called *Henry VI: Part III*. It was by an actor with the hubris to think he could write plays the equal of someone like Greene, a writer by the name of William Shakespeare.

And this playwright was popular – Greene complains that by his "own conceit" he was "the only Shake-scene" in the country. It's the earliest known written reference to Shakespeare as a playwright. Baconians, Oxfordians, and all other conspiracy theorists who doubt the veracity of Shakespeare's authorship should note that Greene didn't doubt Shakespeare was the author of his plays, he just didn't think those plays were any good. But it is Shakespeare's name, not Greene's, that history bequeathed to posterity. Jonson shared some of Greene's prejudice against the workman-like son of a glove maker from Stratford, infamously saying that Shakespeare knew "small Latin, and less Greek." And yet he also said that Shakespeare was "the soul of the age." Greene was ultimately very much of his time, which is in its own way an irreparable literary loss, for our era could be greatly enriched by him. Nobody could credibly claim that he has that talent of the playwright and poet who he so mercilessly attacked in his death-bed confession, but his verse may still be able to speak to us, perhaps even sing.

Greene could marry an educated man's verse with the poetry of the street. His poem "Weep Not, My Wanton" has the cadence and rhythm of the folk ballads which were just starting to be disseminated through cheaply printed broadsheets, some of which would be collected as Child Ballads and played as music for centuries. He writes: "Weep not, my wanton, smile upon my knee:/When thou art old there's grief enough for thee./Mother's wag, pretty boy,/Father's sorrow, father's joy." In content, theme, and scansion it reminds one of the Scottish folk ballad "Lord Randall," which would first be printed less than two decades later, and would more famously become the basis for the chorus of Bob Dylan's "A Hard Rain's A-Gonna Fall."

Indeed with its simple rhymes, its inverted parallelisms ("Father's sorrow, father's joy"), it wouldn't have been surprising if one heard a musical arrangement of this in a Macdougal Street bar or a coffee shop off of Canal or Houston in the late '50s and early '60s. Greene, like Dylan and all other high-culture cannibals of folk and popular culture, had an ear for everyday speech and was able to write poetry that sounds simple but not simplistic.

Greene's misanthropic pose towards the world wasn't new – his lyric from a poem included in *A Groatsworth of Wit* that reads "Deceiving world, that with alluring toys/Hast made my life the subject of thy scorn" expresses an attitude that wouldn't be unfamiliar to Solomon in *Ecclesiastes*. Greene is Oscar Wilde's romantic who may be lying in the gutter but is staring at the stars. In his jaded, hurt, and bruised relationship with the world, Greene sings:

> Oft have I sung of love and of his fire;
> But now I find that poet was advised,
> Which made full feasts increase of desire,
> And proves weak love was with the poor despised;
> For when the life with food is not sufficed,
> What thoughts of love, what motion of delight,
> What pleasance can process from such a weight?

Greene knows he has talent, but now his "gifts bereft" from the "high heavens." Parnassus is inaccessible, the muse does not speak, and Greene sees "the murder of my wit." Well into his thirties, Greene wasn't a young man anymore, especially in an era that saw death call on many so much earlier than in subsequent generations. And yet there is a bit of the Romantic death in Greene as an artist whose excesses pushed him to the edge of creativity and mortality.

If the nineteenth century had Keats and Rimbaud, and the twentieth our "Club of 27" composed of rock stars who expired before infirmity, then Greene is a worthy candidate for the sixteenth century. He writes of poetic inspiration: "Because so long they lent them me to use,/And so I long their bounty did abuse." He begs unsuccessfully that: "Oh that a year were granted me to live,/And for that year my former wits restored!" He ends: "My time is loosely spent, and I undone." If we're to believe the literary critic Stephen Greenblatt, Shakespeare got his final revenge on the dead Greene when he based one of his greatest characters on him: a drunken, cowardly blowhard by the name of Falstaff.

We can't retroactively diagnose what killed Greene at the age of thirty-four. The writer Gabriel Harvey wrote that it was because of "a surfeit of pickle herring and Rhenish wine." Based on what we know of his lifestyle, cirrhosis seems not unlikely, though one can't discount the possibility of venereal disease (even if he didn't bear the trademark physical deformations or madness of syphilis). Perhaps it was a combination of causes. Poets had died young before – Philip Sidney was famously slain by a bullet at Zutphen, Henry Howard the Earl of Surrey was felled by an axe of Henry VIII, and Chidiock Tichborne, whose youth was "but a frost of cares," was executed by order of Elizabeth. But the aristocratic Sidney was a martyr for the Protestant cause in defense of the Dutch during the Eighty Years War, and the other two were killed for political and religious reasons. Greene was simply a hack writer and versifier. He is the first of a type: the artist pushed to extremes, who has the courage to go beyond the edge into excess, but who does not have the strength to return.

The brazen head in *Friar Bacon and Friar Bungay* only speaks three lines: "Time is...Time was...Time is past." Now we have new machines, more powerful than Greene's magical brazen head. Can the poets of the past speak again? Can a new brazen head proclaim that, for Greene, "Time is now"?

One Devil Too Many Amongst Them

Christopher Marlowe's eponymous classic *The Tragical History of the Life and Death of Dr. Faustus* may have premiered in 1594, but they were still talking about those first performances thirty-nine years later. The Puritan pamphleteer and ideologue William Prynne, in his massive 1633 anti-theatrical tome *Histriomastix,* recounted diabolical legends surrounding this most diabolical of plays. He reports that "to the great amazement both of the Actors and Spectators" who were "prophanely playing" in a production, that there was a "visible apparition of the Devill on the Stage." Naturally, some were "distracted with the fearful sight." The good Puritan, who would shortly be imprisoned in the Tower of London and have his ears cropped for implying in that same book that the Queen was a whore, assures us that though he was not himself familiar with such theatrical dens of iniquity, he can confirm the event's veracity as "the truth of which I have heard from many now alive, who well remember it."

This wasn't the only night when it seemed that an extra devil invited itself onto the stage as a member of the cast. A monograph written shortly after Marlowe penned the play, by someone identified only as "G.J.R," recounts that during a performance of the scene where Dr. Faustus begins his conjurations that there suddenly "was one devil too many amongst them." It seems that the hocus pocus nonsense magic of Marlowe's immense Latin learning had accidentally triggered an actual occult transaction, pulling one of Lucifer's servants from hell into our own realm. On that stage in Exeter, there among conjuring circles, chanted invocations, and the adjuring of God's love, the extras playing stock devils with caked-on red makeup and fake horns strapped to their heads suddenly had the opportunity to meet the real thing. G.J.R. informs us that "after a little pause...every man hastened to be first out of doors." A pious ending however – the actors ("contrary to their custom" as he duly informs us) spent the night in "reading and in prayer," making sure to get "out of the town the next morning." But perhaps even that is no match for the premier of the play, at the Rose Theatre in Southwark (which today lie underneath a parking garage) among taverns, brothels, and bear-baiting pits, when some in the audience claimed that they spied Mephistopheles' Master himself among the crowd, having availed himself of the opportunity to travel up to Earth and to see how accurately his old friend Kit Marlowe had presented him. No word on the review.

Of course, discounting the possibility of any immortals dwelling among us, we can't confirm the accuracy of such claims. This is in keeping with the sense that there is something of the medieval in *Dr. Faustus* with its cursed (goat-skin?) grimoires and its personified Sins, with devils and angels on shoulders tempting its main character, and demons dancing on stage. But for all of the medievalism of *Dr. Faustus*, parroting the genre of the morality play, and with its Enochian letters inscribed in Kabbalistic circles (though this sort of magic was always more Renaissance than medieval), Marlowe's text is in some ways one of our first modern plays. Furthermore, "Dr. Faustus" is our first modern man. Strung as he is between faith and doubt, insignificance and omnipotence, sin and salvation, and particularly between freedom and fate. Dr. Faustus is not a medieval man, but rather is a creature, and in part a creator, of our world. For what could be a more Faustian bargain than those contracts that gave us such immense technological power while perennially threatening us to the damnation of complete ecological collapse? In his skepticism and arrogance, but also in his total dependence and painful doubt, Faustus may be our contemporary, but the vision in which an imperfect man is given the power to sell the world seems a particularly modern one. Whiffs of sulfur are not just on those stages in Exeter and

Southwark where Marlowe dreamt of the modern world, they were also in the mustard gas factories of the first world war, the desert plains at Alamogordo, New Mexico where Oppenheimer detonated his gadget, and upon the rapidly melting Arctic ice caps. Of course I hear echoes of Dr. Faustus' screams of damnation over the last century, for "this is hell, nor am I out of it."

Performances of *Dr. Faustus* seem to have a tendency of conjuring an extra devil now and again. But evidence of those hoof-prints of Satan, and of the infernal contract he offered to that poor necromancer, skitter across the pages of history and literature – in short there have been a lot of extra devils over the years. It seems as if *Dr. Faustus,* even if grounded in that occult history of a real man who Marlowe read about, was still the play which launched a thousand others' works and burnt the topless towers of Christendom. There are of course the literary treatments – Goethe, Stephen Vincent Benét's "The Devil and Daniel Webster," Mikhail Bulgakov's *The Master and Margarita,* Thomas Mann's *Doktor Faustus,* even the baseball musical *Damn Yankees.* But supposedly real Faustian bargains are just as plentiful, from the German *Faustbuchs* of the mid-sixteenth-century which Marlowe mined for source material; to Urbain Grandier, the Satanic French priest of the seventeenth century with his devilish pact and his monastic orgies; and his contemporary the Scotsman Thomas Weir who professed to be a loyal and solemn Covenanter, but strolled the winding cobble-stoned streets of Edinburgh with Satan; to Joseph Moulton, the fearsome "Yankee Faust" of Revolutionary New Hampshire; and of course at the dusty crossroads of Highway 61 and 49 in Clarksdale, Mississippi where bluesman Robert Johnson sold his soul to the devil sometime around 1931.

Musicians in particular seem to have a bit of the Faustian about them, something mysterious in the alchemy of melody and rhythm itself. The Italian violinists Giuseppe Tartini and

Niccolò Paganini, and the French composer Phillipe Mussard, all from the eighteenth century, supposedly saw their names on contracts with the devil, and some have suggested that the minor-keyed "Gloomy Sunday," the notorious "Hungarian suicide song" written by Rezső Seress around the same time Johnson went down to the crossroads, has some of the heat of hell in it too. If Dr. Faustus is the first modern man it's because he is the first of a modern type – the artist. No longer is the individual but a conduit for the muse of the Christian God; no, now he moves to the command of a different master, whether his own consciousness or that other being. Or maybe those two are really just the same thing.

That the bohemian persona is a devilish one has of course always been a frequently acknowledged truth. All those late nights plying the creative trade, fortified with poppy, alcohol, and Christ knows what else. Dr. Faustus during the witching hour, with his leather-bound tomes and his scrying mirrors, scribbling furiously on vellum and divinating with the sacred geometry. Faustus is not a mad scientist, he is no Dr. Frankenstein, rather he is the artist – he is Marlowe himself. Marlowe – renegade, rogue, rascal – his real person unknown and unidentifiable and yet his mystique remains consummately attractive. Only seven plays to his name, compared to the thirty-eight of his competitor Shakespeare. The mighty Marlowe whose mighty-line made Shakespeare's career possible, and though Shakespeare penned five times the number of plays, consider how much greater Marlowe's batting-average is! There are some clunkers in Shakespeare's folio (whether one wants to admit it or not) when compared to the sheer concentrated dramatic energy of Marlowe, which is astounding. From 1587 to 1593 he gave us Dido, queen of Carthage pining for her Aeneas; the slinky, sly, hilarious, troubling, reptilian Barabas; blood of the martyred Huguenots flowing through the streets of Paris; terrifying Tamburlaine trampling his way across the Asian steppe into

Europe, caging kings and burning Qur'ans; Edward II laying in the arms of his lover Gaveston and dying for it; and of course Dr. Faustus himself. The plays, when considered alongside Marlowe's shocking poetry and translations, in which he played dirty Ovid next to Edmund Spenser's stately Virgil in this new feminine Augustan Age, are remarkable.

But if the creation of Dr. Faustus is one of the first modern men, in his ambiguities, contradictions, and secrets, the creator is equally among the first modern men. Marlowe, he of the supposed "School of Night," who met with Walter Raleigh and the astrologer John Dee in graveyards to summon their own extra devils. Marlowe, he who potentially shared a bed with his colleague Thomas Kyd and who declared (according to the renegade priest Richard Baines), "That all they that love not tobacco and boys are fools." Marlowe, the first real atheist who supposedly disbelieved, and who declared that Moses "was but a juggler" and that "Christ was a bastard and his mother dishonest" (also as recorded by Baines). Marlowe, possible agent of Sir Francis Walshingham's fearsome Privy Council, who performed God-knows-what-manner of subterfuge and espionage in that employ upon the continent, and who was perhaps assassinated for it. Marlowe, who was accused of nailing a threat to the door of one of London's Dutch-Protestant "Stranger Churches," written in perfect iambic pentameter and signed "Tamburlaine" (another act for which he may have been killed). Marlowe, who may have never seen the face of a God he didn't believe in, but who saw that of the Devil, and was "tormented with ten thousand hells/In being deprived of everlasting bliss." Marlowe, who was stabbed to death through the eye in a Deptford tavern over a bill (at least that was the official story). Marlowe, one of the greatest poets of his age. Marlowe, one of the greatest poets of ours as well.

There are mysteries with Marlowe the person of course, just as there are with the actual text of his masterpiece. From a quarto Text A printed in 1604 a decade after its author's murder to the longer (and funnier) Text B published four hundred years ago this year. Scholars have parsed both texts, asking which ones may more accurately match the undiscovered foul manuscripts of their author, what both versions say about religion in their respective time periods, and whether differences reflected changes in the performance of the play over time – no argument as to whether acting companies were trying to minimize accidental demon conjuration. The version from 1604 has thirty-six lines that the one of 1616 deletes, however that later printing makes up for that cut by adding 676 new lines, lengthening the whole thing by a third with a bevy of dark comic interludes. Did the first printer make some judicious editorial decisions, cutting nearly a third of the play which was later restored in Text B based presumably upon the foul papers of Marlowe? Or did the (different) printer of that subsequent version gather those 676 lines based on over twenty years of performances, elaborations added and refined by the actors themselves, such as Edward Alleyn who so consummately performed the title role night after night? Theater is after all a collaborative art, a player tries something new which works better than something old, things are improvised and discovered to improve the play, ineffective lines are abandoned – it's an exercise in living editing and revision. Drama is a creative act that has a manner of breaking free from the bounds of its creator, to get quickly out of hand and lend itself to unexpected consequences, much like the result of Dr. Faustus' contractual obligations themselves. Academics, as is their manner, have oscillated back and forth as to which version is more "authentic." For years Text A, in its brevity, its unity, and its cryptic elegance was seen as more true to Marlowe's intent. Subsequently, consensus shifted towards Text B with its slapstick and its humor, with the earlier dubbed "the bad quarto," though recent years have seen the shorter version's return to esteem. Ultimately, what the example of the blurry, ambiguous, indeterminate relationship between the two versions and their creator demonstrates is the strange and chimerical nature of creation itself. For in the collaborative endeavor of literature, the "author" has always been a bit of a fiction, for who feels so confident as to fully be able to trace and untangle those rhizomatic complexities where inspiration and the inspired are netted together as a gleaming, silver web?

One difference between the two is crucial though, as always hinging on the question of whether Faustus can or will repent – a massive theological difference. In the 1604 text it is written, "Never too late, if Faustus can repent"; the version whose 400th anniversary we mark this year records it as if "Faustus will repent." What a difference in interpretation one short syllable can make, one change of word? "Can" implies that Faustus's agency may be constrained by some larger force, while the word "will" grants the doctor the ability to choose his own course. "Can" has a connotation of helplessness, that there may be some personal actions beyond Dr. Faustus' command; while "will" preserves the possibility that the individual is still free, that he is freely choosing damnation instead of having it thrust upon him without choice.

Does Dr. Faustus admit that he is powerless? The earlier implies an endorsement of a particularly Calvinist world view, as was the ideology of the English Church in the decade that Text A was printed; the later one embraces the sense of freedom implied by the Arminian theology fashionable among the bishops of ten years later. Those debates among the Reformed divines concerned the issue of God's predestination; the medieval schoolmen had their *Fortuna,* today we have neuroscience, evolutionary psychology, social and economic base and superstructure, and the inevitable teleology of history's march forward, or downward. The tragedy is that the problem remains the same as it ever was, whether Faustus "can" or "will" repent – because the fact is that he never does. He's damned either way – whether we're to be saved or not remains just as uncertain for us as it was for him – yet perhaps already decided. In the contemporary world, since it was born four centuries ago, we've always found ourselves in Dr. Faustus' study, and it's always a half-hour before midnight. The tragedy remains not whether salvation is possible, but whether we can even try.

The Rival Poet's Lover

Richard Barnfield, the forgotten homosexual sonneteer, entered literary consciousness in 1593 as an admirer of another lettered renegade, that of the late, great, dissolute Robert Greene. Barnfield was sixteen years younger than Greene, and indeed he doesn't enter the stationer's register as a printed author until a year after the elder writer's death. It's not known if they met or not, though it was certainly possible in the small literary world that was Elizabethan London (where it is known that Barnfield did meet Edmund Spenser, Michael Drayton, and, of course, Shakespeare). With Greene's body scarcely room-temperature, Barnabe Rich penned a scurrilous pamphlet titled Greene's News from Both Heaven and Hell. The content is largely predictable from the title, and young Barnfield responded a year later with a defense of his fellow bohemian, titled Greene's Funeral.

The former pamphlet is a moralistic, denunciatory condemnation of Greene and his lifestyle, one which charges him with his own early death, and detests the lifestyle he lived and his writing which was produced from it. As is the nature of scolds, moralizers, pedants, and puritans everywhere it took a masochistic happiness in its own schadenfreude, proving that Aquinas was correct when he said that one of the chief joys of heaven was being able to enjoy the suffering of those in hell. The two pamphlets are often paired together, and indeed since textual scholarship can be an ambiguous science, there has been some scholarly uncertainty as to who should properly be attributed authorship of either essay. The evidence that Rich wrote the first pamphlet and Barnfield the latter is inexact. Indeed it has been suggested that the same author actually wrote both, first the diatribe against Greene and then his defense. There is historical precedence for this sort of thing; for example, the so-called "War of the Theaters" between Jonson and Thomas Dekker was largely concocted for marketing purposes. It's certainly possible that a canny professional writer in the 1590s would be willing to spread the literary disease of Greene's News from Heaven and Hell and to then sell its cure in the form of Greene's Funeral. One imagines that confident man that he was, Greene may have even appreciated the gambit, yet the evidence that we do have does seem to indicate separate authors.

Barnfield's work has received little respect over the years. In 1911 A.J. Bell, of the University of Victoria, demonstrated the propensity towards snarky aesthetic critique which characterized the scholarship of his era when he wrote "For Greene's Funeral less can be said, and it must be confessed that the pamphlet is almost entirely without literary value," adding that its only virtue is "the merit of brevity." And yet Bell also points out that "apart from the writings of Nashe, [it is] almost the only attempt in defense of Greene." Whatever the artistic values of Greene's Funeral it has historical importance in this, especially in terms of identifying a generic classification for the transgressive poets of the English Renaissance. If it's correct that Barnfield is the author of Greene's Funeral (and the initials listed on the printing seem to verify this) than it's a biographical thread of admiration and acknowledgment between one underappreciated poet who was influenced by another. Indeed it indicates a shadow canon, a transgressive, alternative, marginalized collection of writers pushed to the edges of English society. They were both members in a sort of fraternity of the outcaste. For if Barnfield was looking for another poet to read and take as sort of a symbolic mentor, Greene would be an exemplary figure. That Greene's Funeral, whatever its actual literary quality, is the only defense of Greene, and that it is most likely by Barnfield, evidences that the young poet was aware of his own threatened identity, and his status as someone as likely to be persecuted as the dead pamphleteer was. What Barnfield may have seen in Greene was a subversive compatriot, a fellow penitent at the limits of English society.

It's notable that otherwise the influence of Greene on Barnfield seems negligible. Indeed despite Dr. Bell's sarcastic estimation of the literary worth of Greene's Funeral, Barnfield has long been acknowledged as a generally superior poet. No less a critic than C.S. Lewis wrote in his magisterial English Literature in the Sixteenth-Century that Barnfield deserved to be categorized alongside Shakespeare as a master-poet, even if Lewis' conservative politics couldn't abide the poet's sexuality. This is how critics have traditionally handled Barnfield; he has in some sense endured as a faint murmur in scholarship, from his own day where he was respected as a Renaissance humanist poet, till the present when there has been a resurgence in interest in him. Recent scholarship has resuscitated interest with the poet, on his own terms.

Anthologies, such as The Affectionate Shepard: Celebrating Richard Barnfield, compiled by Kenneth Boris and George Klawitter, have introduced the author as a subject for critical analysis and appreciation, even if he has yet to permeate the more general consciousness. Barnfield has often constituted a sort of trade-secret among scholars, a poet who on technical acumen alone deserved to have his sonnet sequence included alongside those of canonical writers like Sidney and Shakespeare, but for whom the blatant homoerotic content all but precluded him from inclusion. In 1594, the same year that Greene's Funeral was printed, Barnfield's first major work was also published, The Affectionate Shepherd. He was only 21 years at the time, but had clearly absorbed the conventions of the pastoral mode which was so popular, accounts of shepherds living bucolic lives that are contrasted with the deprivations and decadence of the city. In The Affectionate Shepherd, Barnfield celebrated the love between the Trojan nymph Daphnis, and the hero Ganymede.

Classically-educated Britons were not unfamiliar with the conventions of homoeroticism inherited from Greek and Roman literature. Though sodomy itself was a capital crime (if rarely proven) it was understood that these tropes were utilized as a fictional conceit, a perhaps at times winking understanding that the content of these works couldn't possibly be endorsing actual sexual love between men in the contemporary world. They merely reflected an idealized version of a pagan past which had long since disappeared. Yet something in The Affectionate Shepherd disquieted both author and audience enough that Barnfield felt the need to explain in the preface of his next collection that some "did interpret The Affectionate Shepherd otherwise than in truth I meant, touching the subject thereof, to wit, the love of a shepherd to a boy." Yet while protesting that the subject of his book wasn't personal or advocating for such love, the preface from which these denials emanated was for Cynthia, with certain Sonnets, and the Legend of Cassandra where his enthusiastic dedication to William Stanley, the sixth Earl of Derby, only increased suspicions that Barnfield himself had personally known such love.

Barnfield has always existed in an awkward position in literary criticism concerning the period. In his own era as well as in subsequent ones he developed a reputation as truly talented and exemplary. His works like Cynthia, The Encomian of Lady Pecunia, and The Passionate Pilgrim have been singled out for admiration and praise. Indeed the highest honor that can be given to a poet of this period was bestowed like laurel leaves upon his brow with the misattribution of two of his sonnets to Shakespeare, something that endured well into the twentieth century. Yet the rampant homophobia and conservatism of the official guardians of what is acceptable poetry ensured that Barnfield's name always had to have an asterisk by it. This stigma has in part been removed in our own day, as literary critics have rediscovered Barnfield, and attempted to rehabilitate his besmirched name, not just in spite of his homosexuality, but in part because of it. But before we can understand why Barnfield has been read as gay, and whether that's legitimate or not, it's first necessary to understand how a category like "homosexuality" operated in the early modern period.

It's impossible that Barnfield would have regarded himself as necessarily "gay," and certainly not as "homosexual." It wasn't until 1886 that the German doctor Richard von Kraft-Ebing introduced the second term as a description of men and women who are attracted to their own gender. It marked a transition in society's understanding of same-sex desire. Prior to the advent of the term "homosexuality," gay sex was thought of as something that individuals did, after the introduction of the term it became an intrinsic part of one's individual identity, a sort of immutable essence that we think of as an orientation. Any casual perusal of the historical record demonstrates that sex between men was common from antiquity onward, but the classification of individuals who had homosexual sex as "gay" is largely a modern convention. It's unclear whether Barnfield's homoerotic verse should be taken as evidence that he actually had sex with men, though there were men who obviously did have sex with other men.

But Barnfield would not have thought of himself as having a gay identity in the same way that someone in the modern world might. In short, though homosexuality is universal and has existed as long as people have, how culture interprets it (in both negative and positive ways) is contextual. Foucault charted how attitudes towards sexuality have shifted in his landmark 1976 The History of Sexuality, and this performative aspect of gender identity was explicated by the philosopher Judith Butler in her 1990 Gender Trouble. Queer theorists have argued that gender, as a category distinct from biological sex, is in large part performative and defined by the social constructions of a given culture. When using this theoretical distinction to examine Barnfield's era we see a society that did not understand homosexuality as a hard-and-definite identity that was to be contrasted with heterosexuality, but rather they identified a variety of prohibited sexual practices that they classified as "sodomy." The historical irony is that though these practices were technically a crime (and people certainly suffered for them, especially if they lacked the social capital to protect themselves) the literary conventions of the Renaissance (especially their admiration for the classical past) condoned a fairly liberal expression of male same-sex desire as long as it was subtly couched in the language of the Greek and Roman past.

For teachers of Renaissance literature who wish to focus on gender in the period, Barnfield is perhaps the most literal example of homosexual desire, but he is not the only one. Christopher Marlowe's 1592 masterpiece Edward II depicts the unsubtle erotic love between the medieval king and his male love Gaveston. Though the play concludes with Edward's execution by being sodomized to death with a red-hot poker, the drama is surprisingly ambivalent about the king's predilections. Indeed his downfall is not caused by his homosexual desire, but rather by misplaced trust in his counselors (including the queen). As he wrote in that play, "The mightiest kings have had their minions" for even "Great Alexander loved Hepahestion." Marlowe himself has been identified as homosexual, with his roommate the fellow playwright Thomas Kyd sometimes assumed to be his lover. Indeed the notorious Baines letter which accused Marlowe of atheism among other capital offenses also claimed that the playwright had uttered, "All they that love not tobacco and boies [boys] are fools," though it's worth pointing out that the variable orthography of the period leaves the second noun open to a possible interpretation of actually being the word "booze." Indeed Shakespeare's sonnets have been noted for their potential homosexual themes, with the narrator extolling the beauty of the fair youth to whom a substantial bulk of that sequence is dedicated. That famous sonnet cycle has a number of unnamed characters, including a so-called "rival poet," who because of the implied homoerotic content in Shakespeare's poetry is sometimes identified as Barnfield.

If homoerotic content was not an uncommon convention in the literature of the period, then why has Barnfield been signaled out for particular censure, especially if so many scholars agreed to the artistic quality of his work? In Edward II the monarch's erotic attractions are veiled through the distance of history, in Shakespeare there may be indications of same-sex attraction, but there is never any sex between men and the language of desire is muted and subtle (all the better to engage plausible deniability). Indeed the nature of the poetic persona allows the narrator of Shakespeare's sonnets to not be autobiographical at all, simply a character created by the author. Yet in Barnfield's sonnet sequence we have something new in English literature, and that is an unabashed and full-throated expression of male homosexual desire written in an unequivocal first person. Though Barnfield (unsuccessfully) defended his poems against the accusation of them promoting sodomy, the verse itself is seemingly a proud (if at times heartbreaking) expression of the love between men in the seventeenth century.

Critics have historically been so flummoxed and disturbed by Barnfield's corpus that they've gone to great lengths to explain away the homosexual content of his work before finally deciding to simply ignore it all together. Though Marlowe was a life-long bachelor who lived with another man, and though his writing would seem to indicate some familiarity with same-sex desire, nothing in his work approaches the sheer literalness of Barnfield. And though there are convincing reasons to see Shakespeare's sonnets as in some sense homoerotic, the bard was himself married. In a similar way, literary historians tried to concoct a sort of domestic respectability for Barnfield that would help explain away the gay eroticism of his sonnets as simply fictional artifice. They point to the records which indicated a "Richard Barnfield" had married a younger woman and retired to the life of a respectable country gentleman in Staffordshire. These records demonstrate that he died contentedly married in 1627, attended by wife and surrounded by bourgeois hearth and home. For scholars of a certain disposition it would go a long way to casting doubt on the aspersions that Barnfield was in some sense a gay man, but unfortunately for them subsequent investigation has revealed that the "Richard Barnfield" mentioned in these accounts was actually the poet's father. Barnfield himself died seven years before, very much a bachelor.

Barnfield's poetry haunts, not just because of his talent which has been traditionally ignored, but because he supplies a quiet voice to a community of men denied theirs. Homosexual men of the period lacked a vocabulary to speak of their rights, and were buffeted by the oppressions of church and state. The literature of the time was too toothless to fully express that love, yet Barnfield courageously speaks of his frustrations and sorrows. His posterity was ruined because of it. Take as an example his "Sonnet 8:"

Sometimes I wish that I his pillow were,
So might I steale a kisse, and yet not seene,
So might I gaze upon his sleeping eine,
Although I did it with a panting feare:
But when I well consider how vaine my wish is,
Ah foolish Bees (thinke I) that doe not sucke
His lips for hony; but poore flowers doe plucke
Which have no sweet in them: when his sole kisses,
Are able to revive a dying soule.
Kisse him, but sting him not, for if you doe,
His angry voice your flying will pursue:
But when they heare his tongue, what can controule,
Their back-returne? for then they plaine may see,
How hony-combs from his lips dropping bee.

He writes, "Sometimes I wish that I his pillow were,/So might I steal a kiss, and yet not seen,/So might I gaze upon his sleeping eye." The theme of unrequited love was certainly known to the early modern poet, if not defined by it. One thinks of Petrarch and his Laura, an example reflected in myriad lyric poems. But the male pronoun makes it clear that it is not a Laura for whom Barnfield pines. It continues with, "Although I did it with a panting fear;/But when I well consider how vain my wish is." It's hard not to read this fear as that of the social sanction which forbids expression of this love to the beloved. It is the poet Thomas Wyatt's echo of Christ's "Noli me tangere" but with the added poignancy that consummated love is not just forbidden, but desire as well. Barnfield's sonnet 16 begins, "Long have I long'd to see my love again,/Still have I wished, but never could obtain it;/Rather than all the world (if I might gain it)." He continues with, "Yet in my soul I see him every day...Sometimes, when I imagine that I see him,/(As love is full of foolish fantasies)/Weening to kiss his lips, as my love's fees,/I feel but air; nothing but air to be him."

It's tempting to read these poems as autobiographical, and of course this tendency should be embraced carefully, especially in the early modern period. Barnfield no longer has the agency to define himself; we must be careful to not pull him from a closet he didn't necessarily know he was in. And Barnfield himself at least initially connected the homoerotic language to those same classical conventions one sees in Marlowe and Shakespeare. I do not mean to imply that the unrequited love in a Barnfield sonnet is somehow more tragic than that in a Wyatt verse. Yet it's hard not to feel some of the desperation and secrecy of gay men of Barnfield's era in these lyrics, which adds a level of pathos that sometimes isn't as immediate in more canonical works.

This is most clearly seen in his poignant and wrenching sonnet which begins, "Sighing, and sadly sitting by my love,/He asked the cause of my heart's sorrowing." The very first line indicates everything that is fascinating about Barnfield, and the depth of his poetic ability. The line is largely iambic pentameter, but he begins with a trochaic substitution, which propels it forward with a sense of immediate urgency (much as the first line of Shakespeare's Richard III does a similar thing). In a lesser poet the alliteration could be impotent, but in Barnfield's hand it reminds us both of the English language's special gift at alliteration, as well as pushing the line forward with that sense of sweaty-palmed nervousness. This tension is heightened because the poem indicates that the narrator is by his love's side, and that this man is unaware of the speaker's feelings for him. That it is the unconsummated love between the narrator and the beloved which is the origin of this melancholy is confirmed starting in live five when Barnfield writes, "Compelled (quoth I), to thee will I confess,/Love is the cause, and only love it is/That doth deprive me of my heavenly bliss./Love is the pain that doth my heart oppress." When the poem opens we only know that the narrator is in sorrow and that he is by the side of his beloved. If we are to understand the narrator as equivalent to author than we also know that both individuals are men. And while we may suspect that the cause of Barnfield's sadness is love, this isn't confirmed until the beginning of line five. The unprecedented brilliance of the poem is in the ninth line, which reads "And what is she (quoth he) whom thou dost love?" It is not irrelevant whether we interpret the narrator as literally being Barnfield or not, it is now impossible to read this poem as being written under a feminine persona, this is a male narrator who is writing about his unstated love for another man. Something about the friend's gentle confusion is almost unspeakably sad.

Barnfield, or his narrator, or both, answers the interrogative with, "Look in this glass (quoth I), there shalt thou see/The perfect form of my felicity./When, thinking that it would strange magic prove,/He opened it, and taking off the cover,/He straight perceived himself to be my lover." The possibility of a romantic or sexual relationship between these two friends is so inconceivable to the beloved that he initially finds the possibility that this is a magic mirror which will reveal some woman's face more likely than this being an awkward fumble of the narrator trying to confess his own love for his friend.

But an ambiguity at the end does allow for the possibility of a sort of magic, if perhaps a wishful romantic alchemy. When the friend peers into the mirror, "He straight perceived himself to be my lover." The last word is ambiguous, "beloved" would be more technically appropriate, even if it would alter the correct meter of the line. But if the friend perceives himself to be the narrator's "lover," does that imply that the mirror has somehow bewitched him? In the sixteenth century the word "lover" was sometimes used to connote intense friendship (as with David and Jonathan in translations of the Bible from that time), but the melancholic love-sickness seems to preclude that possible meaning here. In terms of meter and rhyme scheme it is written in the exact structural conventions of a Petrarchan sonnet, which as a genre takes unrequited romantic love as its major theme, as such the poem seems undeniably to be about homosexual romance. The concluding line of the sonnet allows for the possibility that the friend could still be transformed into a lover.

The emancipatory potential of Barnfield's verse is that the possibility of consummated same-sex love is implied, the poignancy is that it requires the almost supernatural to be made possible. Without further historical evidence it's impossible to know if like Edward with his Gaveston, Barnfield himself had romantic companionship, or if these thoughts were all theoretical. But if we're to celebrate Shakespeare for turning the conventions of Petrarchism on their head when he celebrated the Dark Lady as opposed to the standard fair woman of lyrical convention, then Barnfield equally deserves to be celebrated for the still-more radical attempt to write love poetry to a man, as a man.

Notes on John Dee's Aztec Mirror

In the British Museum – away from the Rosetta Stone and Elgin Marbles with their legions of selfie-taking tourists – is a shiny, jet-black obsidian mirror. Not much bigger than any standard hand mirror, the artifact is circular with a hole-bored handle at the top. A beautiful, dark, reflective black, it was forged from volcanic Mexican obsidian which the Aztecs associated with their god Tezcatlipoca, lord of divination (among other things). This is a ritual object, and its exact provenance is unknown. The conquering Spanish brought back things like this by the boatload while they plundered Aztec gold to become the world's first truly global empire (and in the process they imported disease, war, and slavery). The Aztecs had used obsidian stones just like this one for prophetic purposes over the course of generations. Now, spirited away from a destroyed and subjugated civilization they journeyed to a profoundly different culture where they would create new stories, and generate new prophecies. This particular mirror was owned by the eighteenth-century gothic writer, architect, and son of the former Prime Minister, Sir Horace Walpole. He affixed a label to the mirror which simply stated: "The Black Stone into which Dr Dee used to call his spirits..."

Dr. John Dee has long fascinated students of the Renaissance. A sixteenth-century magus, Dee straddled the now-seemingly contrary realms of the occult and science. The great Warburg scholar Dame Frances Yates claimed that his massive library was the very mind of the Renaissance. But his was an esoteric knowledge, even during an esoteric age. Not quite at home in the classical humanism of his fellow rhetoric-minded colleagues, Dee longed to create the English equivalent of the Neo-Platonist and hermetic academies which had thrived in Florence a century before. His was a counter-Renaissance, indebted not to Erasmus and More but rather Ficino and Mirandola. And Dee's sectarian allegiances, seemingly malleable depending on the denomination of whatever land he should happen to find himself in, was focused on a type of positivist magic. He longed for a scientific method of the occult. Dee was notorious in his own time – seemingly respected as brilliant but also chided for his lack of publication and feared for the secrets he may have divined.

Yet while his name is not included among those innovators of what came to be called science – Kepler, Brahe, Copernicus, Bacon – he could include himself among their own slightly-occult circles (indeed he personally knew all of them save for Copernicus). In that shadow-land that is the emergence of modernity, Dee can count himself as being both the last of the Chaldeans and one of the first of the moderns. His fortunes had a tendency to rise and fall as irregularly as *fortuna's* wheel turned. He found himself imprisoned under Mary I and he begged the witchcraft obsessed James I to try him for sorcery (as that was the crime he was most often accused of) so that he could clear his name. Unique unluckiness that he had, he found himself persecuted when he didn't want to be, and not persecuted when he did. And while some courtiers at Westminster were friendly to him, and some were not, he always had the confidence of his most beloved monarch who ruled between that frosty Catholic inquisitor Mary and the fearful Protestant literalist James: the Virgin Queen, Gloriana, Elizabeth. It was Dee who decided the day of her coronation, it was Dee who always had her confidence as astrologer, and it was Dee (perhaps looking into his black American mirror) who first christened a land for Elizabeth across the ocean as being "the British Empire."

Dee endures at the margins of accepted history. Two generations ago he was revived as a subject of proper academic study by Yates, but there is still something unacceptable or ghostly about him. His name appears in just too many weird books in the occult section of the suburban mega-bookstore. He may have traveled in the same circles as Francis Bacon, but Bacon gets credit for identifying and defining the contours of the burgeoning scientific revolution; Dee is associated with "Enochian magic" and speaking to angels through a crystal ball. There is a gulf between him and us today, and because of it he still seems dangerous, still lacks respectability. His vision is at times shockingly contemporary, the sober advocate of calendar reform, an instrumental figure in advocating mathematics as a universal language, the proponent of new cartographic methods. But there are always those pesky angels in our peripheral vision. And while we as scholars are encouraged to not project modern-day prejudices anachronistically onto the past, to not diagnose or pathologize behavior that comes from an incredibly different culture (for the past as they say is a type of foreign country), Dee can try our patience with his seeming naivety. It's hard not to feel a bit of condescension over the man who accepted at face value his scrivening partner Edward Kelley's news that the angels had informed him that God required them to wife swap. And then it's hard not to feel a bit heartbroken when Dee matter-of-factly informs his silent journal that the task was achieved after initial protestations from his wife.

In his curiosity he is intensely admirable. Dee was motivated by a faith that beneath the seeming random nature of everyday life – the tragedies, the violence, and the sadness – there was a universal order and that man could understand it and improve upon his world. We mustn't forget that this is a belief in progress, and whether progress actually is real or not it is intensely modern a faith. But we also must acknowledge that Dee believed this wasn't just achieved through mathematics or natural science, but through his divination, his crystal ball, his obsidian mirror. Dee was the founder of Enochian magic, he invented with Kelley (or discovered depending on your perspective) a divine Adamic language that was spoken by the angels and named after the mysterious figure Enoch who it is written of in the Bible that, "And Enoch walked with God: and he was not; for God took him" (Genesis 5:22). It's the strange language of the Hebrew Scriptures, a culture even more foreign and harder to interpret than Dee's. There is something moving in Enoch, the father of Methuselah, and the first person to not die, to presumably ascend to heaven like Mary mother of Jesus, Christ, or Muhammad after him. Enoch "was not; for God took him." From these few inscrutable lines an entire Apocrypha grew out of Enoch. He appears in Ethiopic scriptures, in Old Slavonic religions texts, in rabbinic Midrash. In the kabbalah it is argued that Enoch was transformed into the "lesser Yahweh," the angel Metatron – God's very voice. It's this, the language of this creature's tongue that whispers in Dee's ear. It's the letters of this angel's alphabet that Dee reads in Tezcatlipoca's mirror.

And yet his seemingly ungrateful fellow countrymen did not distinguish between the good angels and bad demons when it came to the supernatural communications he and Kelley supposedly received through objects like the British Museum's mirror. One can imagine Dee's face staring into that volcanic blackness, "the smoky mirror" (as Tezcatlipoca's name translates from Nahutal). What we would see in that dark reflection is a man who evokes the characters he is often associated with, a cross between Marlowe's Dr. Faustus and Shakespeare's Prospero. Sunken and tired eyes, a long, prominent aquiline nose and any trace of a facial expression hidden under the costume of a pointed wizard's beard. On his seemingly hairless head a simple academic skull-cap, around his neck the frilled collar of the Elizabethan attendant to courtiers that he was, and his clothing the austere black of the Puritans who reviled him. We do not know who had possession of the mirror between Dr. Dee and Sir Walpole, perhaps more provocatively we do not know who had possession of it between its arrival in Europe and Dee's acquiring of it. Other than that antiquarian Walpole's brief note, we do not even know if Dee actually owned it. Tezcatlipoca's reputation as being a god who can only be depicted in a smoky mirror endures, for smoke obscures, confuses, stings the eyes. While a mirror is supposed to clearly reflect smoke smudges into uncertainty. Much like Dee, the mirror exists in a fundamentally mysterious zone. What does the mirror mean? Does it make any argument, or like a carnival mirror merely defer questions and answers back on themselves, providing us with no closure but with an opportunity to ruminate, to divine if you will?

It is important that Dee's possession was an object from a specific place, and that place was the Americas. And it was made by a particular people, by the Aztecs, Indians. Whether defenders or denigrators of the Indians, whether de las Casas or Cortez (or their contemporary proxies), it's often taken as a teleological given, an inevitable outcome that the indigenous would be conquered by Europeans. And yet nothing could be further from the truth, to assume that the Indians' defeat was a guarantee is to assault them and to do violence to their memory. Well into the eighteenth century the interior of America was well under native control. It was the Europeans of the time who saw their own march of conquest as inevitable and we're heirs to that opinion. If any one event can be taken to have enshrined in the European imagination their promised and prophetic future dominion over the fourth part of the world, it was Cortez's destruction of the Aztec. Enhanced by Spanish and generally European propaganda in the five centuries since it happened, the mythopoeic significance of the event shouldn't be discounted as a foundational legend on the creation of our brave new world that has such people in it. To begin with, the discovery, or rather invention, of America (as the critic Edmundo O'Gorman has it) was such a profound shift in the cosmology of the western imagination that arguably even the Copernican Revolution or the Reformation itself seem insignificant in its light.

To learn that an entire undiscovered hemisphere filled with unknown people lay beyond the western horizon must have been shocking to common people in a way that astronomy with its complex epicycles and its orbits couldn't be. It was, as one Spanish explorer had it: "the greatest event since the creation of the world." The old Trinitarian three-continent geography had been disrupted, the very literal existence of the Americas was a challenge, if not a heresy, that demanded an answer. It should not be minimized – the profound affect this land to the west had on the European consciousness. Indeed it was new in a way that could charitably only be understood as mythic. John Mandeville's medieval voyages may have been to a constructed India, but India was always known to be real. China was known by the Romans (who traded with her). Africa may have been a "dark continent," but it was there. And always Prester John was somewhere with the ten tribes of Israel across the boulder-filled Sambation. But America was something different, something that required a new myth but could only be discussed in the language of old: Cockaigne, paradise, Eden.

And in the construction of that myth various beliefs were projected onto this "new" world, which declared it both paradise and fallen world. But that such lands existed was challenging enough, to find such a civilization as the Aztecs with its triumphant city of Tenochtitlan must have strained the cognitive abilities of the Spanish who came upon it. Central to the myth of Spanish dominance has been the old chestnut of Cortez being mistaken as the god Quetzalcoatl by Montezuma. But our evidence for the actuality of this is from second-hand sources, Dominicans and Franciscans recording the syncretic beliefs of a subjugated people a generation later. That this white-skinned eastern god journeying from the east should seem so messianic is not hard to understand. The Aztecs story has never been told in a western tongue; it is just as blank as their obsidian mirror. And as that mirror reflects back what its viewers wish to see the Spanish read their triumphant victory over the indigenous as providential proof of the white-man's inevitable dominion over this new world. That this was accomplished not by a few hundred starving conquistadors but indeed thousands of Indian troops rebelling against Tenochtitlan, and of course with the hidden microbes that would seem like "magic bullets" (to borrow Greenblatt's phrase) to both Cortez and Montezuma is not part of our myth. But it was there, in a land west of More's Utopia (which Vasco de Quinoa would try and make a reality in Mexico the very year More lay his head on the block) where contingencies and mistakes of history happen. It was first here that the Spanish and then the rest of Europe would first fully create an imaginary land they christened America.

It seems prescient that Dee's vision was potentially so shaped by an object from the New World, from America. Dee's historical mirror-image, his oppositional twin Francis Bacon, imagined a perfect society named Bensalem in his proto-novel *New Atlantis*. The citizens of Bensalem – which lay to the west off the coast of Peru – like so many others Bacon envisions utopia as American – are ruled by the empirical discoveries of the scientists who labor in a university known as Salomon's House. In Bensalem the structuring system is one of scientific positivism. Decisions are rationally made by recourse to a combination of both deduction and induction. Theories are formulated, tested experimentally and observationally, discarded if proven wrong and accepted if the evidence is in favor of them. Bacon was a Christian, of course, so his Bensalemites are as well (and a profoundly multicultural group to boot), though almost incidentally and the story of their conversion is secondary, if not borderline comical. It's clear that what rules Bensalem is a form of science. But for Bacon, for whom knowledge was power, this is not a neutral or disinterested science, but a system that exists to utilize the natural world for the benefit of man.

Perhaps more than even a scientific utopia it is a technocratic utopia. Bacon makes clear that his imaginary American "New Atlantis" is predictive of where he thinks technology designed through empirical science could lead humanity. So what does Bacon's America look like, what does his future look like? A Bensalemite explains to their visitors that what is possible are "high towers," and "the producing also of new artificial metals," to make fruit that is "greater and sweeter, and of differing taste, smell, color, and figure." There are "heats, in imitation of the suns," that in New Atlantis it is possible to "represent and imitate all articulate sounds," that there is "flying in the air," and "ships and boats for going under water." Most tellingly there are "houses of deceits of the senses, where we represent all manner of feats of juggling, false apparitions, impostures and illusions." America has oft-been represented as that land of continual, almost garish progress, a technologically addicted society ruled by a never-ending desire for novelty. For a contemporary reader it is eerie to read of Bacon's society with its skyscrapers, its synthetic materials, seeming nuclear power, recorded sound, airplanes, submarines, and most telling of all movie theaters (or TVs, or computers…).

But it's only a mistake of historical perspective that has us seeing Dee as so different from Bacon. After all, Dee believed that the universe was orderly and understandable, that mathematics could describe it, explain it, and predict it, that tools could be developed that changed and improved life. What was his obsidian mirror but a calculating machine, a computer? It was after all a type of technology, a black mirror as enigmatic as the computer screen turned off reflecting our own distorted faces back at ourselves. But Dee, for all of his professional silence, was too outspoken in his private writings. Bacon had the good sense to have faith in future generations to solve these problems and to invent these technologies; Dee's arrogance was such that his system was already complete. Instead of scrivening mirrors we have computers and they operate not on unseen angels but on unseen electrons. Because of his failures Dee remains modernity's dark and forgotten twin. We are able to live in a world that he could conceive of, but one which he could have never invented.

Exile in that Infinity

"If you had found planets circling one of the fixed stars, there among Bruno's infinities I had already prepared my prison shackles, that is, my exile in that Infinity."
Letter from Johannes Kepler to Galileo Galilei, 1610

"I hardly ever read a book without wanting to give it a good censoring."
Robert Cardinal Bellarmine SJ, 1598

"O God, I could be bounded in a nutshell and count myself a king of infinite space."
William Shakespeare, Hamlet, *c. 1600*

According to the Italian, the English were just as unimpressed with him as he was with them. On an Ash Wednesday in 1583 they sat in this dark-wood paneled dining room, tapestries keeping out the chill of late winter even as the cold couldn't help but enter through the leaded window with its multicolored glass diamonds. The Italian's thin, stubbly black beard, his olive complexion and his shaggy dark hair that had grown out from his tonsure distinguished him from the gathering of fair-skinned courtiers who had invited him to supper. Giordano Bruno, of Nola, born in the shadow of Vesuvius and raised on the peaches and lemons which grew in her fertile soil, and whose intellectual training was in Naples' monasteries and chaotic streets, was very far from home here in damp, dark London. Chief among the English was Fulke Greville, author of arguably the first biography in English, who was perhaps dressed in his imposing ruffled Elizabethan collar and the rich satins and velvets of the aristocratic class.

Greville was close friends with Sir Philip Sidney, who admired

Bruno and who the Nolan dedicated a book to. Yet despite his affection for noble Sidney, the cosmopolitan Bruno, who true to the humanist maxim had made wherever he happened to be residing at that moment his home, still found the English to be "disrespectful, uncivil, rough, rustic, savage and badly brought up." While he disparaged their uncouth table manners and their inability to clean themselves before and after they ate, the Englishmen found Bruno to be obtuse and pretentious, answering his declarations about Copernicanism with snotty rejoinders quoted from Erasmus. And yet, in Bruno's fictionalized dialog Ash Wednesday Supper, which recounts the dinner, and which appropriated the form and structure of Plato's Symposium and married it to the vulgar, obscene, practical, and endlessly creative Neapolitan dialect of his youth, Bruno expressed some of the most sublime metaphysical speculation of the sixteenth century. It is as if Pulcinella, the clown of commedia dell'arte, was suddenly able to declare with utmost sophistication and beauty the infinite nature of the universe.

Almost exactly seventeen years later and also on an Ash Wednesday, the short former monk would find himself naked, chained to a bundle of cut faggots, with one spike pierced through both his cheeks and another one finishing a cross through his lips. Here, in theCampo de Fiori – the Roman "Field of Flowers" – he had finally returned to his homeland and faced Michelangelo's massive and still unfinished dome as he was immolated. For what was the Nolan philosopher burnt? He was executed because the Church feared what was printed in his dozens of books, spoken through his lectures at the top universities of Europe from Padua to Oxford, and scratched in the very margins of his personal library, composed as it was with the infernal syllabus that is the Index Librorum Prohibitorum. For several months in 1593 he was imprisoned by the relatively liberal Venetian Inquisition – the Doge always eager to keep his independence from the Pope – and then possibly tortured for the next seven in the dungeons of the Tor di Nona by the Roman Inquisition (for which no records survive, lost in the Napoleonic conquests). Bruno was made a martyr for his beliefs – but it remains difficult to classify those beliefs.

Witnesses for the prosecution (and there was only a prosecution) claimed that he abjured Christianity, that in his earliest days as a friar in Naples he denied the Trinity, stripped his monastic cell of all but a crucifix (reminding his superiors of those iconoclasts beyond the Alps), that he defended the fourth-century heretic Arius, that he had consorted with and attended services among the Lutherans and Calvinists in the great schismatic capitals, that he had bragged about trying to start his own Rosicrucian religion, and that there were already cells among the swayable people of Switzerland and Germany who were attracted to Bruno's hermetic faith with its blend of Christianity and the occult, his mythology as familiar with Thoth and Apollo as it was with Christ. A man who had been imprisoned with Bruno in Venice was brought forth as a witness to the many blasphemies in word and heresies in thought which the Nolan had supposedly uttered as he awaited trial. The prisoner – a cleric himself – claimed that Bruno denied that "bread transmutes into flesh" and "that he is an enemy to the Mass, that no religion pleases him" and that he claimed "that Christ was a wretch...[and] that Christ...was a magician." This witness stated that while awaiting his trial Bruno often ironically compared himself to Christ, and claimed that the Son of God was no better than any of the prisoners, for even Christ wished to resist his execution during that human moment at Gethsemane. Sometimes the blasphemy was less sophisticated than that – sometimes in rage and frustration the philosopher would scream at God the Father, "I despise you, fucked cuckhold, done and undone!" But Bruno also said more sublime things that for all their beauty enraged the Church no less, for he believed that "the world is eternal and that there are infinite worlds."

Like Erasmus, whose books he had hid in his monastic cell when he was young, he made no single town his home, but rather the whole of a rapidly disintegrating Christendom was his study. From a provincial settlement some thirty miles from Naples – which at the time ranked among one of the largest cities in the world – he would travel to, write in, and teach at universities in Paris, Venice, London, Geneva, Oxford, Prague, Wittenberg, Venice, and Padua. He would meet the crowned heads of Europe: Henri III of France, humbled by the violence of the massacre on St. Bartholomew's Day, when the Seine was bloodied by the martyred Huguenots; Elizabeth of England, who for some time seemed to offer the promise of toleration to persecuted Bruno but whose via media was more Machiavellian strategy than intellectual position; and Rudolf II of Prague, with his court filled with not just jesters and magicians, but astronomers and artists, and always with that regent's aching desire to pierce that shadow veil between the world as it seems and the world as it is.

On these journeys, over the course of a short life of only a bit more than a decade of writing, he had printed dozens of arguments, dialogs, plays, pamphlets, poems, and even instruction manuals with exotic titles such as The Song of Circe, The Candlemaker, Ash Wednesday Supper, and On the Limitless and Numberless. In his writing, his lectures, and his private tutoring (to among others Henri III) he argued for a strikingly original interpretation of the universe. And what was this vision? For Bruno reality did not end at the conclusion of the nine crystalline spheres of the Ptolemaic world: it extended indefinitely into pure infinity, and was aged on a scale of eternity and not the prosaic few millennia that organized Christianity believed in. That in this immeasurable universe there are other suns, with other planets, which have their own inhabitants. That our reality is structured by atoms, and that we are unified in our compositional substance, and that as God is somewhere,

God is everywhere. In On the Immense he writes, "Now, if you please, ask me: Where is place, space, vacuum, time, body? In the universe. Where is the universe? In every place, space, time, body. Is there anything outside the universe? No. Why? Because there is no place nor space nor motion nor body."

It would be easy to read this as a scientific world view (and it often still is read this way), but it would be a mistake. Bruno was conversant in the emerging new science, but Bruno was not a scientist. His was not an empirical world – at least not exactly. For Bruno it was the manipulation of numbers and symbols, memory and word, which generated knowledge of the cosmos. It is true that he embraced Copernicus' heliocentrism, but not necessarily because it simplified complex calculations involving epicycle upon epicycle or because it explained the retrograde motion of Mars, but rather because in restoring the sun to the center of the solar system it gave due reference to Apollo. "Sun, who alone bathes all things in light," as Bruno said in his Apollonian hymn, his Copernicanism justified more by a type of Neo-Paganism than by the telescope. Kepler, for his witchy associations, or Tycho Brahe even with his astrological ones, and certainly Galileo (who sometimes seems so modern that he may be a refugee from the future), all began to speak in the language of science. Bruno was a hermeticist: however, his unseen forces were not things like gravity but substances of a more occult sort. Bruno's laboratory was not Brahe's Danish island observatory espying the supernova of 1572, but rather the libraries of Italian occultism. He was the embodiment of the mystical, otherworldly, transcendent perspective of men from the previous century like Giovanni Pico della Mirandola or Marsilio Ficino, or even Plethon who still worshiped the gods of old, and who attended that Medici-funded Florentine conclave in 1438 which was the closest the Catholic Church ever came to suturing that amputation from the Greek east.

None of this is to disparage the Nolan – far from it. It is merely to explain that his was not a modern heresy, but rather a golden thread of a heresy which stretched back to the beginning. Bruno was thinking of that thrice-great Hermes, who the Egyptians believed was baboon-faced Thoth, who first invented writing, and who the Christian kabbalists of Florence and Prague believed had even taught Moses in his youth, when he wrote that, "Egypt is the image of heaven, and to state it more clearly, the colony of all things that are governed and exercised in heaven." In believing that the reality could be infinite, and that time could be eternal, Bruno did not justify his beliefs by science, yet he still may have been right. And regardless, his vision remains beautiful. And he tried to spread that vision throughout that disunited continent. Giordano Bruno's career is a story of cities – Naples, Geneva, Paris, London, Prague, Venice, Rome.

It was Naples that gave the Nolan his tongue. The dedication to his Expulsion of the Triumphant Beast reads "Giordano speaks the common language, he names names freely...He calls bread bread, wine wine, a head a head, a foot a foot, and other parts by their proper name." Neapolitan is a frank, no-bullshit dialect, which trades freely in wit, insult, obscenity, and casual blasphemy. At Oxford they laughed at him when he lectured because his accent was so thick, and even in Venice fellow Italians had trouble understanding what he was saying. But it was in that low dialect that he was able to express that which was highest. He would learn not to fear authority in Naples, whether among his own Dominicans, or later among the Calvinists of Geneva who would excommunicate him from a faith which wasn't even his, or among the fearsome and brilliant new Jesuits. He once quipped that Naples was a paradise inhabited by devils, and indeed life was not always at a premium in a city that existed under the threat of continual volcanic annihilation (and which still does). This was the dirty but also the beautiful city, where that fellow heretic, the utopian Thomas Campanella would dream of his City of the Sun and of an Age of Spirit which would commence in 1600, and where half a century after Bruno's death the fishmonger Masaniello would expel the Iberians in Europe's first modern revolution. In Florence there was magic practiced in the institutes of the Medici, and the hermetic corpus and the Sibylline oracles were consulted as Plato's Academy was reopened. But Naples was a different city, full of not just philosophers and monks, but pick-pockets, prostitutes, and murderers. Where Pico della Mirandola consulted the writings of Plotinus and Pseudo-Dionysius the Areopagite, the young Nolan would have seen magic of a more practical manner – the buttara la fava of men forecasting the future by throwing beans, of women scrying oil floating on water. Here, in Naples, the Renaissance was maybe not always the high-class affair it would be in Florence, but it was a crowded, dynamic, confusing, and violent one. It is only appropriate that in the heat-blanched fields of the Mezzogiorno that a man like Bruno could turn his eyes to that celestial orb and see infinities of light. And yet the Church did not take to Bruno's philosophical improvements upon Catholicism, and so they expelled him from the community of the faithful, and he exiled himself from Italy.

It was Geneva that gave him division. The Inquisition would make great purpose out of Bruno's attending of Calvinist services in that Swiss city, but the philosopher had always maintained that he was simply following local custom. It was an unusual town for him to migrate to. Though Italian Protestants had been crossing the mountains now for two generations to find amnesty here in Beza's theocracy, it was not a place conducive to the temperament of a scholar like Bruno. Surely he knew the cautionary tale of the Spaniard and possible marrano Miguel Servetus. Some decades before Bruno, that unfortunate had come to Geneva fleeing from the Spanish Inquisition only to find himself the first heretic ever condemned and executed by a Protestant regime. Some say that his incineration was a sort of perverse favor that the Catholic Church had asked of their

Calvinist enemies. That earlier heretic, whose life and fate so mirrors that of Bruno's, was guilty of Socinianism, of denying the Trinity, something which Bruno had flirted with since he was a teenager. Servetus' prosecutor was John Calvin, who had failed at everything he had ever tried – be it the Parisian legal trade, or a career as a rakish, humanist dandy penning homoerotic poetry. And so, since he had failed at everything to that point, he decided to move to Switzerland and redefine God. And some half-century before Bruno's arrival, Calvin had looked at Servetus and with those cold eyes with their cold gospel he sentenced the Spaniard to a burning flame. The only reason Servetus' work survives is because a sole copy not consigned to the bonfire of the vanities was maintained by that old scholar himself, whose name was once Jean Chauvin, and who ironically couldn't part with the Spaniard's book. When the Nolan arrived, Geneva was still a city dictated by Calvin's interpretation of biblical law, and for Bruno with his exultation of human freedom the dark theology of double predestination was as psychologically restrictive as the town's puritanism was socially. The Calvinists excommunicated the Italian for the second time in his life: once an exile from the faith of his fathers, he was now an exile from those that had rebelled against the same fathers Bruno had.

It was Paris that gave him memory. Henri III had invited Bruno to be his personal tutor, to explain to him the Ars Magna, the art of memory, which he traveled the continent teaching at universities. Bruno had been inspired by the medieval Catalan Ramon Llull, a thirteenth-century Franciscan who invented a complex calculus of intellectual interconnectedness, finding parallels between disparate phenomena and ideas to generate new concepts. Llull's method of intellectual computation involved a simple yet ingenious mechanism – paper wheels turning within wheels marked with a complex set of symbols representing various forms and thoughts, with different categories lining up and generating new concepts, and intricate tree-like diagrams that he used to create a type of spiritual physics, hoping to generate the doctrine of Christianity through calculation and pure reason and thus to demonstrate to Jews and Muslims the intellectual superiority of the Catholic Church. The Muslims of North Africa were less than impressed with his theological calculating machine, and ended up stoning him to death. But from his Ars Magna came the earliest articulation of what could be thought of as a computer, and Bruno's inspiration for his own great art, a complex mnemonic system for improving one's memory. Inspired by how Llull's rotating circles within circles made connections between different phenomena, Bruno invented a method of combining various divergent concepts so as to better commit to memory tremendous amounts of information and text. Drawing not just from Llull, but from classical rhetorical theory as well, Bruno developed a system whereby ideas and words were metaphorically associated with elements of actual physical buildings, and in recalling the details of their architecture one could almost magically bring forth the memorized works in question. It was a system of memorization by divide and conquer, texts broken down into their smallest elements, and then perhaps arbitrarily wed to some element of a place so that when the student mentally returns to said building, they only need to imagine themselves walking throughout to recall all of the stored information. Brought to Paris by the king, Bruno may have taken a concrete space such as Notre Dame Cathedral to explain to Henri how a given text, say something from Bruno's long-dead yet respected sparring partner Thomas Aquinas' Summa Theologica, could be memorized as effortlessly as the ancient druidic bards were once able to recall their epics. A few sentences may be associated with one stained glass pane, a whole chapter with the window, a book with the side of the nave, the conclusion with the altar. Bruno converted text into space, and made calling forth whole books as simple as visiting a place in your imagination. With all the enthusiasm of some sort of back-woods confidence man, Bruno advertised his amazing skills by writing: "This art required much less work, industry, and practice than all the others you might read about, so that within three or four months it offers an easier, more certain method for those who choose it than those who follow other methods will attain in three of four years." But for Bruno this was no parlor trick, this was, as it was for Llull, the very physics of thought, the means by which the great code of reality could be interpreted.

It was London which gave him debate. That northern city was cold, and was unlike Apollo's hazy land of the midday sun which had birthed the Nolan. It may have been a few decades since the Thames had frozen over and it was possible to walk from Fleet Street to Southbank without crossing at the city's only bridge, but that early March Ash Wednesday when he dined with Greville there would have still been the unfamiliar chill which marked this planet's last mini-ice age. For Bruno, London seemed encased in cold, though in other ways it was not dissimilar to Naples – it had the same mélange of cut-throats and cut-purses – a canting underclass with a colorful vocabulary who crowded the just-opening theaters across the river from London, as well as her brothels and her bear-baiting pits. Ruling over that island was Spenser's Gloriana, the Virgin Queen, Elizabeth. She was the monarch of a small island at the very western edge of the world, speaking a honking, guttural, monosyllabic branch of West Germanic, and like Bruno's fellow countrymen under constant threat of attack by the seemingly omnipotent Spanish with their treasures of Aztec and Incan gold. And despite these seeming limitations, Elizabeth had apparently created a very Golden Age, her courtiers had taken the fourteen-line parsimony of the sonnet (so amenable to the easy rhymes of the Romance languages) and hammered earthy English into something that would perfect that form. The theaters south of London began to stage dramas by Marlowe, Shakespeare, and Jonson which conveyed a type of interiority no literature had achieved before, and the difficult reformations she inherited from her sister, her brother, and her father made this Protestant island a surprisingly fertile field for all manner of creative thought. Here Bruno met and immensely admired the great Sir Philip Sidney. They shared a name – Giordano was his confirmation name, his birth name was Filippo. And both Sidney and Bruno were named for the same Philip, ironically the one who sat on the Hapsburg throne at El Escorial. Many of Bruno's teachers at the monastery of San Domenico Maggiore died in the Neapolitan revolt against Spanish rule; Sidney would be felled by a bullet at Zutphen as he aided the Dutch in their war of independence against Spain. There were other connections between them, Bruno and Sidney were like two divergent categories on concentric wheels of Llull's apparatus rotated onto one another. How could Bruno not appreciate the aristocratic courtier-poet, whose magnificent sonnet cycle took that most astronomical of titles, Astrophel and Stella? But on the whole Bruno did not enjoy the English – their island cold, their people unappreciative. It is possible that he, like other continental refugees, could have found a home among the British. Despite the growing Puritan faction within the Church, Hooker's burgeoning live-and-let-live latitudinarianism was at least for some a matter of genuine Anglican policy. But Bruno, who always loved the sun, could not abide this kingdom of short winter days, and he began his way back southward. Some believe, however, that before his departure he was recruited as an espionage agent by Sir Francis Walshingham, the reptilian head of the Privy Council. Knowing how he remained unwelcome by the inquisitions of many of the city-states of Italy, Bruno cheekily and ultimately appropriately took the codename "Faggot," after the bundle of sticks that heretics were burnt alive on.

It was Prague that gave him magic. Here the eccentric Holy Roman Emperor Rudolph II forged a strange and occult kingdom, very different from the Counter-Reformation police state that his cousin Philip ruled over in Spain. Rudolf, who some saw as mad, was obsessed with oddity, aberration, and the spectacular. Here he assembled collections of Wunderkammer filled with ancient artifacts, exotic taxidermy, shells, minerals, and curiosities collected from around the world. Rudolf fancied himself as a type of Prospero, and true to his desire to be both king and wizard he had summoned the greatest scientific and magical minds to Prague in an era in which the demarcation between those two spheres of knowledge was less clear than it is today. This claustrophobic capital of winding cobbled streets snaking over the Bohemian hills and of mist falling on the red-tiled roofs of its small stone houses was for a time the most occult city in all of Europe. Here, in the shadow of its gothic cathedrals and synagogues, were gathered at a time not just Bruno, but also the astronomers Brahe and Johannes Kepler, the English-court astrologer and communicant with angels John Dee and his assistant Edward Kelley, and the Italian painter Giuseppe Arcimboldo with his fantastic paintings of men composed of books, fruits, and mechanical devices. It was in sixteenth-century Prague that the great kabbalist Rabbi Judah Loew ben Bezalel had taken mud from the Vlatava and fashioned a golem, using incantations to imbue this pile of dust with life, taking motes of adamah and making his own Adam. The creature was to protect the Jews of the Prague ghetto, and was controlled by the inscribing and erasure of a single Aleph on his forehead, that primordial letter being the simple difference between the words for "truth" and "death." Supposedly the remains of Yoselle, the Golem are still entombed in the attic of the Prague synagogue. Less evidence remains of that other necromancer, the historical Johann Faust, who though he mostly resided in that capital of division that was Wittenberg, spent some time in Prague decades before Bruno would be a resident.

It was Venice that gave him prison. Returning to Italy should have never been considered an option by the Nolan, and yet years living among the descendants of Goths in the lands of cold winters, warm beer, and bland food had convinced him to return to Italy. Still, that most Serene Republic of Venezia was not necessarily an inappropriate place for Bruno to take up residence, even if it was on that Catholic peninsula. It was a transitional place, between east and west, buffeted by the Holy Roman Empire, the Spanish, and the Ottomans. The Venetians had grown rich on massive trade, opening up the orient centuries before, and in the marketplaces of the Piazza San Marco there were artifacts from the Levant, spices from India, textiles from central Asia, and cloth from China all being haggled over. The canals of that wedding-cake city were traveled by not just Catholics, but Protestants, the Orthodox, Jews, and Muslims. Venice was nominally Catholic, but her true faith was trade, and in the ecumenical spirit of capitalism the Other was mostly welcome within her watery byways. Despite the worst intentions of the papacy, Venice remained the capital of southern European publishing, now rivaled only by Frankfurt, and the city honored the long-dead printer Aldo Manuzio who saw accessible books as a birthright for all scholars. Venice had an independent and liberal spirit, and she had buffered herself against the political machinations of Rome as effectively as the dams which kept the city from sinking. The Venetian Inquisition was more to pay lip-service to Rome, being comparatively forgiving. And the doges, always careful to never acquiesce too much to any foreign power, either sultan or pope, ordained their own bishops without intercession from the Vatican (which is why many Hussite heretics received the collar in Venice). But Venice's fortunes were falling – the defeat of the Armada off the coast of England began to move the center of sea-faring commerce from the Mediterranean to the Atlantic – and the memory of her spectacular vanquishing of the Turks at Lepanto was beginning to fade into history. The doge needed the support of the Papal States as the Spanish began to hem him in, and so Bruno was arrested by the Venetian Inquisition. And in the course of his deposition, shadow diplomacy secured the Nolan's extradition from Venice to Rome.

And it was Rome that gave him death. In a lifetime of traversing many rivers – the Seine, Danube, the Thames – he now faced the Tiber. Giordano – Jordan. He was obsessed with waterways almost as much as he was with the sun, but unlike in the conclusion of his poem The Heroic Frenzies he would not find baptism at this Jordan. Instead he found Robert Cardinal Bellarmine. Bruno's career intersected with virtually every important intellect of the late sixteenth century, and while many of them were geniuses and were his equals, perhaps no piercing intellect understood him and took him as seriously as Bellarmine did. He was the first Jesuit cardinal, made so by Pope Clementine VIII, and often when he explained why he joined the Society of Jesus he said it was because it precluded the possibility of his ascending higher office since before him Jesuits had been barred from being made princes of the Church. But for all his stated humility, he was also a dogged and zealous enforcer of orthodoxy who fully lived the Ignatian zeal to affirm that black is white if the Church so decrees it. But Bellarmine also belied the old and naïve slur that the zealous are always stupid, for in the cardinal Bruno ironically may have found the first equal who truly absorbed and understood his system and what precisely was so dangerous about it. There were scores of heretics not just in Rome and Italy, but throughout Europe. Men and women were routinely brought in by the inquisitions, and overwhelmingly acquitted and released. Eccentric aberrations in proper theology were in some ways tolerated, punished just enough so that everybody would remember who was actually allowed to write doctrine. But Bruno was a different matter: here was a well-traveled and well-connected man who preached a strange gospel of pantheism and apocatastasis, who denied all miracles so as to enshrine the world itself as the only miracle, who saw organized faith as superstition and her clerics as ignorant asses.

Using the analytical prowess that to this day has rightly earned the Jesuits their reputation as the intellectual vanguard of the Church, Bellarmine encapsulated the Nolan's philosophy into eight positions untenable to Catholic orthodoxy, which Bruno was asked to repudiate. By the conclusion of the trial, after six years of imprisonment, and possibly torture with devices that had names like thestrappado (which wrenched your limbs from your sockets as you were hoisted upon a pulley) and the Judas Chair (in which one was partially impaled upon one's anus), Bruno refused to recant and couldn't explain away the seeming heresy, and so his execution was ordered in that Roman field of flowers on an Ash Wednesday, in that jubilee year of 1600. According to one witness the philosopher told Bellarmine and the Inquisition that, "Maiori forsan cum timore sententiam in me fertis quam ego accipiam," that is, that he thought that they feared delivering the execution sentence more than he feared hearing it. If Bellarmine was troubled by this seeming curse from the Neapolitan magician, we do not have a record for it. And yet sixteen years later, perhaps haunted by the memory of the little monk being burnt alive in that Roman square, the once fearsome inquisitor would be uncharacteristically charitable when presented with another heretic, the astronomer Galileo, whom the cardinal spared from the auto da fé.

The question is still unanswered: what was Bruno a martyr for? It's been cliché for centuries that he was the original sacrifice for the new science, a scapegoat delivered by the hands of a backward and superstitious church. But none of it is as easy as that, for, as I have said, Bruno was no scientist. And his own biography denies that he had a personal opposition to the very church which would ultimately condemn him; after his excommunication Bruno attended Mass every week (and when in non-Catholic countries attended the services of those lands), while faithfully and respectfully abstaining from the Eucharist, in accordance with the terms of his expulsion from the Church. Several times in his life he tried to have the bill of excommunication reversed, pleading with confessors that he be readmitted, but with these cases only able to be nullified by a bishop or the pope. In 1889 a group of Italian free-thinkers emboldened by the anti-clericalism of Garibaldi's Risorgimento commissioned the sculptor Ettore Ferrari to place a statue of the Nolan in the Campo de Fiori as a monument to early science and secularism. In his hooded cowl, which the historical Bruno had not actually worn for years, and which made him look like a character from one of Mathew Lewis' gothic novels, Bruno seemed to face accusingly in the direction of the Vatican. At least that's how his directional stance has usually been interpreted. Who is to say that the look on his face isn't one of longing?

It is an inconvenient fact that while Bruno was certainly a heretic in his era, he'd remain one today as well, albeit one not sacrificed in a public square. In the sixteenth century he perhaps naively and unintentionally existed outside the strictures of normative Christianity. But today his strange world view and his esoteric epistemology would mark him as separate from the prevailing intelligentsia's positivist orthodoxy. Despite modern declarations that canonize Giordano Bruno as a martyr for science, he was not. There was not yet a "science," not even a word for it. The Renaissance is a foreign and confusing nation. Its laws are different from ours; its rules are different from ours; its thoughts and dreams are different from ours. They speak not just a different language, but the very definitions of words are different. Bruno lived in a twilight world, not quite antiquity and not quite modernity. He was not against it, but he was not a martyr for science. He was a martyr for something else. In his own words, his belief was that there was a "harmony with all nature, and…a general philanthropy by which we love even our enemies, lest we become like brutes and barbarians, and are transformed into his image who makes his sun rise over good and bad, and pours out a rain of grace upon the just and the unjust." Perhaps he was a martyr for a faith that is not yet ready to be born? But in the end, he was a martyr for something. And maybe that, in its own way, is enough.

But a Walking Shadow, or: The Metaphysics of Shakespeare

Prospero famously says towards the conclusion of *The Tempest,* "We are such stuff/As dreams are made on; and our little life is rounded with a sleep." I argue that this sentiment – that our lives are somehow illusory, and that fiction and reality are closely intertwined – constitute William Shakespeare's central philosophical position. Colin McGinn, author of *Shakespeare and Philosophy,* is in agreement. He explained to me that "Skepticism is Shakespeare's main theme." He continued by explaining that "the possibility of error about people and the world...in its many forms" is the central epistemological subject of the plays. Furthermore, Shakespeare argues not only that life, like theater, is fundamentally a fiction, but also that it is the task of the individual to self-fashion themselves in light of that realization.

I would not argue that Shakespeare was somehow a professional philosopher – after all, his first duty was always to the construction of artifice. And yet in 1817 William Hazlitt claimed that Shakespeare "was as good a philosopher as he was a poet." Indeed McGinn agreed when he wrote to me, "How could Shakespeare not be a philosopher – he was everything else?" Perhaps it behooves us, especially today on the four-hundredth anniversary of his death, to reflect on the ways that our most singular and all-encompassing author consistently conveyed this particular philosophical perspective – how he was the proponent of his own skeptical-minded Shakespearean Platonism.

The question of the gulf between appearances and reality is arguably the central project of metaphysics. As an issue of ontology it has motivated Kant, Descartes, Berkeley, Hume, the great pre-Socratic philosophers like Parmenides, Pythagoras, and of course Plato, for whom as Alfred North Whitehead noted, "all of western philosophy is but a footnote." If this is true, then Shakespeare wrote some of the most illuminating commentary (and critique) in that collection of annotations. Shakespeare has Imogene in *Cymbeline* take part in a moment of dark ironic Platonism when upon waking next to a decapitated corpse she remarks, "I hope I dream'/For so I thought I was a cave-keeper." In her own literal, and perhaps Platonist cave, she mutters "'Twas but a bolt of nothing, shot at nothing,/Which the brain makes of fumes: our very eyes/Are sometimes like our judgments, blind."

The sentiment would not be out of place in The *Republic*. In his allegory of the cave the philosopher famously compared our reality to being but shadows on a wall. But there is a problem for any artist who wishes to express this view, for if the world of human experience is simply an artifice, how much more so incomplete is that of the work of art? Plato and Shakespeare are in some sense in agreement that art and theatricality are a system of lies, but where the Greek wrote that "there is an ancient quarrel between philosophy and poetry," Shakespeare's cumulative approach to questions of artifice, reality, illusion, experience, and fiction across his thirty-six plays is to dramatize this fundamental paradox of life and literature.

Writing about the hallucinatory world of *A Midsummer Night's Dream* with its "rude mechanicals" and its gossamer sensibility, McGinn observed that the play "is all about the difficulty of distinguishing dreaming from wakefulness, illusion from reality, what is merely imagined from what is veridically perceived." This is not just the central theme of that play, but indeed it is the perspective of several of Shakespeare's works, from the ambiguous ghost in *Hamlet* to the statue of Imogene at the conclusion of *A Winter's Tale,* and the enchanted Forest of Arden in *As You Like it* (whose very title could grant a degree of epistemological relativism). Indeed it is from that last play where Jacque says that "All the world's a stage,/And all the men and women merely players." While it is of course not wrong to read this as a comment on the innate performativity of human social interactions, we can also take it in more radical ontological directions, or as A.D. Nuttall put it in his indispensable *Shakespeare the Thinker*, "An incipient Platonism is at work within the dramaturgical art."

Yet this is a Platonism that is combined with a certain Pyrrhonic skepticism (very much in the air at the time of composition). As Macbeth memorably utters, "Life's but a walking shadow, a poor player/That struts and frets his hour upon the stage/And then is heard no more." If Plato worried that literature was but a pale imitation of life, which was in turn but a pale imitation of the world of the Forms, then for Shakespeare the center holds even less. For it is not that theater is similar to our lives, but rather that our lives are similar to theater. Ah, but there is the rub, for in Macbeth's formulation if this drama is "Signifying nothing," than the actors (who are all of us) have the ability to endow their performances with their own meaning even if they mean nothing in and of themselves.

Shakespeare turns Plato's denunciations of art and poetics on their head to argue that it is the fictional narrative that is somehow more true than reality, or as McGinn writes, "fiction has *greater* longevity than material things, since Shakespeare's plays, say, will last longer than any building erected in his time; immortality belongs, if anywhere, to the characters of fiction, not those of real life." This is the central argument of "Shakespearean Metaphysics," though its origins are not with the playwright, even if he gives them their fullest dramatic encapsulation. Indeed the greatest Elizabethan literary critic Philip Sidney a few decades before the height of Shakespeare's career claimed something similar when he wrote that, "Now for the poet, he nothing affirms, and therefore never lies."

The presence of this sort of sentiment in an Elizabethan critic's writings is not historically surprising, and it should be kept in mind lest one take it as my argument that this particular perspective was unique to Shakespeare. Indeed Renaissance England was home to a diversity of philosophical positions that are reflected not just in the Bard's plays, but throughout the literature of the period. Continental Neoplatonism which was so central to the continental humanist project developed its own domestic flavors in the form of the Cambridge Neoplatonists, and a certain bemused skepticism celebrated in writers like Montaigne (who Shakespeare would have read in John Florio's translation) were widely explored by authors. Indeed questions of reality, illusion, truth, and artifice were common in not just the culture, but in the popular theater as well. Yet Shakespeare's contribution to this tradition remains the most culturally enduring.

As the critic Julia Briggs writes that "Elizabethan drama made no attempt to conceal the medium in which it operated. More often playwrights deliberately exaggerated its artificial qualities." She explains that authors "employed a wide range of techniques that openly acknowledged or even emphasized the mechanics of stage illusion, including prologues and other framing devices, asides, soliloquies, and plays-within-plays." In many ways early modern audiences had a sophisticated, metafictional and borderline "post-modern" approach to theater that when rediscovered by modern playwrights like Bertolt Brecht with his *Verfremdungseffekt* come across as experimental. This sense of the uneasy (and sometimes relative) relationship between artifice and reality underscored what Briggs has called the "stage-play world" of the period, where an uneasy relationship between reality and its representation defined experience from the theater to politics to religion.

But central to this "stage-play world" is what the critic Stephen Greenblatt calls "self-fashioning." He explains that the Renaissance upper-classes were able to construct a persona or identity according to a variety of social standards including behavior, fashion, and education. Self-fashioning is a form of both imitation, and performativity. In Shakespeare this social concept is certainly enacted, but there is an implication of more radical questions of illusion and reality as well. Antonio says in *The Merchant of Venice,* "I hold the world but as the world...A stage where every man must play a part." This is of course a metaphor, but it's a potent one and one where the more literal representations of dream and reality expressed in plays like *The Tempest* demonstrate Shakespeare's investment in this theme. This is, in part, the origin of Shakespeare's exceptionality. As McGinn explained to me, Shakespeare was "original in seeing that skepticism is part of life, not just an abstract philosopher's question" and that this is especially true "concerning other minds."

For all of the author's diversity in narrative subject, it is remarkable how consistently he engages with an argument for the illusory nature of observed reality. In that same monologue quoted earlier Prospero breaks the fourth wall of the theater, saying, "These our actors,/As I foretold you, were all spirits and/Are melted into air, into thin air." Drawing attention to the possibly literal location of the play's performance, the Duke of Milan says that "the great globe itself.... shall dissolve" once the enchanted trickery of the drama has ended. Of course the "great globe" could refer to the world itself.

In acknowledging both the fictive power of the theater, but also the fictive qualities of "real life," Shakespeare takes part in what philosopher Simon Critchley and Jamieson Webster call the "Gorgiastic Paradox of Theater" (named after the ancient Greek rhetorician). They ask "Is the truth best said or perhaps only said in a fiction; that is, in a lie and a falsehood? Might not the dubious legends of tragedy and the fake emotions they induce leave the deceived spectator in the theater wiser and more honest than the undeceived philosopher..?"

Indeed this seems to best express Shakespeare's metaphysics, that to paraphrase Picasso, "Art is a lie that reveals the truth," but also that life itself is a type of lie. The playwright's *Ars Poetica* finally is not just his demonstration of this deeply artificial reality we live in, but also his own talent and ability to construct such deeply affecting and powerful fictions which are still completely artificial. Almost every single possible personality type that one could encounter in everyday life has an analog in the thirty-six plays; that Shakespeare uses words alone to construct these brave new worlds with such people in them is a trick worthy of his Prospero. In the end it is the plays themselves that are the conclusion of his dramatic syllogism; their very existence is the "Q.E.D." of his argument about fiction and reality.

The Other Folio

Renaissance playwright Ben Jonson: sacred and profane, bawdy and holy, contrite and arrogant, dramatic and boorish. Examine Abraham van Blyenberch's painting of Jonson that hangs in London's National Portrait Gallery. Jonson does not cut a particularly handsome figure: His nose looks like it was broken in a fight (it probably was), his mouth hangs open, his hair is messy, and he seems hungover (he probably was). But it's hard not to see a keen intelligence and sarcastic humor in that intense, bemused, skeptical stare – not to mention a bit of pathos from a man who had his share of sorrow during his own life. When compared to the face of William Shakespeare, whether the balding, bourgeois shopkeeper of the first folio's engraving or the bohemian sporting a piratical earring in the Chandos portrait, Jonson's picture is largely invisible today. Ironically, if he's widely known for one thing, it's predicting his competitor's enduring popularity. He has become a victim, as he would put it, of "That old bald cheater, Time."

In the dedicatory sonnet he wrote in 1623 for the collected works of his sometimes-friend and all-the-time nemesis Shakespeare, he claimed that the latter was, "Not of an age, but for all time." Rarely is literary horserace betting so spot-on, as one only need look at the commemorations and reflections about the 400th anniversary of Shakespeare's death (I wrote my own article, in fact). Of course, Jonson's prediction was accurate, and in some sense it was correct to the detriment of the man who made it, for that little bit of verse about Shakespeare is probably the most widely quoted fragment of Jonson. Yet 1616 saw not only the death of Shakespeare, but also the publication of the first major folio of dramatic work, predating the more famous folio of Shakespeare's. At the ripe age of 44, and with his career only half over, Jonson took the unprecedented and unusual step of collecting his poetry (a respected form) alongside his masques and drama (relatively not respected forms), and compiling them in the large, expensive, prestigious form of the folio. Jonson's folio brought new legitimacy to the stage, and in the process he revolutionized English literature. Last April, Shakespeare had his day of commemorations; now, let this other folio and the man who made it have their moment, no matter how modest – even if Jonson was himself anything but a modest man.

Outside of academic circles, where there has been a resurgence in interest, Jonson is a distant third in the contemporary popular imagination about the time period, after canonical Shakespeare and sexy Christopher Marlowe. When it comes to Renaissance theater written by people other than Shakespeare, you're lucky to see Marlowe's *Dr. Faustus* performed, and some edgy directors will give us John Webster's *The Duchess of Malfi* or John Ford's fantastically titled *'Tis Pity She's a Whore*. Jonson, though it's not unheard of, isn't produced as often. Yet Jonson was the great showstopper of the age, revolutionizing the theater every bit as much as the others, writing in every major genre from domestic and revenge tragedy to city comedy, and penning verse that despite its deceptive simplicity is among the most moving of that age. Moreover, while Shakespeare is in some sense a cipher onto which a variety of positions and opinions can be projected, Jonson in his imperfections can seem more real. Shakespeare may have been for all time, but Jonson was so of his own age that he remains more tangible as a personality.

Like Shakespeare, Jonson was from a relatively working-class background (his step-father was a bricklayer). Accepted to Cambridge, finances precluded him from attending. But Jonson was still proud to the point of conceitedness when it came to his deep humanistic reading. After all, it was in that same sonnet to Shakespeare where Jonson jabbed that the Bard knew "Small Latin and less Greek." Like his counterpart, Jonson made a reputation in Southwark, across the Thames from the City of

London, which was governed by anti-theater Puritans. Jonson worked among the first commercial theaters in English history, surrounded by taverns, brothels, and bear-baiting pits, with the river acting as perdition's boundary. In the Middle Ages, theater had been an extension of the Catholic Church, with massive pageants like the Corpus Christi Cycle dominating the dramatic imagination. Upon the Reformation and with the stripping of the altars and the closing of the monasteries, theater was forced out of the cloister and into the entertainment business. There was already a coterie of playwrights writing on secular themes in blank verse before Jonson and Shakespeare would become famous, but it was Jonson's generation (and in large part Jonson himself) who would elevate the grungy, grubby, dirty medium to the realm of true art. Writers like Thomas Kyd, Thomas Dekker, John Fletcher, Richard Beaumont, Robert Greene, John Webster, and John Ford transformed the stage into a platform for exploring complex narratives, difficult characters, and immaculate turns of phrase.

In plays like *Every Man in His Humour* (1598), *Sejanus His Fall* (1603), *Eastward Ho!* (1605), *Volpone* (1606), *Epiocene, or the Silent Woman* (1609), *The Alchemist* (1610), *Bartholomew Fayre* (1611), and *The Devil is an Ass* (1616), among dozens more, Jonson perfected a distinctly English voice. He could shift from learned erudition to puckishly working class, a diction that could be estimably holy while also ribald, verse where the tavern's lanterns and the cathedral's candles burn your eyes simultaneously. Of his corpus there are masterpieces that can stand alongside Shakespeare and Marlowe, plays like the "beast fable" *Volpone,* a satirical account of the Court of St. James's diplomat in Venice, Jonson's friend Henry Wotton. In *Volpone* human personalities are endowed with bestial characteristics, from the titular character, who is a "Sly Fox;" to his sycophantic servant Mosca, who is as drawn to his master as a fly is to shit; Corbaccio "The Raven;" and Voltore "the Vulture," who is of course a lawyer. A similar sensibility concerning the foibles of human vanity regarding wealth, religion, and almost everything else is also demonstrated in *The Alchemist* with its cast of conmen, cut-purses, prostitutes, and credulous Anabaptists. But no play in Jonson's body of work, or indeed that of the English Renaissance's, is as unmitigated a triumph of narrative complexity, earthy dialog, and experimental finesse as his masterpiece *Bartholomew Fayre*. A "city comedy" that attempts to demonstrate the complex, chaotic, fetid, and glorious reality of everyday life in England's capital.

Jonson creates characters who ply their wares at the massive carnival-like fair at the edge of the city, where different classes and occupations all mingle, with the play presenting as complete a tableaux of the city as ever depicted on the stage during the Renaissance or any other era – Samuel Taylor Coleridge thought it among the most perfect plots ever created. Figures like Win Littlewit, Justice Overdo, and the unsurpassed Ursula the Swine Woman deserve to be resurrected on our stages more frequently, if at least for the weirdness of seeing the puritanical kill-joy Zeal-of-the-Land Busy intellectually humbled by a puppet during a theological argument centering on the genitals of marionettes. Jonson took every opportunity to get one over on his Puritan persecutors (who would ultimately close the theaters during the years of Interregnum, from 1649 to 1660). The author's irreverent cheer, as displayed in scenes such as the puppet-genital-disputation in *Bartholomew's Fayre*, establishes Jonson's fusion of learning and humor, always the most potent alliance against puritans either then or now.

A failed actor with the Admiral's Men, he became one of their star playwrights at the Rose Theater (and in turn Shakespeare performed as an actor in Jonson's early hit *Every Man in His Humour*). Paid £100 a year by King James I, Jonson is credibly the first Poet Laureate of England (placing him as the first in a line that would include William Wordsworth, Alfred Lord Tennyson, and Ted Hughes). Yet he also served prison time in

1597 for his role in writing a "Leude and mutinous" play entitled *The Isle of Dogs* (which is now lost), and then again a year later for murdering an actor in a duel. He received a comically light sentence by utilizing a loophole called "benefit of the clergy," where his knowledge of Latin supposedly demonstrated an immunity from civil courts.

In keeping with Jonson's wild contradictions, the scurrilous, libelous, banned, and imprisoned playwright found an intellectual home not just at Newgate Prison, but later at the Palace of Whitehall, where he helped to develop the genre of the masque. The aesthetic precursor to opera or the musical (or maybe even more appropriately the Vegas dinner show), masques were spectacular pageants of performance, music, and special effect pyrotechnics that demonstrated the Stuart Court's wealth and power. Often featuring "performances" by royalty themselves (including some of the first by English women upon the stage), Jonson entered a fruitful, if often contentious, creative partnership with the architect Inigo Jones. In masques written for Queen Anne, such as *The Masque of Beauty* (1608), *Oberon, The Fairy Prince* (1611), and *The Golden Age Restored* (1616), Jonson wrote dialog to be spoken among the technically dazzling mechanical sets of Jones, featuring marvels such as mermaids riding in on seahorses and the ladies of the court traveling upon a giant clam shell pulled by aquatic monsters across a raging storm. That latter effect was used in *The Masque of Blackness* (1605), which also has the dubious distinction of being among the first performances to use blackface in the depiction of African characters; the English had just begun their horrific role in the trans-Atlantic slave trade. If Jonson's legacy is one of creative brilliance, we must also reckon with the fact that it includes the Queen of England, Scotland, and Ireland standing aloft a palatial stage with burnt cork upon her face.

The charged, neon, electric luminescence of spectacle hangs about Jonson and his work. In short, Jonson was one of the inventors of creative marketing, with a sensibility that would be perfectly attuned to the gimmicks of the modern social media universe. For example, there was the publicity stunt whereby he spent several months in 1618 walking from London to his ancestral homeland of Scotland. He lodged in Edinburgh with the famed Scottish poet William Drummond who then wrote a popular account of the feat, a description of the new "British" Poet Laureate exploring a rapidly emerging terrain where England and Scotland were unifying. Jonson's reflections on his encounters were pithy and human; if Twitter had existed he'd have no doubt presented an entertaining collection of hashtagged reflections on his journey north (as indeed the University of Edinburgh did when they transformed Jonson's accounts into tweets a few years ago). Even more audacious than his walking tour to Scotland was the so-called "War of the Theaters" two decades earlier, which ran from 1599 to 1602, and featured Jonson in possibly mock-competition with the playwright Thomas Dekker (among others) in a rhetorical fight across several plays that seems to almost prefigure modern-day hip-hop feuds. Whether the whole thing was a legitimate display of grievances between writers or a cagey mutually beneficial marketing ploy to increase ticket sales is arguable, but this delineates precisely what's so fascinating and current about Jonson.

But if Jonson's plays were enjoyed during his lifetime, it was his poetry that was expected to achieve true posterity; though for the last century, Jonson's verse and that of his protégés have seen their regard fall in favor of more sophisticated poets. The eighteenth-century lexicographer Dr. Johnson (of no relation – notice the "h") defined the metaphysical poetry of Jonson's friend John Donne as poetry where "heterogeneous ideas are yoked by violence together," a verse that revels in contradiction and paradox. By contrast, Dr. Jonson identified the "Cavalier Poets" (or "Tribe of Ben") in opposition, with a more conservative aesthetic. It should be clarified that these categories are ever malleable, and that strictly speaking most literary historians classify Jonson less as a member of the Cavalier poets than as their guiding influence. But if Dr. Johnson was one of the first literary critics to distinguish between these two movements (ones that the poets themselves might not have recognized), then it wasn't until T.S. Eliot's 1921 essay "The Metaphysical Poets" that the critical regard of the "Tribe of Ben," and by proxy the man whom they drew inspiration from, would see a precipitous decline, from which the Cavaliers have never really recovered.

In Eliot's (accurate) estimation Donne and those influenced by him were poets of unique ability, exhibiting intellectual daring displayed with provocative metaphors, conceits, and wit. The Cavaliers, by contrast, were poets whose verse was as conservative as Eliot's politics – lyrics that were all *carpe diem*, gathering one's rosebuds while one can, drinking, carousing, and pining for some aristocratic golden age. Where the metaphysics were daring and mature, the Cavaliers were seen as traditional and childish. Where the metaphysics concerned themselves with the complexities of faith and doubt, the Cavaliers wrote poems about some comfortable, pastoral fantasy. Jonson's estimation of Donne was that, "for not being understood, [he] would perish," the irony being that it was Jonson who perished and precisely because he was understood too well. There is difficulty in simplicity, though; it's hard work to make a poem seem easy.

Still, Jonson, of course, was no Donne. Jonson's poetry may have had enough wit, cleverness, ingenuity, and immaculate phrases that his verse deserves to be anthologized next to Donne's *Holy Sonnets* or "To His Mistress Going to Bed," but ultimately there is a reason why Eliot canonized the metaphysical poets over the Cavaliers. As the Victorian critic John Addington Symonds observed of Jonson, "His throne is not with the Olympians but with the Titans; not with those who share the divine gifts of creative imagination and inevitable instinct, but with those who compel our admiration by their untiring energy and giant strength of intellectual muscle." With Donne's compasses, his globes, and his interrupting sun, the poet constructed an entirely novel little world, made cunningly. By contrast Jonson was less an initiator of a radical movement than he was an incredibly talented and competent writer of verse, albeit an often-brilliant playwright. And with such an outsized, Falstaffian personality (how he might despise that adjective being associated with him), it's easy to forget those closest to Jonson.

While writing poetry and staging those plays, Jonson and his wife had to bury three children. We aren't even exactly sure of the name of the woman whom Jonson described as "a shrew, yet honest," his wife who probably went by the appellation Ann Lewis. Despite Jonson's barb about her, by all accounts their matrimony was relatively warm. But the heartbreaks of life can take their toll; despite affection, they didn't live in the same house for Jonson's last five years.

Even if his inner life can sometimes be obscured in bombast and anecdote, more the raconteur with a glass of sack in one hand and a barbed comment on his tongue than a figure poised for introspection, the most moving of his poetry makes Jonson the human more closely available to us. If poetry is truly a fragment of emotional singularity, a warm and holy sanctuary providing organization to experience and meaning to life, then Jonson was nothing less than completely, and truly, a poet. Writing in elegy of his dead son, who shared his name, Jonson says, "Rest in soft peace, and, asked, say here doth lie/Ben Jonson his best piece of poetry." One should resist the cynicism that observes how Jonson equates his child as being simply another production of the poet's brilliant mind (even if "his best piece of poetry"), for a man of Jonson's ambition and ego that claim is not insignificant nor empty. But the poignancy and pathos of "On My First Sonne" is in its heartbreaking conclusion, "For whose sake, henceforth, all his vows be such,/As what he loves may never like too much." In that one line we get as much sense of the traumas and the losses of Jacobean London (where losing your children at a young age was no rare incident) as we do in all of *Bartholomew Fayre,* and we see the human at the center of Jonson's own self-mythologizing. Consider the pain that must accompany this self-imposed distance, this moratorium on feeling, whereby he must resist liking that which he loves due to the inevitability of its loss. The confessional is implicit in this 12-line masterpiece, and hiding among its letters and punctuation is a father's loss, preserved and passed down for four centuries.

Having written verse such as this, Jonson has no need to be celebrated with the biggest monument in the Poet's Corner, or to have his bust displayed in the lobbies of libraries, or to have his plays produced every month of every year in every major English-speaking city in the world. He has no need of those things because he has already perfectly accomplished what it is that a poem is supposed to do, whether that poem is known by everybody, anybody, or nobody. And we should be grateful to Ben Jonson for letting us share in his loss. And we should be thankful to Ben Jonson for writing poetry such as this. And we should remember Ben Jonson, this, the 400th year of his first folio.

The Dark Lady Inscribed in the Book of Life

In 1597 Amelia Lanyer visited the astrologer and physician Simon Forman several times at his practice on Philpot Lane in Westminster. Across thousands of pages, Forman, for whom the appellation "physician" is significantly less rigorous than it would be today, recorded his interactions with the residents of London. Forman has long been of interest because of the records of his attendance at plays from the Globe to the Blackfriars, his prodigious sexual conquests (for which he invented the odd noun "halek," as in "I had halek today"), and his testimonies about life outside of the noble coterie. Forman is also interesting because of Lanyer, who some critics have claimed inspired the infamous "Dark Lady" of William Shakespeare's sonnets. The evidence, as with many things from what is the undiscovered country that is the past, is incomplete and sometimes difficult to read (often literally, as with Forman's awful penmanship which has caused critical problems in past scholarship). But what is apparent is that Lanyer wasn't Forman's regular sort of client. While she may or may not have been Shakespeare's Dark Lady, she was most definitely the first professional woman poet in the English language. She is the author of an epic, feminist, mystical rewriting of Genesis entitled *Salve Deus Rex Judaeorum*, published in 1611, and which has only recently been given critical attention.

And just as fascinating, she is perhaps the first "Jewish" poet in English as well.

She was the daughter of a court musician and the wife of another, former mistress to Henry Carey, the Baron Hunsdon (who was first cousin to the queen) and some years after her associations with the magician Forman, her literary patron would be Margaret Clifford, Countess of Cumberland. It was to the last that she dedicated her *Salve Deus Rex Judaeorum*, attaching several patronage poems to her single volume, taking part in the complex economics of negotiation and validation existing between a poet and her patron. Among these poems was her admittedly treyf-sounding *A Description of Cooke-Ham* (the name is that of the estate it describes), written in the Augustan conventions of the "country house poem," celebrating the space of Clifford's residence which Lanyer made her home when widowed. Never an aristocrat herself, Lanyer was of the middling yet rising gentry. Her mother, Margaret Johnson, was aunt to Robert Johnson who wrote many of the musical settings for Shakespeare's plays, her husband Alfonso was a second-generation Huguenot who performed for Elizabeth, and her father Baptista Bassano played for Henry VIII.

It is from Baptista's side that Lanyer has her Jewish associations, for some scholars with varying degrees of certainty have claimed that the Bassano line were *marranos*, converted Jews maintaining connections with their ancestry. Some argue that the family were originally Moroccan Jews, a Sephardic complexion used to claim Lanyer as the Dark Lady. Susanne Woods, Lanyer's most complete biographer and one of the scholars who has done more than anyone to kindle an appreciation of her poetry, finds the evidence compelling but inconclusive. Baptista Bassano was from Veneto, a holding of Venice, where the surname "Bassano" was commonly Jewish, and where Jews were frequently employed as musicians. Lanyer's nephew was even married into an English *converso* family, perhaps indicating a community of converted Jews who kept social associations with each other. Tellingly the Bassano coat-of-arms depicts silk worms, hosiery being one of the few occupations granted to Jews in Veneto.

The title of her magisterial poem *Salve Deus Rex Judaeorum*, with its prominent placement of the word "Jews," could indicate her Jewish background. A literal translation of the title being "Hail God, King of the Jews" would seem to indicate it less so.

And yet I would argue that a close reading of the poem demonstrates not just the probability of Lanyer's Jewish connections, but that she had some knowledge of the faith as well, specifically the Kabbalistic traditions so associated with Renaissance Sephardim like Isaac Lauria. It is the idiosyncrasies of this heterodox tradition that may have supplied material she used to launch her feminist defense of Eve in that poem. To be clear – I am not arguing that Lanyer herself was secretly Jewish. There are baptismal records at Bishopgate for her, and her father's relationship with the vehemently Protestant Seymour family implies that they may have been Protestant refugees from Italy (though the father's name of Baptista would be characteristic of recent converts proving their new Christian bona fides). Rather, what I am arguing is that Lanyer was able to use a particular manifestation of Judaism to produce a borderline heretical Christian rereading of women's religious role.

But why the connection to the Dark Lady? Most of what we know is contained in the records of Dr. Forman. She consulted him after her husband had traded in the lute of the ensemble for the sword of the navy, as he journeyed to Cadiz on Essex's expedition against the hated Spanish. She was not particularly close to him and their marriage was an issue of professional convenience. Wanting his future read wasn't an issue of sentiment, it was to divine if a title was to be granted (it would not be). Forman also poignantly records she suffered several miscarriages (only one son survived, who would also become a musician) and feared for her current pregnancy, which she would also lose. Less poignant is that the consistently unethical Forman wondered if Lanyer's precarious emotional state would lend her to being an easy mark for his sexual advances. As with so many men of his kind, when she demurred, he labeled her a "whore" in his diaries.

The British historian A.L. Rowse in his 1973 *Shakespeare the Man* controversially (and for many unconvincingly) claimed that Forman's writings proved that this supposedly raven-haired, black-eyed, olive-complexioned woman was the adulterous companion of the greatest writer in English, and was the Dark Lady of his sonnets. The sonnet was invented in the Middle Ages by Catalan troubadours, perfected by the Italian Petrarch whose influence emanates through the Renaissance, introduced into English by Henry Howard who was the final execution of Henry VIII's reign, and explored in cycles by Wyatt, Sidney, Spenser, Drayton, and Donne. But Shakespeare's sonnet sequence is the penultimate one, and the Dark Lady is its beating heart. The Dark Lady's ghost has haunted English literature ever since. As a game of puzzle solving, scholars have obsessively tried to identify the "characters" in the 154 sonnets which comprise the greatest compendium of lyric poetry in English. For critics of an autobiographical bent (which is largely out of fashion) the narrator is obviously Shakespeare. The "fair youth," whom he often describes in homoerotic terms, is often thought to be the young aristocrat William Wriothesley, the third earl of Southampton. The rival poet's identity? For these critics it must be Christopher Marlowe, the brilliant, tortured, sexy author of that most diabolic of texts, *Dr. Faustus*, stabbed through the eye in a Deptford tavern at the age of 29. And the Dark Lady, the most enigmatic of these already faint shadow identities, who was she?

She whose "eyes were nothing like the sun," whose "heart torments" with her "false-speaking tongue," and yet whose dark complexion proved that black is "beauty's successive heir." The Dark Lady, mistress of the poet whose dalliances with both the fair youth make a cuckold out of the narrator. The Dark Lady is simultaneously evocative, independent, intelligent, sensual, loving, and cruel. The Dark Lady who is slandered with that ancient slur against women, which impugns sexual desire and desiring, and which perhaps owes more to the perceived sin of Lilith than Eve. The Dark Lady, who is an example of Shakespeare's genius in creating characters who seem to actually live. It is impossible to not see what is intensely attractive about the Dark Lady – and it's hard not to sympathize with the inclination to try and uncover who she was based on. But this is assuming that she was indeed based on someone. Though we don't know her name, her personality is viscerally, almost materially conveyed through the subtle language of the poet. Elizabethan and Jacobean England valued physical fairness in a woman, strawberry blonde hair and stereotypically rosy cheeks. Exemplified by Laura in Petrarch's *Il Canzoniere,* or by Stella in Philip Sydney's eponymous sequence of c.1580, or in the pale visage and red hair of the female regent who oversaw this Golden Age. Yet Shakespeare subverted this ideal, describing his beloved as "dusky," "dun," "dark," and most provocatively as "black." He took the generic convention of the *blazon* (in which the anatomical perfections of a woman were enumerated) and turned it upside down, celebrating what would have marginalized the Dark Lady during the period.

Early modern Europeans tended to be prejudiced more on theological difference than perceived racial ones (this period saw the origins of describing people as "white" and "black"). Catholics, various dissenting sects of Protestants, a conflation of Turks, "Saracens," and Moors into one amorphous Islamic menace (not so different from today), so-called "Blackamoors" (or people of African descent who Elizabeth tried to expel from her kingdom), and of course, the Jews were all marginalized people in England. Although the Bassanos may have had Jewish ancestry, the Jews were a people who were seemingly mentioned everywhere and who existed nowhere. Officially expelled in the thirteenth century, it seems unlikely that men like Shakespeare, Marlowe, or Donne had ever met a practicing Jew. And yet Shakespeare gave us his Shylock, Marlowe his Barabbas in the anti-Semitic *The Jew of Malta,* and Donne said (at least metaphorically) that the Jews did "Buffet, and scoffe, scourge, and crucifie" him. Yet communities of Jews lived within London, mostly exiles from the *Reconquista* in Portugal and Spain, and all converted Protestants.

The most famous was the queen's personal physician, Roderigo Lopez. He fell afoul of Elizabeth, and was implicated in a conspiracy to have her assassinated (historians have subsequently exonerated him). Before he was hanged, drawn, and quartered at that bloody field of traitors and blasphemers known as Tyburn, the *converso* who most likely remained true to his adopted faith screamed that he "loved the queen as well as he loved Jesus Christ." The crowd, assuming him to be ironic, erupted into laughter. Shakespeare scholar Stephen Greenblatt has conjectured that the playwright may have been witness. Only four years later Shylock would prowl and slink on the stage of the Globe, wearing the kinky red fright wig and the over-sized fake nose that were standard costuming for Jewish characters.

But the Bassanos were different in other ways as well, for the English had a conflicted relationship with Baptista's homeland. Italy was the origin of the Renaissance and in regard to fashion and literature was to be emulated. But it was also the home of that fabulous beast, the Whore of Babylon who all good Protestants associated with the pope's throne of St. Peter. Italians were physically and perhaps spiritually dark, impetuous, violent, scheming, Machiavellian, overly physical, and superstitious. We can sense the English sentiment about Italians when we read Thomas Nashe's 1594 *The Unfortunate Traveler,* possibly the first novel written in English, which depicts an Italian nobleman forcing his enemy to pray to Satan and then killing him immediately. The blood-soaked plays of Jacobean revenge drama were replete with over-the-top Italian names, defined as such by simply ending in a vowel more than because of any verisimilitude.

The malleable borders of whiteness can be seen if you look at the globe that sits behind two staid French diplomats in Hans Holbein's 1533 masterpiece *The Ambassadors.* Europe is surrounded by the white-space of all the continents separate from Christendom – North Africa, the western border of Asia, the recently uncovered lands of the Arctic north and the eastern fringe of America – all a neutral white. Europe alone, and her partner island Britain at her western edge, is a blazing, celestial gold. The only exceptions to this are two other more unfortunate islands off of Europe's coast, who we are to assume aren't part of Europe and her civilization – Ireland and Sicily. Venice in particular held a special fascination. In that independent, liberal, and perhaps licentious city-state the English saw a dark mirror-image. Also a powerful naval state defined by trade, Venice's churches and bishops operated semi-independently of Rome. It had been a way-station for Italian Protestants who had made their way to London's so-called "stranger churches." Venice fascinated with its claustrophobic alleyways and canals, its grand squares and opulent palaces, its ominous masked balls and its printing-houses willing to trade in any manner of heresy. Lanyer's family may have been Jewish, but they wouldn't have had to have been to be outside the mainstream, no matter how successful they were at their trade. Still, the Bassanos were non-dissenters, which is to say that they were faithful attendees of the Church of England. But even if her baptismal certificate said she was an Anglican, and even if her own beliefs were faithfully Christian, I believe that her prayers were still uttered in a Jewish tongue.

Lanyer's only book of poetry appeared in an auspicious literary year. The printing presses of London also inked three Shakespeare quartos, Chapman's translation of Homer, a Jonson play, Donne's *Anatomy of the World,* the complete works of Edmund Spenser, a reprint of *Dr. Faustus,* and perhaps most monumentally of all, the first edition of the King James Version of the Bible. Lanyer's slim book of verse would have competed in the book stalls crowding the square in front of St. Paul's and in the print shops lining Grub and Fleet streets along the river Thames from the City of London to Westminster. And yet nothing in the corpus of English literature was quite like Ms. Lanyer's accomplishment. Women had certainly written in England before, the fourteenth century had authors like Margery Kemp and Julian (ne Jillian...) of Norwich, closer to Lanyer's era Anne Lok reflected on the penitential psalms in a magisterial sonnet sequence, and Mary Sidney, the sister of Philip, produced an almost unparalleled version of the Davidic songs configured in every single poetic form available. Mary Wroth had written her massive romance *Urania,* and even Queen Elizabeth composed verse. But all of these women were noble in some way, Lanyer was something new, a woman who professionally wrote. Noblewomen were willing to pass their poems about in manuscript form, all of them steadfastly avoided the "stigma of print," like an author disdaining the internet. Among the coterie of working-class authors like Jonson and Shakespeare, Lanyer's writing was sold for money, in the book stalls of the metropolis.

What was just as surprising was the content of her book. In her prescript to *Salve Deus Res Judaeorum* she writes, "this have I done, to make known to the world, that all women deserve not to be blamed." She targeted the Augustinian view of original sin being Eve's fault, and blames this orthodoxy on "evilly disposed men, who forgetting they were born of women, nourished by women, and if it were not by the means of women...would quite be extinguished out of the world." She defends Eve from the accusation that she was responsible for man's fall by explaining that if Adam had full knowledge of the prohibition that ultimate responsibility must lieay with him; furthermore if she was supposedly made from the material of Adam, than that initial sin must be traced ultimately back to him. Considering that the bulk of the poem then focuses on Christ's passion, what is particularly Jewish about all of this? There is a precedent for the appropriation of Judaism in an act of creative subversion. Theresa of Avilla, the sixteenth-century Spanish nun, was of *converso* progeny, a fact which ran her afoul of the Inquisition before she would find herself celebrated by those who attempted to persecute her.

Though a fervent Catholic (she is a saint obviously) she consciously utilized the rhetorical tropes of Kabbalistic texts like the *Zohar* in her baroque writings. Lanyer does something similar, when she writes, "This honey dropping dew of holy love,/Sweet milk, wherewith we weaklings are restored...Lilies and with roses...Your constant soul doth lodge between her breasts,/This sweet of sweets, in which all glory rests" (all spelling has been modernized by the author). The references to honey, milk, dew, roses, and the bridegroom (whom she references three times in the poem) seem distinctly Solomonic. The Hebraic parallelism of "sweet of sweets" conjures the biblical poetics of the Jewish scriptures which Christian rhetoricians were only beginning to categorize. This Jewish poetics of the erotic was common in Laurianic kabbalah, indeed compare the following fifteenth century Spanish poem *Shiur Qomash* which is narrated by a woman to her beloved (who is God) with a passage from *Salve Deus Rex Judaeorum*. First the section from *Shiur Qomash*:

My beloved is fresh and ruddy,
To be known among ten thousand.
His head is golden, purest gold,
His locks are palm fronds
And black as the raven.
His eyes are doves
At a pool of water,
Bathed in milk,
At rest on a pool;
His cheeks are beds of spices,
Banks sweetly scented.
His lips are lilies,
Distilling pure myrrh,
His hands are golden, rounded,

Set with jewels of Tarshish.
His belly a block of ivory
Covered with sapphires.
His legs are alabaster columns.

The imagery is unmistakably similar to that from *Song of Songs*. Not only that, but the convention of a bride writing a love letter to her bridegroom who is God is a mainstay of Kabbalistic poetry from the middle ages. It's hard not to see Lanyer as working in this exact same tradition when she writes:

This is that Bridegroom that appears so faire,
So sweet, so lovely in his Spouses sight,
That unto Snowe we may his face compare,
His cheeks like scarlet, and his eyes so bright
As purest Doves that in the rivers are,
Washed with milk, to give the more delight;
His head is likened to the finest gold,
His curled locks so beauteous to behold;

Black as a Raven in her blackest hew;
His lips like scarlet threads, yet much more sweet
Than is the sweetest honey dropping dew,
Or honey combs, where all the Bees doe meet;
Yea, he is constant, and his words are true,
His cheeks are beds of spices, flowers sweet;
His lips like Lilies, dropping down pure myrrh,
Whose love, before all worlds we do prefer.

Or take the section where she writes, "Long may thou joy in his almighty love,/Long may thy soul be pleasing in his sight,/Long may though have true comforts from above,/Long may thou set on him they whole delight" with its uncanny similarity to the priestly blessing of the kohanim. Not only that, but there are phrases where she seems to reference the *Shekhinah*, God's indwelling presence within the tabernacle, which in Hebrew is grammatically feminine and which she may have understood as functioning like the Holy Spirit in the Christian Trinity. She writes of "…an immortal Goddess on the earth/Who though she dies, yet Fame gives her new berth," a possible allusion to the *Shekhinah*, which after all would take the form of an "immortal Goddess on the earth." There are strikingly Jewish images, including the bridegroom, the tabernacle, possibly the *Shekhinah*, and the Book of Life where she writes, "By his deserts the foulest sins to clear;/And in the eternal book of heaven to enroll," a sentiment that many Jews may recognize from the *Yom Kippur* liturgy. Though the Book of Life does appear in Christian writing such as the Pauline Epistles (though Paul was a Jew of course) its association with the High Holy Days makes it seem particularly Jewish. Lanyer mentions it six times, a notably high amount for a Christian author. And what would being enrolled in the "eternal book of heaven" be but being inscribed in the Book of Life? And what Zion was Lanyer dreaming of when she wrote, "Yay, look how far the east is from the west," eerily similar to the most celebrated line of the medieval Jewish poet Judah Halevi who wrote, "My heart is in the east, and I am in the uttermost west?"

When A.L. Rowse conjectured that Lanyer may have been the Dark Lady, he claimed that the only record of her existence was in Forman's diaries. It's true that the Ashmolean Museum at Oxford where Rowse was working contained Forman's writings but none of the nine surviving copies of *Salve Deus Rex Judaeorum*. Yet a short walk to the Bodleian Library and Rowse could have found this book by a woman he claimed was silent, only speaking through Shakespeare's sonnets. Thankfully literary scholars have given the "Dark Lady" an afterlife; professors like Susanne Woods, David Bevington, Marshall Grossman, and Barbara Lewalski among many others have ensured that Lanyer will occupy a place in the cannon she was denied because of her gender. Conservative critics like the always-pugnacious Harold Bloom attribute this widening of the cannon to "political correctness." Far from it, the inclusion of a poet like Lanyer is not a denigration of the cannon, it's an acknowledgment that she should have always been included. Did Lanyer have Jewish ancestry? I believe that a biographical reading as well as a literary analysis demonstrates that she probably did. Was Lanyer the Dark Lady? Anyone who argues that with any degree of certainty is being purposefully naïve or disingenuous. Now, 370 years after her death, what's important is that she doesn't need to be the Dark Lady. It's already impressive enough that Amelia Lanyer is herself.

East of El Dorado

Before his execution on October 29, 1618, Sir Walter Raleigh enjoyed one last pipe of tobacco. Then, before laying his head upon the block, he engaged in a polite disputation with his executioner. According to William Tyler Olcott in his 1914 compendium *Sun Lore of All Ages*, "There was a discussion as to the way he should face, some saying he should face the east. Raleigh then remarked: 'So the heart be straight it is no matter which way the head lieth.'" It's an anecdote that presents the explorer as calm, courageous, scholarly. One imagines Raleigh staring toward the direction of golden sunset, toward that mythic city of El Dorado, which he'd repeatedly failed to find in the South American jungles. There's a certain poetry in his response as well; in addition to his reputation as courtier, explorer, adventurer, and war criminal, he's also one of our greatest poets.

Raleigh's artistic stock has waxed and waned, even if his lean, muscular, and plain style appealed to a certain imperial Victorianism. Even today, any comprehensive period anthology will include Raleigh's most notable lyrics, especially his 1592 "The Nymph's Reply to the Shepherd," a response to Christopher Marlowe's pastoral "The Passionate Shepherd to his Lover." The pair were so popular that the biographer Izaak Walton would record some half-century after the poems' composition that two milk maids would repeat the conjoined lyrics back and forth from memory, having "cast away all care, and sung like a nightingale...the ditty fitted for it."

It's hard to categorize "verse for milk maids." Literary historian Michael Schmidt describes Raleigh's "preferences for plain style and brusque, masculine utterance." Schmidt sees Raleigh as a nascent metaphysical poet, not unconvincingly arguing that his verse "rich in verbal texture and in metaphor extended" implies that Raleigh is most properly classified alongside John Donne and George Herbert. C.S. Lewis noted Raleigh's propensity for Anglo-Saxon affectations, his rejection of the humanistic optimisms of the sixteenth century, and as such he classified the poet as an anti-Petrarchan, as holding a vehemently English, almost anti-Renaissance position. Raleigh rejected the flowers of rhetoric, save for those simple (but not simplistic) tropes of the plain style: contrast, antithesis, anaphora, alliteration, parallelism, and the monosyllable. Lewis claimed that such opposition merited Raleigh's inclusion among the "drab poets," such as John Davies or Michael Drayton. Despite Raleigh's continued anthologizing, his reputation as a relatively minor poet endures.

By contrast, the idiosyncratic American poet-critic Yvor Winters saw great value in Raleigh's rejection of Petrarchism. The so-called "Winter's Canon" endures as a counterfactual literary history, valorizing poets whom he saw as unfairly marginalized. Winters presented a shadow canon existing in tandem with Shakespeare, Marlowe, Donne, and so on. A teacher of poets including Philip Levine, Donald Hall, and Robert Pinsky, Winters exacted a crucial, if obscured, role in what we talk about when we talk about Elizabethan verse. For Winters, a rejection of the excesses of Romanticism necessitated a recovery of plain style poets who'd long been passed over, a coterie of writers for whom verse was defined with the almost Puritanical parsimony of simply being "the art of saying something about something in verse," where the poem is nothing more complicated than a "statement in words about a human experience." In *The New Criterion*, David Yezzi explains that Winters' "greatest single essay" was a piece for *Poetry* magazine were Winters argued that the Elizabethan era was "the most versatile in the language... unequaled, the peak from which he perceived a long decline."

According to Yezzi, Winters' "critique of the poetry of the late sixteenth and early seventeenth centuries flouts convention," especially in his reclamation of plain style in opposition to the intricate beauties of Petrarchism. Critiquing Lewis's language surrounding the "Drab Poets," Winters writes that the former had blamed "modern scholars for approaching the period with Romantic prejudices" while conceiving of the "entire poetry of the period in terms of a Romantic prejudice." Winters' condemnation of Lewis, and by proxy the academic establishment, was withering; the problem with Lewis is that "he likes the pretty so profoundly that he overlooks the serious." In arguing that plain style was superior to the "sugared" affectations of those inheritors of Petrarchism (including Shakespeare), Winters rejected "rhetoric for its own sake" and identified an enduring strain of minimalism which has defined much of subsequent canonical literature, particular American and Modernist writing. For a fine example of Raleigh's proficiency in the plain style, take the prefatory sonnet for Edmund Spenser's *The Faerie Queene*, an epic dedicated to Raleigh, who was Spenser's commanding officer during the atrocity at Smerwick during the Second Desmond Rebellion. Raleigh's sonnet is a brief in favor of both Spenser's mythmaking, as well as of the plain style:

> Methought I saw the grave where Laura lay,
> Within that temple where the vestal flame
> Was wont to burn; and, passing by that way,
> To see that buried dust of living fame,
> Whose tomb fair Love, and fairer Virtue kept:
> All suddenly I saw the Fairy Queen;
> At whose approach the soul of Petrarch wept,
> And, from thenceforth, those Graces were not seen:
> For they this queen attended; in whose stead
> Oblivion laid him down on Laura's hearse:
> Hereat the hardest stones were seen to bleed,
> And groans of buried ghosts the heavens did pierce:
> Where Homer's spright did tremble all for grief,
> And cursed the access of that celestial thief!

Raleigh enacts a sort of *translatio studii et imperii*, whereby the cultural significance of the Italian Renaissance will pass onto Britain as the site of future greatness. Spenser's epic simultaneously built upon and rejected Italian models, such as Ludovico Ariosto's *Orlando Furioso* or Torquato Tasso's *Jerusalem Delivered*. Both the epic itself and Raleigh's sonnet make an argument for nascent English literature, in opposition to models then in vogue. Raleigh imagines the burial place of Petrarch's unrequited lover for whom *Il Canzoniere* drew its inspiration; the explorer sees "the grave where Laura lay," and though hers is of a "living fame," her mortal remains are so much "buried dust." The metaphorical significance in Raleigh's nationalist argument is obvious.

Raleigh's reveries are interrupted by the appearance of Spenser's Fairy Queen, for even whom "At whose approach the soul of Petrarch wept." The graces which inspired Petrarch have left, just as surely as the spirit of history moves in a westerly direction, where even "Homer's spright did tremble all for grief,/And cursed the access of that celestial thief!" There is something apocalyptic in the sonnet, where "hardest stones were seen to bleed/And groans of buried ghosts the heavens did piece"; it conjures up nothing less than the raptures of Judgment Day itself, of the dead arising after the crucifixion, and as such it connects the project of English literary greatness to a millennial project. The sonnet is crafted with a certain parsimonious, minimalist elegance. An argument could be made that poems are best evaluated by how visceral their first lines are; as such, the memorable "Methought I saw the grave where Laura lay" would place Raleigh within the caliber of Donne or Emily Dickinson. His initial line is perfectly wrought.

His range was impressive, more impressive than has sometimes been claimed. Consider his unfinished "The Book of the Ocean to Cynthia," probably written while he was first imprisoned, possibly reconstituted by him from memory, and only rediscovered in 1860 among the papers of William Cecil, Elizabeth's chief adviser. At an intended 15,000 lines, Schmidt describes it as "his longest and most ambitious poem," best understood as "essentially autobiographical epic romance." Schmidt explains that Raleigh has "moved beyond the aphoristic style, pithy and spare" and that the piece "traces English poetry's transition from plain to aureate style," arguing that the poem "can be read as 'modernist' *avant la lettre.*"

Written from the perspective of the Ocean addressing the Moon, the symbolism involves a rather obvious declaration from the sea-faring Raleigh to the Queen. These poems must be read as part of the project of bolstering British literary and imperial greatness; they should, of course, be understood as part of that hagiographical scripture for Elizabeth's Cult of Gloriana. It would be apt, though, to also read something like "The Book of the Ocean to Cynthia" as a primogeniture of "American" literature, both because of who wrote it and because of its thematic concerns. Raleigh writes, with America in mind, that, "To see new world for gold, for Praise, for glory,/To try desire, to try love sever'd far,/When I was gone, she sent his memory,/ More strong than were ten thousand ships of war./To call me back." If there was any constant in Raleigh's mind it was this "new world of gold," this constructed El Dorado to which he would ever sail, and that image of a land overflowing with material opportunity that has been an American myth since the beginning.

Scholar William Spengemann explains that the "writings we call Early American Literature enact and document" that discovery itself, "standing as they do at the crucial point where the geographical history of English, previously confined to a corner of Europe, first crosses the eastern shoreline of the New World." In Raleigh's poetry one sees intimations for elements of American literature from Herman Melville to Ernest Hemingway, arguably the genesis of a tradition where appropriately enough

Raleigh is himself the first "American" writer. For Spengemann, Raleigh's writings mark the "beginning of a long process of geographical expansion, demographic redistribution, and linguistic change," and as such one could classify "The Book of the Ocean to Cynthia" as a type of "American" epic.

Yet his most arresting poetry lay elsewhere. Raleigh's considerations of mortality rank him alongside Donne as one of the most perceptive in a particularly melancholic era. Schmidt describes "The Passionate Man's Pilgrim," supposedly written on the eve of execution, as "the most amazing confrontation with death in English verse." The explorer writes:

> And this is my eternal plea
> To him that made heaven, earth, and sea:
> Seeing my flesh must die so soon,
> And want a head to dine next noon,
> Just at the stroke, when my veins start and spread,
> Set on my soul an everlasting head.
> Then am I ready, like a lamer fit,
> To tread those blest paths which before I writ.

His unadorned style conveys homespun piety, where God is simply addressed as He that "made heaven, earth, and sea" (note the descent downward, and the end stop with that geographic feature that made Raleigh's name). Part of what's so remarkable is the thought of Raleigh envisioning the promise of "an everlasting head" the evening before he was to lose his; the Christian hope that his "soul, like a white palmer,/Travels to the land of heaven." It's like a Protestant version of *jisei,* the Japanese death poems written by Zen monks prior to their passing.

Far from Raleigh's reputation for impiety, the libertine quaffing drams at the Mermaid Tavern, or the supposed member alongside Marlowe of an infernal "School of Night," his death poem reconciled him to orthodoxy. In fairness, there is also that other Raleigh, the radically skeptical one; the poet who described, "Our mothers' wombs the tiring house be/Where we are dressed for this short comedy"; the Raleigh who condemns, "Heaven the judicious spectator is/That sits and marks still who doeth act amiss"; the dour cynic who preaches that, "Our graves that hide us from the searching sun/Are like drawn curtain when the play is done." This is the Raleigh who in his *History of the World* would describe God as "the author of all our tragedies," for whom, "there is no other account to be made of this ridiculous world than to resolve that the change of fortune on the great theater is but as the change of garments."

His contention is as old as Ecclesiastes and as recent as existentialism. Raleigh arguably expresses a conventional *contemptus mundi* pose in keeping with the melancholia of the age which produced Robert Burton and Thomas Browne, yet there is still something arrestingly modern about it. Even more so a translation of Catullus: "The sun may set and rise,/But we contrariwise/Sleep after our short light/One everlasting night." No intimations of immortality, nor succor of God; understandable that some would impugn Raleigh with the charge of "atheist," even as he speaks through the deniable persona of a long-dead Roman.

I've no idea to Raleigh's personal atheism; the record is contradictory, and besides, overly autobiographical readings of literature are avoided for a reason. I suspect, like all of us, he tended to be a little bit of both, to varying degrees, depending on circumstance, despite Schmidt's contention that "He speaks for and as himself." Hard not to want to read Raleigh that way, this ever evocative, ever vital, ever romantic, ever troubling man. An innate attractiveness in this poetic explorer whom Schmidt reminds us had to live by "talent, wit, chicanery, and strength," who "writes not out of habit but necessity."

If I can conjecture about Raleigh's spiritual orientation, however, I wonder if not his variable agnosticism was born out of a desire not to necessarily see a Paradise in heaven, but to find one on earth. America, after all, was that which he pursued unto the very gates of mortality, the failed expedition to an El Dorado cause of his final misfortune, for it was that which spent his life. In "Farewell to Court," he writes of a "country strange without companion," using prescient language eerily prefiguring his circumstances in 1617, stranded on Trinidad after seeing his son killed, and awaiting transfer back to London to be punished for violating the terms of his agreement with the King.

William Carlos Williams, in his 1940 response to Raleigh's response to Marlowe, writes that, "We cannot go to the country/ for the country will bring us/no peace." Williams used the word "country" in the same pastoral sense as the original pair, but we'd be apt to think of it in the sense of the Americas as well, for America certainly brought Raleigh no peace, even as he prayed that the discovery of some temporal Eden would earn him respite from the punishment to which he'd been condemned. The poet was no atheist when it came to belief in America, though that god had ultimately betrayed him, as he placed his head upon the block towards the westerly direction of paradise, a country from which no explorer, not even Raleigh, may return.

The Destroyer of Worlds in His Newfoundland

On July 16, 1945 an assembled group of scientists saw a false sun rising in the west. Here, in the *Jornardo del Muerto*, scientific myths of progress and religious myths of the last days were finally fused in a terrifying transmutation of mass into energy. They witnessed an alchemical nightmare at Alamogordo, New Mexico where man's fear and desire for apocalypse was finally matched by man's technical ability. It is hardscrabble country, desolate, alien, foreign, uninviting, inhuman. "Single Day's Journey of the Dead-Man" is the translation of the name of this barren basin that was a northern edge of colonial New Spain. The Spanish supposedly named it after a German prisoner that perished while trying to escape the clutches of the Inquisition, death marking its earliest days. It is a country where the twin dreams of New World millennialism ambivalently exist alongside the apocalypse that naturally awaits any journey into not just a New World, but the Last World. It was here that the Spanish searched for the utopian paradise of the Seven Cities of Cibola, but also where Franciscans and Dominicans were killed in the Pueblo Revolt. Here, towards the far west of the North American continent, life and death exist in reciprocal accord. El Dorado and the Seven Cities of Cibola do not exist in the *Jornardo del Muerto*, but the Trinity Test Site did. It was there, long after this land had been indigenous, Spanish, or Mexican, that the United States – that inheritor of millennial expectations and apocalyptic desires – tested its first atomic bomb.

Years later J. Robert Oppenheimer, the learned, cultured, cosmopolitan physicist who headed the Manhattan Project, was asked by its military director, Lieutenant General Leslie Groves, why he had chosen to name the test site "Trinity." Groves had assumed that Oppenheimer chose the name arbitrarily, just another generic religious place name that would throw off any suspicion that something special was happening in the New Mexico desert. The physicist answered:

> There is a poem of John Donne, written just before his death, which I know and love. From it a quotation: "As West and East/In all flat Maps – and I am one – are one,/So death doth touch the Resurrection." That still does not make a Trinity, but in another, better known devotional poem Donne opens, "Batter my heart, three person'd God."

And so this site – where the intense heat of man's first nuclear explosion would transmute sand into glass – would forever be known as "Trinity." Less than a month later 129,000 Japanese civilians would die at Hiroshima and Nagasaki.

Scarcely more than a year before the Trinity test, Oppenheimer's mistress, the psychiatrist Jean Tatlock, had committed suicide. Her father, John Tatlock, was a prominent literary scholar and had introduced his daughter to Donne right as the first generation of New Critics and modernist writers began his rediscovery as a poetic voice (and not just as the author of the sermons for which he was also rightly celebrated). It's been conjectured that Oppenheimer first read Donne while living at Los Alamos, given a copy of his poems by Tatlock. If he named Trinity in honor of his dead mistress, he scarcely could have picked a more appropriate writer. In Donne we see not just the combination of radically discordant metaphorical images "violently yoked together" (as Dr. Johnson famously had it) but also the conflation of the individual with the cosmos, a life with all of human history. Microcosms and macrocosms endlessly reflect one another so that a person can be the universe and a single death the apocalypse. In his splitting and combining of metaphors we have a type of literary fission and fusion and in the atom bomb we have the most sublime of this metaphysical poetry writ gargantuan. As Donne could see the whole world in a room, the apocalyptic destruction of the bomb from the tiniest of atoms shows us a little world made cunningly: it is a combination of elements, of angelic sprite and black sin.

That Donne should be connected to Oppenheimer is one of those illuminating oddities of history that, given the physicist's incredible breadth of knowledge, should ultimately not be seen as surprising. In this, Year 70 of the Newfoundland that was discovered by men like Oppenheimer, it is worth considering the correspondences that exist between Donne and he. This may not provide answers but rather questions; there may be no argument but perhaps reflection. It would be untenable to argue that Donne influenced Oppenheimer. "Trinity" is merely the name Oppenheimer chose – an atomic bomb test by any other name would be as destructive. But this synchronicity across time does provide us seven decades later with a way of examining the metaphorical, or perhaps even allegorical, connections that exist between poetry and reality. The two were after all not just masters of paradox in their respective domains – Donne with the wit of the metaphysical conceit, Oppenheimer with the enigmas of quantum mechanics – but in their own lives as well. The seventeenth-century poet was both Jack Donne, libertine seducer of women, and Dr. John Donne, Dean of St. Paul's. Oppenheimer was both the American patriot and the political subversive denounced as un-American by his own government; and he was the sensitive pacifist who constructed the most violent weapon in humanity's arsenal. It was a tool that could melt both poles at once, and store deserts with cities, and make more mines in the earth than quarries were before. In the consilience of Oppenheimer and Donne, science and literature, there are shadows of the ever-receding sun in the west, premonitions of that last day to come.

Indeed if America is the nation which may have provided the first actual means for a man-created apocalypse then Donne's

"Holy Sonnet XIV" is an appropriate baptismal name for that moment zero in human history. As mentioned earlier, both Donne and Oppenheimer were fascinated with the transformation of space. The tiny and the large, the atomic and the cosmic, exist in a more malleable relationship than common sense would assume. For Donne "one little room could be an everywhere," and Oppenheimer demonstrated how the rapid splitting of atomic nuclei could unleash enough energy to level a city in a second. But Donne saw in the declining West a prophecy – for as history ever moved forward into the future it also moved geographically to the west – the prediction of the classicists' *translatio studii et imperii* or the biblical Daniel's visions. In America, history had reached its conclusion, its westernmost terminus. The circle had been closed where the occident collapsed into the oriental, and *Revelation* must be fused with *Genesis*. Donne's logic – in fact many people's logic, spread across poetry, sermons, and pamphlets – had it that America's westernmost status signified it as the site of our play's last scene. The irresistible logic of history and the arc of teleology signified the new lands at the western edge of our maps as the site of Judgment. Indeed Donne himself preached in a sermon from 1628 at St. Paul's that:

> In a word, whether we be in the Easterne parts of the world, from whom the truth of Religion is passed, or in the Westerne, to which it is not yet come; whether we be in the darknesse of ignorance, or darknesse of the works of darknesse, or darknesse of oppression of spirit in sadnesse, The world is the Theatre that represents God, and every where every man may, nay must see him.

For Donne and many others the natural course that history must take was the transition of faith from the eastern world where the "truth of Religion is passed" to the western, to "which it is not yet come." Indeed, Donne himself harbored an obsession with America: he had attempted to immigrate to Virginia but been unable to do so, and this very sermon was preached before the stockholders of the Virginia Company. For Donne, America was the site of mankind's last act. With such a prophecy, whose poetry would have been more appropriate to christen that nuclear testing site in the western desert?

If we were to construct a new calendar system to reflect a new world, one would start with July 16, 1945. Donne wrote that, "We think that Paradise and Calvary,/Christ's cross and Adam's tree, stood in one place." Alamogordo, New Mexico was the Adam's tree of our new error, the atomic apple plucked as part of the Faustian bargain of pure knowledge manifested in terrifying violence. It's the first moment and also paradoxically the last, a Calvary of sorts, though it remains doubtful whether this New Golgotha offers any promise of salvation.

Some of the physicists harbored a worry that the intense heat of the nuclear explosion would cause a chain reaction in the atmosphere, atoms fusing together and engulfing the whole planet in the equivalent of a massive hydrogen bomb. Hans Bethe – the man who figured out how stars actually shone while the poets were just observing that they did – performed a few calculations on the back of an envelope and decided that that fear was probably unfounded. That day they did not go and catch a falling star. To wrench a lyric of Donne's from its original context and to invert it, the scientists had feared, "There I should see a Sun by rising set,/And by that setting endless day beget."

The physicist Richard Feynman recounted desperately trying to get his radio communication working with others assembled to watch the test, and finally freakishly hit the frequency of a classical music station out of San Francisco just as the bomb detonated, the desert eerily filling with the sound of arias as the horizon became a blinding light, the music only to be silenced by the tremendous sonic blast of the bomb itself as sound caught up to light.

Enrico Fermi, who first constructed a fissionable nuclear pile under the squash courts at the University of Chicago, reported that: "Although I did not look directly towards the object, I had the impression that suddenly the countryside became brighter than in full daylight. I subsequently looked in the direction of the explosion through the dark glass and could see something that looked like a conglomeration of flames that promptly started rising."

A 13-year-old boy named Jim Madrid, driving with his mother to Hollman Air Force Base where he often did odd jobs for extra money witnessed the blast as he traveled west:

It rose from the heavens, so bright, so extremely bright. My mother said in Spanish, *"El sol esta arrimando. El mundo se va a acabar."* The sun is coming close. The world is coming to an end...She told me to drop to my knees, but I kept looking... That light was horrendous. As high as the heavens. I expected to see God coming out from under it. If it's the end of the world, I wanted to see.

As Donne wrote, "Yesternight the sun went hence,/And yet is here to day." A few hours after the blast a bewildered farmer found one of his donkeys standing, dead, with his eyes open. It seems he had been frightened to death by the blast, the first casualty of the nuclear age.

In 1721 the Puritan divine Cotton Mather – who was an inheritor of Donne's eschatological hopes in the redemptive promise of America – had a vision from the comfort of his Boston manse: "We have seen the sun rising in the west." At 5:29:21 July 16, 1945 – half an hour before God's dawn – a new sun rose in the west of Alamogordo. It signaled the emergence of man's dawn. Donne and Mather had been correct: the means of apocalypse had been created here in the uttermost west, but whether redemption would follow remained unanswered, and seems increasingly unlikely.

It was Oppenheimer's reaction that would be the most famous. Not only a dutiful student of science, but a prodigy trained in languages, history, religion, literature, he claimed that a line from the *Bhagavad Gita* emerged in his mind like the flash to the west. "If the radiance of a thousand suns were to burst at once into the sky, that would be like the splendor of the mighty one…Now I am become Death, the destroyer of worlds." It was unclear whether the United States had killed God or merely created a new one. The bomb was a "quintessence even from nothingness,/From dull privations, and lean emptiness"; it was a thing "Of absence, darkness, death – things which are not." It had the power to bend, force, break, blow, burn, and make the world new. Months later – after thousands of Japanese had been instantly incinerated, thousands more dying in hideous physical pain from radiation sickness, and still thousands more permanently handicapped – the physicist told President Harry Truman that he felt like he had blood on his hands. The president told him to wash them. And then he privately told an adviser that he never wanted to see Oppenheimer again.

It was in 1962 that Groves asked his odd-couple civilian partner in the birth of the atomic age why he had chosen the name "Trinity." By that point HUAC had hounded Oppenheimer over tangential relationships to suspected communists during his student days, he had lost his security clearances and had effectively retired to the directorship of the Institute for Advanced Study where to the chagrin of the mathematicians and physicists, he hired that other apocalyptically minded poet (and champion of Donne) T.S. Eliot, falling into alcoholism and despondency over his ruined reputation and the nuclear age he had inaugurated. It was at this point in his life that Oppenheimer reflected "Trinity" took its name from a conflation of two Donne lyrics, "Hymn to God, my God in my Sickness" and "Holy Sonnet XIV."

Oppenheimer's explanation of the choice performs its own close reading of the poems by the light of a nuclear flash (we'll leave Tatlock's role to theorists of a more Freudian disposition). "Hymn to God, my God in my Sickness" says "As West and East/ In all flat Maps – and I am one – are one, so death doth touch the Resurrection." On a sphere, a globe, there is always more east or more west to travel to as one converts and conflates into another. It is only on a map (Donne's "Imagined four corners") that there are definite edges to the east and to the west, and that all four cardinal directions' most extreme definitions are the edges of the paper. East and west are positive and not merely relational qualities in the fiction of the map. It is these "flat Maps" which produce the illusion of a definite east and west. For Donne, death and Resurrection are similarly illusory, ultimately being one. In the "flat Map" of a human life, death and resurrection seem real and final. For Donne, in the spherical reality that is actual life, death and resurrection merely mingle into one another, as east and west do in reality. In this way Oppenheimer seems to betray an optimism that his famous quotation of Krishna from the *Mahabharata* didn't indicate – that this death should signal a resurrection. For Donne – and for Oppenheimer? – east is always touching west just as death is always touching rebirth. And yet batter our hearts' nuclear bomb; no resurrection seems to have come from those New Mexico sands.

It may have been that the bombing of Hiroshima and Nagasaki prevented a hideously violent invasion of the Japanese homeland. But the great fear of the promethean nuclear demon released from bondage is that it will verify Chekhov's principle of narrative – if you see a gun on a table in the first act of a play you can be guaranteed it is going to go off in the last.

A dark vision – it is the midnight of our age, and the world's last night. New York, Washington, Moscow, Beijing, Berlin, London, all the great cities of the world destroyed in whatever war is to come. St. Paul's Cathedral once laid waste in the Great

Fire of the late seventeenth century and almost destroyed again in the blitz of 1940 finds itself in ruins. In the debris one can make out the remains of a chapel built in honor of the men that perished in that last world war. It is dedicated to the Americans who fought alongside the British, and facing that chapel is a statue of John Donne, the base of which is still black from the flames that almost destroyed London in 1666. In this way Donne stares at an America to which he always wished to journey and to which he never did. The statue is based on a drawing of Donne in his death shroud, made while he was still alive, and which he hoped would depict how he would look upon his resurrection at the Day of Judgment.

Now I ask, J. Robert Oppenheimer may have convinced us of the reality of apocalypse, but how many of us are naïve enough to still believe in Donne's millennium which would follow? Can Donne's grave be broken up again, can any of ours, can the world's? After such death who can still believe in resurrection? Who among us has faith that on that last day the dead eyes of Donne's funeral statue will be able to finally open, and that if he could, he would be able to see anything left in that west? Can we still believe in spite of it all?

Evidence of hope: after the destruction of Hiroshima the official United States military report predicted that the soil in the city would be so radioactive that nothing would be able to grow there until the year 2020. Yet in the autumn of 1945 a photographer took a photo of a single red canna flower growing through the rubble of the destroyed city. Donne writes: "And Death shall be no more, Death, thou shalt die."

Et in America Ego

"Raleigh is telling how he discovered Earthly Paradise in Guyana the previous year, over there where El Dorado lies hidden. He licks his lips recalling the flavor of iguana eggs and closes his eyes describing the fruits and the leaves that never fall from the treetops...Raleigh's friend, a baldhead with mischievous eyes, knows that this Guyana is a swamp where the sky is always black with mosquitos, but he listens in silence and nods his head because he also knows that Raleigh isn't lying."
Eduardo Galeano, Genesis (1985)

Four centuries ago, Sir Walter Raleigh, last of the Elizabethans, of those adventurers, of those deeply problematic plunderers who endure now more in place name than in posterity, placed his head upon the block and went on his last journey to the west. One imagines Raleigh staring towards the direction of the golden sunset, its color reminding him of that mythic city of El Dorado, which he'd repeatedly failed to find in the South American jungles, and to where he was sailing when he attacked the Spanish galleons, the immediate cause of his final misfortune.

Prior to that, he'd been imprisoned for more than a decade by King James I, unfairly implicated in an assassination conspiracy known as the Main Plot. Occasionally the favorite of Queen Elizabeth I (save for when he wasn't), Raleigh had initially been received by her replacement, with one contemporary reporting that Raleigh was capable of making James "laugh so that he was ready to beshitt his Briggs." Such laughter wouldn't last, however, as Raleigh became inconveniently implicated in the supposed plot, the rare accused crime which he was not actually guilty of. Regardless of the merits of the man's character, Raleigh's thirteen years imprisoned in the Tower of London gave him time to write some of the most startlingly beautiful Renaissance verse, poetry which in its plain style often approaches perfection. What more appropriate way to mark the quadricentennial of his death than to commit to his rediscovery as one of our great poets, compromised though he may be?

The explorer is often remembered as a dignified refugee from the Elizabethan world of courtier scholars, who was abandoned by a Stuart monarchy that represented an increasing capitulation to a world less romantic than that of their predecessors. That's the license we see displayed in the pre-Raphaelite painter John Everett Millais' 1870 The Boyhood of Raleigh. In Millais' imagination, a young, blonde-haired Raleigh sits in drab black, chin cradled in hand, listening in concentrated attention to a swarthy, exoticized Genoese sailor who tells tale of navigable lands west of the sunset.

Almost as obvious in symbolism as the toy ship at the lower left of the canvas is that Genoese sailor, whose impartation of adventure stories signifies a passing of colonial destiny from the Mediterranean to the British, a visual enactment of translatio studii et imperii. What Millais' painting also inadvertently enacts is another, subtler transition, for Raleigh was not just an explorer, but indeed a poet as well, for whom those two vocations had more in common than might first be assumed. As Peter Linebaugh and Marcus Rediker argue in The Many-Headed Hydra, "the cause of a New World empire depended on not only the colonist's trifling beads but also the poet's trifling books."

Appropriate that Millais has as his subject the mediation of stories, for Raleigh's hidden contribution has always been his poetry, often projected onto the very land itself. Raleigh is a veritable incarnation of his age, "the archetypal imperialist adventurer" as Linebaugh and Rediker call him, observing that Raleigh "served as a model for the exploration, trade, conquest, and plantation of English mercantilism." Millais' painting flatters Raleigh and exemplifies our culture's dominant perspective on a complicated man whose name is widely known, but whom the public rarely considers.

Raleigh, as he is memorialized, is a kind of English conquistador, an adventurer associated with the mysterious lost colony at Roanoke and the courtier of apocryphal pablum who prevents Queen Elizabeth's slippers from being muddied by throwing his coat into a puddle, of whom literary historian Michael Schmidt remarked that the explorer was the sovereign's "favorite because he exceeded all the other courtiers in the inventiveness and extravagance of his courtesies," a figure whom his seventeenth-century biographer John Aubrey described as a "tall, handsome and bold man...he was damnable proud." Historians, however, have complicated this myth, with Raleigh's military actions during the 1580 Siege of Smerwick during Ireland's Second Desmond Rebellion being rightly understood as an atrocity.

Raleigh would oversee the slaughter of six hundred surrendering Italian, Spanish, and Irish troops, with his half-brother Sir Humphrey Gilbert writing that "the heads of all those (of what sort soever they were) which were killed in the day, should be cut off from their bodies and brought to the place where he encamped at night, and should there be laid on the ground," explaining that "none could come into his tent for any cause by commonly he must pass through a lande of heads." Historian Daniel K. Richter recounts that a contemporary observer noted that this caused "Greater terror of the people when they saw the heads of their dead fathers, brothers, children, kinsfolk and friends."

Irish heads on pikes foreshadowed Raleigh's ultimate fate, just as surely as Milais' toy boat prefigured his career. If post-colonial theorists and historians have necessarily complicated Raleigh's legacy, seeing not the dashing privateer, but the pirate; not the sophisticated courtier, but the war criminal; not the explorer, but the importer of a dangerous narcotic, then the general public thinks barely of Raleigh at all. Such are the vagaries of a *Washington Post* article from 2011 which reported that a fourth-grade textbook entitled Our Virginia soberly repeats the common error that Raleigh himself charted the North American mainland, a landmass he never set foot on. Raleigh, for most it would seem, is more the capital of North Carolina than a Renaissance man.

Yet despite his myriad sins and crimes, Raleigh would still be considered the Renaissance man exemplar, as sullied as that designation may now be. While I'd argue that the recovery of his poetic verse is an important scholarly and editorial project, his "non-fiction" prose writing alone confers upon him the status of one of the most important writers of the English Renaissance, where the relative factuality of some of his accounts merits the square quotes in the description of that genre as practiced by him.

With an almost Borgesian wisdom, Raleigh understood maps to be their own type of fiction, writing that the "fictions (or let them be called conjectures) painted in maps do serve only to mislead such discoverers...but to keep their own credit, they cannot serve always." Sometimes unfairly categorized by his contemporaries as a notorious atheist, Raleigh at least did understand the contingencies of truth and falsehood when writing an engaging narrative, where one must exonerate those colorful, lying maps with their terra incognita, for they don't always serve the truth, but sometimes illustrate an itinerary to that more colorful country of imagination. Raleigh's motto would aptly be a line of verse from his contemporary Sir Philip Sidney's romance The Countess of Pembroke's Old Arcadia, where though the latter may be speaking of Elizabeth, the sentiment (as with the explorer) could also be oriented towards the world of fantasy in contrast to the dreary particulars of reality: "Reason looke to thy selfe, I serve a goddess."

This goddess of Wonder might as well be the dominant

presence in the narratives of exploration which stud English Renaissance literature. Critic Jeffrey Knapp has convincingly argued in An Empire Nowhere that "the discovery of America spurred the English to write," claiming that England's relative colonial belatedness when compared to her Catholic neighbors encouraged the production of a fantastic literature that imagined "America," while the Spanish and Portuguese explored the actual thing. Pointing towards works as varied as Thomas More's 1516 Utopia, Shakespeare's 1610 The Tempest, and Francis Bacon's 1624 New Atlantis, Knapp argues that the Golden Age of English literature was born both as a means of compensation and as an expression of wonder, which Stephen Greenblatt describes in Marvelous Possessions as the "central figure in the initial European response to the New World, the decisive emotional and intellectual experience."

Raleigh's contention about the accuracy of maps is from his massive, unfinished compendium The History of the World, written in fits and starts while imprisoned for more than a decade in the Tower. That volume would be impressive enough, but it's his short 1595 travel account The Discovery of Guiana which more than solidifies him as a particular, cracked type of epic poet. Elizabeth's 1584 patent charged Raleigh "to discover, search, find out, and view such remote, heathen and barbarous lands, countries, and territories, not actually possessed of any Christian prince, not inhabited by Christian people... to have, hold, occupy & enjoy," and his colonialism was writ in the very language of possessive romance, for as scholar Roland Greene argues in Unrequited Conquests, "Petrarchism is part of that imperialist project." Raleigh forged his actual experiences alongside invention in the smithy of his imagination and produced a slender little thing which did as much as any other book from the Age of Exploration to invent a particular, paradisiacal dream of El Dorado – of America.

Raleigh describes a country along the Orinoco River as "the

most beautiful country that ever mine eys beelf: and whereas all that we had seen before was nothing but woods, prickles, bushes, and thorns, here we behelf plains of twenty miles ineght, the grass short and green, and in diverse parts groves of trees by themselves." Protestant that he was, he was also inheritor of a certain medieval typological thinking, with Raleigh's account seeing him pass from that fallen world east of Eden into the veritable Garden itself. Based on his own highly embellished experiences of the South American jungle, it wouldn't be out of place to imagine an account of passing the Seraphim's flaming swords which guard the entrance to Paradise, for in the rain forest it is "as if they had been by all the art and labor in the world so made of purpose: and still as we rowed, the Deer came down feeding by the water's side, as if they had been used to a keeper's call." In heaven even the wild are as if tame.

The Discovery of Guiana is a chimerical book. Categorizable alongside other masterpieces of early modern exploration literature, such as Richard Hakluyt's 1582 Diverse Voyages or his massive Principle Navigations published in various editions from 1589 to 1600, or Samuel Purchas' 1614 Purchas, his Pilgrim (both of whom incorporated Raleigh's accounts), Raleigh's pamphlet also evokes more archaic, romantic associations. In a proto-scientific era obsessed with filling in the gaps, Raleigh understood the evocations of colorful, cartographic sea monsters painted deftly. Other sixteenth century accounts of exploration, such as Thomas Harriot's 1588 A Briefe and True Report of the New Found Land of Virginia, penned after an expedition to the Raleigh-financed Roanoke colony, eschewed the fantastic in favor of the sober, almost scientific recounting of flora, fauna, and people.

Such is Harriot's objectivity that anthropologists still praise the accuracy of illustrator John White's depictions of the Lenape, who were ultimately felled by both disease and genocide. Raleigh, though he actually saw the New World himself, eschewed verisimilitude in favor of poetry, finely wrought. Where Harriot presents detailed ethnography about the Virginians, Raleigh's account owes more to the fabulist tradition of medieval travel, such as the fourteenth century narratives of the concocted "Sir John Mandeville." In that medieval classic, credulous Englishmen read about monstrosities and miracles in Africa and Asia, by a man who claimed to be a knight traveling among the sundry lands. Raleigh similarly populates his newly found lands with terrifying cannibals, fierce Amazons, and the headless akephaloi – the difference between the two accounts being that Raleigh actually lived, and also that he knew his tales to be exquisitely wrought deceptions. What Raleigh offered was the promise of El Dorado, a land more akin to the medieval realm of Cockaigne, or Utopia, than it was of the fetid jungles which he had actually found.

Rather than providing explication of folkways, vocabulary, and societal organization as Harriot did, Raleigh writes that, "the Incas had a garden of pleasure...which had all kinds of garden herbs, flowers and trees of gold and silver, an invention and magnificence till then never seen." Harriot was producing science, while his employer was content to still write in the idiom of myth, cataloging not the rain forest, but rather the very Garden of Eden. In The Stage Play World, historian Julia Briggs describes Raleigh's exploratory discourse as "Riven with inconsistences" as mingling a "factual account of his travels with a fictional discourse of exotic and idealized lands."

But it would be a mistake to divide mythos and logos too radically from one another in the genre conventions of the early modern travel narrative. Raleigh merely made explicit what was often subconscious in those other texts, for as Greenblatt reminds us in Renaissance Self Fashioning, "descriptive terms are shared in the Renaissance by literary romance and travelers' accounts... because the two modes of vision are mutually reinforcing." In that sense, Raleigh was not merely a discoverer of American lands, he was their inventor too, and as a poet writing in the idiom of those discoveries he must rank as one of the most vital of the era. Vitality is not synonymous with morality, however, and as we collectively face our own rapidly heating west, brought about in part by the very "America" whom Raleigh was so instrumental in penning the epic of, we must confront the possibility that it is a dark poem for which we'd perhaps be better off had it not been written. Erasure, however, is impossible (and besides, if it were, none of us would be here to consider it). Better to remember that poetry is always amenable to revision and editing.

The Unfortunate Invention of White People

The Jacobean playwright Thomas Middleton invented the concept of "white people" on October 29, 1613, the date that his play *The Triumphs of Truth* was first performed. The phrase was first uttered by the character of an African king who looks out upon an English audience and declares: "I see amazement set upon the faces/Of these white people, wond'rings and strange gazes." As far as I, and others, have been able to tell, Middleton's play is the earliest printed example of a European author referring to fellow Europeans as "white people."

A year later, the English commoner John Rolfe of Jamestown in Virginia took as his bride an Algonquin princess named Matoaka, whom we call Pocahontas. The literary critic Christopher Hodgkins reports that King James I was "at first perturbed when he learned of the marriage." But this was not out of fear of miscegenation: James's reluctance, Hodgkins explained, was because, "Rolfe, a commoner, had without his sovereign's permission wed the daughter of a foreign prince." King James was not worried about the pollution of Rolfe's line; he was worried about the pollution of Matoaka's.

Both examples might seem surprising to contemporary readers, but they serve to prove the historian Nell Irvin Painter's reminder in *The History of White People* (2010) that "race is an idea, not a fact." Middleton alone didn't invent the idea of whiteness, but the fact that anyone could definitely be the author of such a phrase, one that seems so obvious from a modern perspective, underscores Painter's point. By examining how and when racial concepts became hardened, we can see how historically conditional these concepts are. There's nothing essential about them. As the literature scholar Roxann Wheeler reminds us in *The Complexion of Race* (2000), there was "an earlier moment in which biological racism...[was] not inevitable." Since

Europeans didn't always think of themselves as "white," there is good reason to think that race is socially constructed, indeed arbitrary. If the idea of "white people" (and thus every other "race" as well) has a history – and a short one at that – then the concept itself is based less on any kind of biological reality than it is on the variable contingencies of social construction.Bottom of Form

There are plenty of ways that one can categorize humanity, and using color is merely a relatively recent one. In the past, criteria other than complexion were used, including religion, etiquette, even clothing. For example, American Indians were often compared with the ancient Britons by the colonizers, who were descendants of the Britons. The comparison was not so much physical as it was cultural, a distinction that allowed for a racial fluidity. Yet by the time Middleton was writing, the color line was already beginning to harden, and our contemporary, if arbitrary, manner of categorizing races began to emerge.

The scholar Kim Hall explains in *Things of Darkness* (1996) that whiteness "truly exists only when posed next to blackness": so the concept of "white people" emerged only after constructions of "blackness." As binary oppositions, "whiteness" first needed "blackness" to make any sense. The two words create each other. The scholar Virginia Mason Vaughan writes in *Performing Blackness on English Stages, 1500-1800* (2005) that: "Blackfaced characters in early modern dramas are often used...to make whiteness visible." "Black" and "white" have never referred to defined groups of people; they are abstract formulations, which still have had very real effects on actual people.

There is little verisimilitude in describing anyone with either term, which explains their malleability over the centuries. How arbitrary is it to categorize Sicilians and Swedes as being "white," or the Igbo and Maasai as both "black"? This kind of racial thinking developed as the direct result of the slave trade. Hall explains: "Whiteness is not only constructed by but dependent on an involvement with Africans that is the inevitable product of England's ongoing colonial expansion." As such, when early modern Europeans begin to think of themselves as "white people" they are not claiming anything about being English, or Christian, but rather they are making comments about their self-perceived superiority, making it easier to justify the obviously immoral trade and ownership of humans.

Hall explains that the "significance of blackness as a troping of race far exceeds the actual presence" of Africans within England at the time. Before Middleton's play, there were a host of imagined "black" characters, such as in Ben Jonson's *The Masque of Blackness* (1605), which featured Queen Anne performing in blackface, as well as Shakespeare's "noble Moor" in *Othello*, staged a couple of years before Middleton's play. Understandings of race were malleable: in early modern writing, exoticized characters can be described as "dusky," "dun," "dark," "sable," or "black." Depictions of an exoticized Other weren't only of Africans, but also Italians, Spaniards, Arabs, Indians, and even the Irish. Middleton's play indicates the coalescing of another racial pole in contrast to blackness, and that's whiteness – but which groups belonged to which pole was often in flux.

Consider the Dark Lady of Shakespeare's sonnets. In sonnet 130, he says of his mysterious paramour that "her breasts are dun"; in sonnet 12, he references her "sable curls"; and in sonnet 127 he writes that "black wires grow on her head." As is commonly understood, and taught, Shakespeare subverted the tradition exemplified by poets such as Petrarch who conceptualized feminine beauty in terms of fairness. Part of this subversion lay in pronouncements such as the one that states that black is "beauty's successive heir," a contention of Shakespeare's that can seem all the more progressive when our contemporary racial connotation of the word is considered. Thus, how much more radical is his argument in sonnet 132, that "beauty herself is black/And all they foul that thy complexion lack." Shakespeare's racialized language connoted a range of possibilities as to how the Dark Lady's background could have been imagined, and the conjecture that she was based on women variously European or African indicates this racial flux in the period.

Or take Caliban, the native of the enchanted isle colonized by Prospero in *The Tempest*. Often sympathetically staged in modern productions as either an enslaved African or an American Indian, there are compelling reasons to think that many in a Jacobean audience would rather understand Caliban as being more akin to the first targets of English colonialism, the Irish. By this criterion, Caliban is part of the prehistory of "how the Irish became white," as the historian Noel Ignatiev put it in 1995. None of this is to say that Caliban is actually any of these particular identities, nor that the Dark Lady should literally be identified as belonging to any specific group either, rather that both examples provide a window on the earliest period when our current racial categorizations began to take shape, while still being divergent enough from how our racialized system would ultimately develop.

Yet our particular criteria concerning how we think about race did develop, and it did so in service to colonialism and capitalism (and their handmaiden: slavery). Bolstered by a positivist language, the idea of race became so normalized that eventually the claim that anyone would have coined such an obvious phrase as "white people" would begin to sound strange. But invented it was. With the reemergence today of openly racist political rhetoric, often using disingenuously sophisticated terminology, it's crucial to remember what exactly it means to say that race isn't real, and why the claims of racists aren't just immoral, but also inaccurate. Middleton demonstrates how mercurial race actually is; there was a time not that long ago when white people weren't "white," and black people weren't "black." His audience was just beginning to divide the world into white and not, and, unfortunately, we remain members of that audience.

Race might not be real, but racism very much is. Idols have a way of affecting our lives, even if the gods they represent are illusory. In contemplating Middleton's play, we can gesture towards a world where once again such a phrase as "white people" won't make any sense. In realizing that humans were not always categorized by complexion, we can imagine a future where we are no longer classified in such a way, and no longer divided as a result of it either.

Monarch of Letters: "Rabbi" John Selden and the Restoration of the Jews

"Rabbi" John Selden used to spend many evenings enjoying a glass of sack or a pint of ale (or several) at the Mermaid Tavern located between Friday and Bread Street. Drinking within distance of the bells of St. Paul's, the good "rabbi" would share the insights of his brilliant jurisprudential mind with Jacobean England's intelligentsia; here, the Inner Temple legalist argued over bitters with the playwright Ben Jonson (who called his friend the "Monarch of Letters"), or heard from William Strachey about the dramatic crash of the *Sea Adventurer* off the coast of Bermuda. In fact, when he was younger he may have had a drink at the Mermaid with that establishment's most famous regular who based a play called *The Tempest* on Strachey's story about that Atlantic shipwreck, possibly recounted to him in that very pub. William Shakespeare would tie one on after a performance at the Globe, and when the explorer Walter Raleigh wasn't imprisoned he would frequent the tavern too, as would the poet John Donne. There were many nights Selden could have spent in conversation, from when he entered the Inner Temple to train as a jurist in 1604, through the reigns of James, Charles, and then the years of civil war and Cromwell. An informal gathering of writers and intellectuals called the "Sireniacal Gentleman" often met at the Mermaid (alongside a group with the similarly unlikely name of the "Damned Crew"), certainly an unusual synagogue; what conversations did "Rabbi" Selden have with them? Did he discuss his suggestion that Parliament (of which he would eventually become a member) should organize itself along the lines of the ancient Jewish Sanhedrin? Or the possibility that the Karaites of Turkey were a type of "Jewish Protestant?" Or did he share a letter he received from another scholar, Johannes Rittangel, which was addressed from a "yeshiva" of no small renown called Cambridge University?

"Rabbi" Selden was of course not one. He was a dutiful member of the Church of England, baptized at the parish church of St. Andrews in West Sussex, a faithful Protestant who tended towards more High Church affectations. While not a rabbi, or even a Jew, Selden was the first Englishman to write comprehensive Talmudic scholarship, fluent in Hebrew and Aramaic (among others) and composing thousands of pages of *Midrash*. He was also one of the greatest historians in England before-or-after he lived, and probably its finest legal theorist. Selden's studies of Judaism were accomplished without personally knowing any practicing Jews (though he corresponded with many learned rabbis by letter), for they had been expelled during the thirteenth-century reign of Edward I. With a small community of mostly Sephardic crypto-Jews living in London at the time, scholar Jason Rosenblatt convincingly argues that Selden was the most knowledgeable person concerning Judaism anywhere in the British Isles, if not simply "the most learned person in England in the seventeenth century." In his seminal study of Selden's Hebraism and its relation to English Renaissance literature, Rosenblatt writes that, "England, after all, unlike some other European countries its size, never produced a great medieval or early modern rabbinic sage." This sceptered isle, this field of green, had no Maimonides, and it had no Rashi, but Selden alone.

Christian Hebraism was a subject of discussion beginning at least two centuries before, with the Renaissance reading of Judaism in a Christian or secular context something that could anachronistically be called "Jewish Studies." Selden may have been the most prominent example of this type of scholar in England, but he was by no means the first in Europe, or arguably even in the wider Western world. Relations between Jews and gentiles generated an equivalent interest in cultural difference far back into antiquity, through the Middle Ages, and into the

Renaissance. The Hellenistic Pharaoh Ptolemy II's quasi-mythic commissioning of seventy-two Jewish translators to prepare the Greek text of the Septuagint three centuries before the Common Era is one early example of non-Jews expressing an intellectual curiosity about Judaism. Greco-Roman fascination with Judaism was enduring and deep, some four to six centuries after the translation of the Septuagint and during the early Common Era, the Roman literary critic Pseudo-Longinus in his *On the Sublime* presents the Jewish God as a potent example of the philosophical and aesthetic concept which his treatise expounded upon. He writes that, "the lawgiver of the Jews – no mean genius, for he both understood and gave expression to the power of the divinity as it deserved...wrote at the very beginning of his laws... 'God said,' – what was it? – 'Let there be light, and there was. Let there be earth, and there was.'" Note the evocative misquote – yet even if Pseudo-Longinus may have been a Hellenized Jew (as indeed both the Egyptian philosopher Philo and the Roman historian Josephus were), his example demonstrates a gentile interest and appreciation for the study of Jewish subjects.

The *Tanakh* itself shows evidence of Greek and Jewish syncretism, *Ecclesiastes* bares similarity to Epicurean philosophy (even as *epikoros* became the Hebrew slur for an apostate), and *Job* arguably follows the dramaturgical structure of classical tragedy at its height. By the era of Roman domination of Judea during the time of the Second Temple there is ample evidence of large communities of gentile *yir'ei Hashem,* or "God-fearers," in the Mediterranean world. These were gentiles who did not convert to Judaism, but still recognized the religious authority and validity of the Noahide covenant (as indeed Selden would), and lived ritually and morally in conjunction with it – and if evidence from the book of *Acts* is taken as authoritative, they seemed fairly content that this covenant did not require them to be circumcised. In the classical world Jewish practice and thought was one intellectual option among many which included

Epicureanism, Stoicism, various mystery cults, and eventually Christianity (who it can be assumed many of that earlier group may have eventually converted to). In many ways the God-fearers were first in a long tradition of groups that would be slurred as "Judaizers," that is gentiles who were understood by their coreligionists as being a bit too Jewish in their practice. What marks the God-fearers as so fascinating is that they were ethnically, linguistically, and culturally clearly not Jewish, yet felt a pull to Hebraic tradition and theology. Groups such as the early Christian Ebionites, who believed that the entirety of Mosaic Law must be followed even if one is a baptized Christian, were almost entirely ethnically Jewish. The God-fearers, in coming from a gentile cultural background, signify something different, a distinctly non-Jewish fascination and respect for Judaism.

The God-fearers, however, were a religious community, and in identifying the emergence of Jewish Studies as an academic discipline we need to separate out intellectual curiosity from doctrinal piety. This is no easy task in a world where secularism was still an impossibility, as it would indeed be until Selden's day. Academic disciplines and departments, like all aspects of our contemporary secular period, evolved from earlier religious antecedents. As such, especially as Christianity emerged as the dominant ideological system in late antiquity, discussions of Jews and Judaism couldn't be theologically neutral, and so these scholarly writings almost always had the gloss of Christian apologetics, whether the standard anti-Judaism of patristic thinkers like Augustine, or the vociferous, teeth-gnashing bigotry of a writer like Marcion (who it should be said was ultimately condemned as a heretic, even if instrumental in the development of the New Testament canon). Any account of non-Jewish intellectual curiosity about Judaism must of course take into account those separations between Jew and gentile. Rabbinic Judaism and Christianity both developed as intellectual approaches to conceptualizing the relationship between God and man in a post-Temple world. Perhaps dating from the first century Church Council of Jerusalem, the two groups would increasingly define themselves in different ways. For Jews the new Temple would in many ways be the Torah itself, and for Christians the person of Christ. This distinction is important for conceptualizing what Jewish Studies could be, because it sets the contours of who exactly was a Jew and a non-Jew.

Anti-Judaism was central to most Christian discussions of Judaism from late antiquity through the Middle Ages. Outside of the relatively tolerant Islamic world, the scholarly study of Jews was overwhelmingly polemical in its denunciations.

Often this hinged on Christian attacks on the veracity and morality of the Talmud, with centers of Jewish Talmudic thought often subject to attack both intellectual and physical throughout the Middle Ages. Christian theologians of the period had difficulty with both their faith's relationship to Judaism, as well as the continued existence of the Jews who maintained their religious beliefs and practices despite Christianity's existence. Since a variation of the Hebrew Scriptures lay at the center of Christianity, it was the post-biblical rabbinical Talmud that was attacked. In part the Talmud was such a convenient locus of polemic because its sheer length and complexity all but guaranteed that even the most learned scholastic and monastic authorities would have been unfamiliar with its contents, and thus accusations of its immorality or "anti-Christian" nature could be spread among a populace who had no means of evaluating the veracity of such claims. Rosenblatt describes the first printed Babylonian Talmud, produced under papal license by Daniel Bomberg in the liberal environs of Venice in 1520, consisting of "forty-four tractates approximately two and a half million words on 5,894 folio pages, unadorned by either vowel points or punctuation."

Three years later and Bomberg published the Jerusalem

Talmud in its entirety, ultimately many copies would find themselves burnt in Rome's *Campo de Flori*. As it wouldn't be until a century after this first printing that Christians like Selden would even begin to gain mastery of the Talmud, it existed in the Christian imagination as a dangerous book which set the Jews apart in their perfidy. There would be attacks on the Talmud from the time of the fifth century Byzantine emperor Justinian through the next millennium, including a thirteenth-century Spanish disputation where it was defended by Nahmanides, public burnings in France during the same century, accusations against it in fifteenth century Aragon, and throughout the rest of the period as well. In Christian apologetics of the time the Talmud could be marked as distinctly Jewish, while the Bible was understood as the preserve of Christians alone, having supersessionally passed into their hands away from those who first wrote it.

One of the first great Christian defenses of the Talmud (and there had been intermittent ones in the past) was delivered by Selden's precursor in Jewish Studies, the German scholar Johannes Reuchlin. A faithful German Catholic, Reuchlin's defense of the Talmud was against scurrilous accusations leveled by a converted Jew named Johannes Pfefferkorn. The "Pfefferkorn Affair" became a seminal event in Renaissance history, as intellectual luminaries like Desiderius Erasmus weighed in on the apostate Jew's proposal that copies of the Talmud needed to be immolated. It was in 1509 in a Europe on the verge of Reformation that Pfefferkorn, a man of dubious background (having been imprisoned for robbery and if anything an opportunist), claimed that, "The causes which hinder the Jews from becoming Christians are...because they honor the *Talmud*." The Dominicans of Cologne agreed. As a result, authorities confiscated Jewish books to be burnt. The Holy Roman Emperor Maximilian wasn't so sure, and so Reuchlin, master philologist and consummate humanist, was enlisted to examine the matter and to ascertain the validity of Pfefferkorn's claims.

Reuchlin was a practitioner of Renaissance humanism as it spread from its origins in Italy through the rest of Europe. He is among that earliest generation of citizens in the "Republic of Letters," who could be seen as precedents for academic scholarship as it came to be practiced in the West. A half-century of historiographical triumphalism has commonly taught that the Renaissance was a profound rupture between the medieval and the modern; the reality is both more mundane and more interesting. Fundamentally humanism was a pedagogical approach, and a method of scholarship defining itself against the Aristotelian scholasticisms of the previous centuries.

If the humanists of the fifteenth and sixteenth centuries were anything, they were academics who approached the questions they investigated by recourse to a set of methodologies and guidelines that strike us as if not modern, at least as anticipating the modern. This was after all the period when the great universities of Europe – Oxford, Bologna, Salamanca, Paris, Valladolid, Basel – first began to distinguish themselves in the disciplines of the liberal arts. And this is the first period where something like contemporary Masters and Doctoral degrees first emerge. Scholars like the fifteenth century Lorenzo Valla who marshaled detailed linguistic arguments to demonstrate why *The Donation of Constantine* was a forgery, or Erasmus' historical explanation of why the *Comma Johanneum* was an interpolation into the New Testament, embodied this free-ranging and fearless approach to texts. This approach in large part was based on a sober and rational consideration of the linguistics and philology of classical languages like Greek and Latin – and ultimately Hebrew. This is not incidental to the development of Jewish Studies, indeed Reuchlin was perhaps the progenitor of that discipline as it emerged out of the new scholarship of the Renaissance, and thus was the perfect individual to defend the Talmud against the accusations of Pfefferkorn.

Reuchlin studied what came to be called the Christian kabbalah under the tutelage of the occult philosopher Giovanni Pico della Mirandola at his Neo-Platonic academy in Florence. This Christian Kabbalah would become one of the central metaphysical systems of the Renaissance, and a source of an enduring fascination concerning the Jews. From della Mirandola the German scholar derived a deep knowledge of Hebrew texts beyond simply that of the *Tanakh,* but of the Talmud and even the *Zohar* as well. His *De Rudimentis Hebraicis* arguably stood as the ultimate example of Renaissance Jewish exegetical thought penned by a non-Jew. No Christian Hebraist would surpass Reuchlin in their knowledge of Judaism until Selden; there is no doubt that despite Pfefferkorn being raised as a Jew that Reuchlin understood the religion far more, and was more sympathetic towards it as well. Rancorous pamphlet wars which would put any contemporary internet fight to shame marked the intellectual life of the era (as a perusal of the correspondence between Thomas More and William Tyndale can substantiate), and Reuchlin and Pfefferkorn did not disappoint, with the latter even accusing the former of being bribed by the Jews for his support. Reuchlin's campaign on behalf of the Talmud was difficult, he was called before the Inquisition several times, and faced severe denunciations by other academics. He would ultimately be victorious, however, and then some – one result was that Maximilian ordered that every German university should have at least two professors of Hebrew, arguably the beginnings of contemporary academic Jewish Studies. There remained a dark irony in his victory, however; in part it was suspicion about Pfefferkorn's own Jewish ancestry and all the implied markers of supposed essential duplicity, which tainted his denunciations of the Talmud as untrustworthy. Witness Erasmus' characterization of him as "a criminal Jew who had become a most criminal Christian."

While professors in Germany argued either for or against the Talmud, and while it was being printed in Venice, no copy of it existed in England, which after all supposedly had no Jews. England's lack of a Talmud changed in 1529, shortly following the settlement of the Pfefferkorn Affair in a Germany now being roiled by the earliest years of the Reformation, when none other than Henry VIII requested the importation of Bomberg's printing of the Talmud for his personal library. Its purpose? Research – to find rabbinical justification to aid in his annulment from Catherine of Aragon and his marriage to Anne Boleyn. It was a different copy of the Talmud which Selden references a century later in 1621 when imprisoned for his role in drafting a protestation about the rights of the House of Commons. He cheekily wrote to his compatriot Sir Robert Cotton, "I have much time here before me, and there is in Westminster Library the Talmud of Babylon in diverse great volumes. If it be a thing to be obtained, I would beseech you to borrow them." Although an estimably respected scholar already, it was Selden's reading of this Talmud acquired during his brief imprisonment that would transform him into the greatest Christian Hebraist of the age. Already celebrated for *De Diis Syris* (1617), as Rosenblatt enumerates, his writings following his imprisonment included:

six works, some of them immense, that add to the scholarship remarkable competence in the Babylonian-Aramaic texts of the Talmud: *De Successionibus ad Leges Ebraeorum in Bona Defunctorum* (1631), which covers every phase of the Jewish law of the Hebrew priesthood; *De Jure Naturali et Gentium juxta Disciplinam Ebraeorum* (1640), which conceives of the imperatives of natural law in terms of the rabbinic Noahide laws, *or pracepta Noachidarum,* divine voluntary universal laws of perpetual obligations; *De Anno Civili* (1644), a lucid and methodical account of the Jewish calendar and its principles as well as a treatise on the doctrines and practices of the Karaite sect; *Uxor Ebraica seu De Nuptiis et Divortiis Veterum Ebraeorum* (1646), a thorough survey of the Jewish law of marriage and divorce and of the status of the married woman under Jewish law and the massive *De Syedriis,* in three books (1650, 1653, 1655, the last, incomplete and published posthumously), a study of Jewish assemblies, including the Sanhedrin, with parallels from Roman and canon law.

Rosenblatt's *Renaissance England's Chief Rabbi* (2006) published by Oxford University Press (housed at Selden's alma mater) is the authoritative study of the Hebraist's outsized influence on seventeenth-century England, and the ways in which that influence can be seen in writers like Jonson, Andrew Marvell, and John Milton. That last listed poet, one of the most learned men of the century, deferred to Selden's immense knowledge of Hebrew, and it was from the Hebraist that Milton drew the massive list of demonic names which populate the parliament of Pandemonium in *Paradise Lost's* first and second books.

There is a telling and fascinating correspondence between Selden and his drinking buddy Jonson which demonstrates the intellectual finesse of the scholar, his acute, analytical, rabbinical mind arguably exhibiting that style called *pilpul,* that is of "peppery reasoning." In 1614, seven years before Selden would acquire his Talmud, Jonson wrote to his friend concerning the question of cross-dressing in the theater. With secular theater being an innovation only a generation old, religious authorities, in particular the Puritans, had condemned the practice of boys performing in women's clothing as immoral and indecent. Massive tomes such as 1633's *Histriomastix* by the Puritan William Prynne, which got its author's ears cut off after declaring that actresses were "notorious whores" (one of the few actresses on the stage at the time being Queen Henrietta Maria), were a common genre. Jonson, who despite his popularity was always in a precarious religious position as he oscillated between Anglican and Catholic and back again, consulted Selden on what the actual biblical interpretation regarding cross-dressing would be.

The playwright, whose livelihood depended on a theater that was being attacked for supposed "monstrous androgyny, boys in delicate dresses worshipping Venus with bears," needed the analytical expertise of a rabbi to explain how theatrical cross-dressing and the Bible could be reconciled. He writes to Selden specifically about the proper interpretation of Deuteronomy 22:5, which was commonly marshaled by Puritans in condemnation of the theater. The poet inquires to "the literall sense and historicall of the holy text usually brought against the counterfeiting of the sexes by apparel." On the continent, the practice of Jews sending letters to learned rabbis for insight into the proper application of *Halakha* was a common genre called *responsa,* of which hundreds of thousands of examples survive. Rosenblatt and his fellow scholar Winfried Schleiner convincingly argue that Selden's reply to Jonson is a type of *responsa,* where Selden specifically utilizes the reasoning of Maimonides to assure Jonson that theatrical cross-dressing is biblical permitted.

Selden's nimble and rigorous logic is based on a historically contextualized understanding of the Bible, which avoids the unsophisticated literalisms of the theater's critics by embracing the nuanced interpretation of Maimonides. The verse in question reads, "The woman shall not wear that which pertaineth unto a man, neither shall a man put on a woman's garment." Selden explains to Jonson that what seems straightforward is not so, based on his knowledge of Hebrew he explains that Deuteronomy 22:5 refers not to women in men's clothes, but rather to specifically armor, and as such is not a condemnation of cross-dressing but of specifically ancient pagan rites which involved the worship of Venus and Mars, making theatrical cross-dressing kosher. Jonson took this explanation to heart, when later that year in his experimental masterpiece *Bartholomew Fayre* he mocked the fussy Puritan condemnations of the theater by having a ridiculous character Zeal-Of-The-Land Busy lose a disputation to the puppet Dionysius, who ultimately finds victory in the debate by dropping his puppet-pants and demonstrating that his kind have no genitals, and are thus not guilty of cross-dressing. While played for laughs, Dionysius' act is meant to show the ridiculousness of religious zealotry. In this, Jonson was inspired by the tolerant and liberal understanding that Selden inherited from the Rambam. As Rosenblatt writes, "Selden's letter on cross-dressing a rare and important example of calm tolerance." In this, our season of homophobic anti-queer rhetoric and violence, it is humbling to remember that four hundred years ago Selden acknowledged the naturalness and reality of gender fluidity, basing his reading on correct biblical etymology and not cold literal misinterpretation, and furthermore he did this in defense of Renaissance England's greatest cultural contribution, it's stage art.

True inheritor of Renaissance humanism and humble student of a culture not his own, Selden was one of England's finest cosmopolitans for whom wisdom was found where it was found. His worldview was expansive and generous, as he wrote:

> Tis much the doctrine of the times that men should not please themselves, but deny themselves everything they take delight in; not look upon beauty, wear no good clothes, eat no good meat, etc., which seems the greatest accusation that can be upon the Maker of all good things. If they are not to be used, why did God make them?

This humane perspective, and sense of religious toleration and flexibility, marked Selden's political writings, which alongside his continental equal Hugo Grotius were instrumental in the development of a philosophy of international law. From his readings, the Noahide Covenant in particular fascinated Selden; the same contract that the God-fearers fifteen centuries before him had believed designated the behavior of Jew and non-Jew alike. These are the seven laws given to Noah that the Talmud claims are binding on all of humanity, from their existence Selden developed a theory of the universal nature of law. Grounded in an exegetical reading of Genesis, the Talmud argues that the entirety of humanity was given this universal covenant that included injunctions against murder, theft, and animal cruelty among others, and the requirement for each people to establish courts suited to the needs of their individual culture. Based on his reading of the Talmud, Selden argued that the legal systems of every country (say the system in England, France, the Holy Roman Empire, and so on) can vary in certain matters of custom and tradition, but that ultimately these courts must be grounded in certain universal principals. In Selden's perspective the law cannot be arbitrary, and violations that contradict this universal covenant are not legally justified.

Selden's legal and ethical vision in many ways anticipates the Enlightenment of a century later. While "natural rights" were very much an eighteenth century concept, Selden's argument for basic, universally binding ethical precepts existing beyond nation, language, or religion anticipate the rationalist political and moral shifts to come. There is something appropriate in the fact that the progressive political movements of the coming revolutionary age, which would find Europe's ghettos liberated and Jews accepted in their nations as citizens for the first time, in part had their precedent in the thinking of a Christian inspired by rabbinical thought. What John Selden offers is a fascinatingly respectful, if not deferential, reading of Judaism on its own terms. While the problematic nature of cultural appropriation is raised, one must still marvel at the unprecedented ecumenical esteem that Selden held the Jews in. As Rosenblatt writes, "One might argue that Selden is precious precisely because he is uncommon, like the courageous few who throughout history have refused to be swallowed up by the mob."

In 1655, crowds in London would have seen a sight of which they may have been expected to be curious, save for how surprisingly unremarkable it must have been. The English populace had long been familiar with the *idea* of a Jew, Shylock and Barabas creeping upon the stage with fake nose and red fright wig, and the Christ-killer slur of Holy Week sermons.

But here, in the increasingly massive and cosmopolitan English capital, walked an actual, practicing, open Jew for the first time in 365 years. A Dutch rabbi, Menasseh ben Israel, strolled through the capital on a fall day that year, perhaps past the Mermaid Tavern, or through the East End which would one day be populated with many Jewish immigrants, or maybe he perused the book stalls of St. Paul's whose massive dome would not be built for a few more decades. But for anyone paying attention to that man in the crowd, they would not see fake nose and red fright wig, but rather a staid, unassuming man. Ben Israel, with his long, dark Van Dyke and his plain starched white collar and wide brimmed hat in the Dutch style, looked more like an engraving by Rembrandt (who did, indeed, draw him) than the stock Jewish character of anti-Semitic stereotype whom the English crowd was familiar with. If anything, in his simple black cloak, the rabbi looked like nothing so much as a sober, conservative Protestant parson.

A decade before and the rabbi had met a Portuguese Jew who had returned from the Brazilian colonies, convinced that the Indians were remnants of the ten lost tribes of Israel. Among Jews as well as Christians the seventeenth century was a messianic era, and the reports from the mistaken Jew convinced the Dutch rabbi that the Jewish people must be fully dispersed to all corners of the globe to hasten the arrival of the *Mashiach*. But America was very far away, England only across the North Sea. And so Menasseh ben Israel decided to initiate negotiations with the English government to secure the passage of his people to that isle. With the Interregnum government of Oliver Cromwell, ben Israel's diplomacy took on a new immediacy, as the Puritans sometimes viewed themselves as the New Hebrews, and were thus theoretically amenable to the rabbi's request. The Lord Protector had his own millenarian hopes for Christ's return in his lifetime, and he may have been swayed by ben Israel's arguments. Cromwell, always a cagy operator, may also have been enticed by the possibility of Jewish merchants transferring their lucrative connections to Spanish traders from Holland to England. And so the rabbi was dispatched to Westminster to argue before this English Pharaoh on behalf of the Israelites.

The possibility of Jewish readmission was hardly unequivocally supported. None other than William Prynne, he of the denunciations against theatrical cross-dressing and the now exiled Queen, vociferously argued against the Jewish admittance into the Commonwealth. Ben Israel summoned his considerable scriptural knowledge to argue the religious necessity that England should lift the ban on the Jews (while his congregation in Amsterdam ironically took his absence as an opportunity to excommunicate a student of his, a meddlesome *epikoros* named Baruch Spinoza). But ultimately the conference decided that there was no legal cause to continue barring the Jewish people from England. And so one writer simply recorded in his diary, "Now were the Jews admitted." If Cromwell expected Christ to come, he didn't; and if ben Israel expected the *Mashiach* to arrive, he also didn't. But the Jews did come, and England was better for it. In those chambers, surrounded by the political and religious luminaries of Commonwealth England, the spirit that presided was that of Selden, whose advocacy and defense of both religious liberty and the Jews had made ben Israel's arrival possible. Selden had corresponded with Jews on the continent throughout his half-century career in becoming the great "rabbi" of England; now his labors had made this moment of admittance possible. But Selden never got to converse with ben Israel, or any other Jew in the flesh for that matter, never seeing the fulfillment of his work. The scholar had died the year before.

Of Canons and Marginal Poets

In 1630 the entirety of the poet John Taylor's work up until that point was printed in the relatively expensive folio form, something that had only previously been done for the historian and poet Samuel Daniel, the playwright Ben Jonson, and of course seven years earlier with the complete plays of William Shakespeare. These printings of Daniel, Jonson, and Shakespeare (whose folio was published posthumously and at the urging of Jonson who financially benefited from it) were in some sense avant-garde, for while religious and classical works were often distributed in this format, the seemingly ephemeral media of vernacular poetry and especially drama did not seem to warrant such lavish packaging. Jonson's folio contains his classic plays such as 1605's *Volpone* and 1610's *The Alchemist*, Shakespeare's listed in its contents, the thirty-six plays which have made him the most celebrated writer in the English language. But what of this John Taylor, the self-styled "water poet" of Jacobean London?

He was a proud Thames boatman ferrying thousands of passengers across the river from Westminster to Southwark, where theaters, bear-baiting pits, and brothels lay beyond the reach of the Puritan leadership in London. A life-long boatman, he worked in a trade which employed at its height close to 20,000 men ferrying politicians and preachers, actors and writers, prostitutes and cut-purses, laborers and aristocrats over the fetid, stinking, putrid slog that was the early modern Thames. The table of contents for Taylor's folio included accomplished verse as well as doggerel on the working-class life of the city which now found itself the largest in Europe, as well as the earliest examples of what could be called investigative journalism when his brother and he traveled to Prague following that city's infamous defenestration at the outbreak of the Thirty Years War.

Readers were entertained by publicity stunts such as his trip to Edinburgh in pursuit of Jonson (with Taylor relying entirely upon strangers for support), and compendiums of useful information such as London tavern reviews. In 1630, fourteen years dead, Shakespeare was of course already in the process of being established as "not of an age, but for all time" (as Jonson put it in that folio's dedicatory poem). Taylor was most certainly of his age, and yet we may stand to gain something if we try not necessarily to make him of our time, but to perhaps listen a bit to what he said of his.

Unless you are a scholar of sixteenth- and seventeenth-century literature you have probably never heard of John Taylor the Water Poet. Or for that matter Robert Greene, the bohemian university wit, or Richard Barnfield, the sodomitical sonneteer. Even if you are a scholar of early modern literature Greene is the only name you'd most likely be familiar with, and you would probably have to be a gender theorist to be familiar with Barnfield. These men, considered marginal writers, existed at the limits of their society. If not transgressive then they at least subverted some expectations of literary decorum, but not necessarily the decorum of their era (though sometimes they did that too). Rather they subvert our expectations of what we have come to consider canonical. One could add to this list writers like Thomas Nashe, the religious-propagandist for hire and author of the first novel in English, *The Unfortunate Traveler*. It's a thrilling picaresque bildungsroman whose Jack Wilkins is forced to travel through the burnt-over country of the European wars of religion, and it deserves to be more widely read. Or Amelia Lanyer, who had the audacity to rewrite Genesis in defense of Eve. Or Robert Braithwaite, an early modern de Quincy who unapologetically celebrated his alcoholism. Or Robert Southwell, arguably the earliest metaphysical poet, who was also a pious Jesuit and found himself upon Queen Elizabeth's pyres at Tyburn and whose skin was used to bind a book about his blasphemies.

I do not mean to suggest the existence of an unidentified school with these incredibly varied figures. Rather I would suggest that then, as now, there is a certain wisdom to be found in those marginal places, a certain beauty in the in-between liminal spaces. These writers are marginal poets, and in some cases they are transgressive ones. There is something to be gained by moving them from those margins. The canon of Renaissance English literature has always been a variable list, from Dr. Johnson in the eighteenth century who first conceptualized the imaginary war between metaphysical and Cavalier poets, to Francis Turner Palgrave in the nineteenth century whose Golden Treasury set the rough contours of the canon as we've come to think of it, to the twentieth-century renegade critic Yvor Winters who extolled little known poets like George Gascoigne and Thomas Campion as the equals of Shakespeare, and who divided the poets into Petrarchan and anti-Petrarchan.

In the twentieth century, feminist and queer critics helped to expand the canon while conservatives like Harold Bloom guarded the fortress of "Dead White Males" who constituted that list. And who are the standard names we see? A good approximation of it would be that Shakespeare, Jonson, Christopher Marlowe, Philip Sidney, Edmund Spenser, John Donne, and John Milton (depending on how "Renaissance" a given scholar considers him) are permanently on that list. Even Donne is a relatively recent addition with the enthusiasm of the New Critics and poets such as T.S. Eliot a century ago. Poets like Greene, Barnfield, and Taylor seem automatically of a different class to the exalted names which fill syllabi and comprehensive examination lists. Yet some of them had their moments of popularity in the past. C.S. Lewis, though disgusted by Barnfield's homosexuality, acknowledged the genius of his verse, and Robert Southey thought Taylor a minor genius. Canons are ever malleable things, a given poet's stock can both rise and fall. That writers like Greene, Barnfield, and Taylor are on the outs now doesn't mean that they always were, or that they always will be. That they are today marginal may seem a given, but how are they transgressive?

Translated into our vernacular, can we say that Greene was a bohemian, Barnfield was gay, or that Taylor was working class? To do so risks pushing us into that fallacious presentism that flattens the distance between them and us, generating a category mistake in imposing our perspective onto that foreign country that is the past. Seemingly generations of high school teachers have tried to make Shakespeare more appealing to disinterested students by claiming that he was the equivalent of a Hollywood screenwriter, but to make this claim is to ignore the perhaps very literal but also very pertinent fact that movies didn't exist in early modern England. This is not a small issue; denizens of the past were not just like us only covered in more dirt and with less sophisticated technology. Their head-space was different from ours. The twentieth-century French philosopher and historian Michel Foucault claimed that time periods were defined by what he called *epistimes,* ideological structures which dominate and circumscribe what sorts of ideas are possible within a given cultural context. To take an example from religion, atheism that is vociferously materialist and makes positive denials of the transcendent or supernatural doesn't seem to really exist before a relatively modern moment. The term "atheist" existed, but it didn't mean what it means today, and scholars like Lucian Febvre doubted whether it could exist in the past. "Atheist" could mean "atomist," or "heretic," or "Epicurean," or even "skeptic," but it didn't mean what it means today because what it means today was impossible to think in a past dominated by religious faith. In the same way, concepts like the bohemianism I associate with Greene don't really emerge until the nineteenth century. They are reliant on certain requirements, like the emergence of a capitalist economic order to rebel against, or Romantic aesthetic theories of inspiration. It's the same with the concept of homosexuality as a static and essential identity. This perspective doesn't really emerge until almost the turn of the twentieth century. And yet to read the writings of Greene and Barnfield one finds oneself respectively reading the work of a bohemian and a gay man.

Some helpful critical terminology can be borrowed from the twentieth-century Marxist critic Raymond Williams, who argued that these sorts of ideological constructs can be dominant, residual, or emergent in our society. That is to say that in any given time period a range of conceptual possibilities do exist, but what marks a given period as different from another one is the proportion of these various conceptual possibilities in relation to one another. As such, we can think of my "movement" as not just marginal, and not just transgressive, but emergent as well. Greene, Barnfield, and Taylor did the things people had always done, but in expressing them they provide clues to the ways perhaps universal human activity was localized in a particular time and place, namely in early modern England. They offer us a transgressive poetics of the emergent marginalized, a prehistory of identities we associate with the contemporary world.

We can take this ferryman Taylor, this self-declared "water poet," as representative of these marginal poets. Considering his conservatism, it may seem contradictory to argue that there is anything transgressive about him. Taylor, who liberally sprinkled his pamphlets with jokes at the expense of his wife, seemed almost achingly conventional when it came to matters of family. Indeed Taylor was a solid traditionalist, equally denouncing Jesuits and Puritans, a stalwart defender of God's Church at Lambeth, and though working-class a committed royalist who denounced Parliament throughout the years of civil war. He was a not untypical breed of English reactionary, the sort one can still find over a pint of warm lager in many pubs today. He had been to Europe and Scotland, but regardless of what he saw or did on his travels the culture of England was always superior. The Catholic Church was the home of the antichrist, but he had no patience for separatists and Puritans. He knew what he liked

– kneelers, prayer books, the king, and sack. And ferrymen.

At times, however, he did have a hearty, Falstaffian ecumenicism, declaring that all were allowed on his boat, regardless of their confession. Indeed if Greene is a marginal poet because of his bohemianism, and if Barnfield is one because of his sexuality, Taylor is among that group precisely because he was so conventional. To a Marxist he wouldn't quite be a member of the lumpen-proletariat; he was more appropriately understood as at the bottom of the rung of the bourgeois, right at the moment of history when it becomes possible to talk about such a class. But in his poetry, reportage, pamphlets, and reviews Taylor provided a voice so common that it was overlooked in his own time and sadly still often overlooked today. Taylor was not particularly talented – though he still remains entertaining – but that was his great strength. Reading Taylor is like reading Falstaff if that character wrote the *Henriad* rather than his creator.

As the driver of a passenger-boat, Taylor got to meet some interesting friends. These associates included the playwright Thomas Dekker whose "canting pamphlets" supplied dictionaries for the respectable to understand the vocabulary of London's criminal underworld, and where he displayed an ear for regular speech that made him the David Mamet of the day. Or Edward Alleyn, the greatest actor of the Elizabethan and Jacobean stage who had been so spooked by the seeming appearance of an actual demon during one of the incantation scenes in Marlowe's *Dr. Faustus* that he donated 35,000 pounds for the founding of Dulwich College, but who was not so spooked that he had any problem collecting payment from a brothel he owned at Southwark. For that matter, neither did his father-in-law, who required a portion of those profits as part of his daughter's dowry, and who happened to be the Dean of St. Paul's. This father-in-law was a poet himself (of no small fame) named John Donne. And of course, among all of his compatriots which included actors, writers, members of court, bishops, and ministers, there was chief among them all the great Ben Jonson.

The poet Alexander Brome wrote of the two friends, "Jonson and Taylor in their kind were both/Good wits, who like one, need not t'other loathe./Wit is like beauty, Nature made the Joan/As well's the Lady," comparing Jonson as "Lady," to Taylor as mere "Joan," understood as a common hum-drum sort of woman, but one who is not without her own charms. There were similarities of course, such as Jonson's experimental 1614 masterpiece *Bartholomew Fair* with its bawdy, cockney characters like Littlewit, Quarlous, and Winwife, it's anal-retentive Puritan Zeal-of-the-Land Busy, and of course his ultimate triumph, Ursula the Pig Woman. They are all mixed together on one day in the city's eponymous fair. The play demonstrated an ear for common speech, just like Taylor in the best of his writing. But there was no mistaking the two in terms of literary station. Jonson may have also come from modest origins, but he was a graduate of Cambridge who exhibited great classical learning in his translations of Horace. Taylor on the other hand would seem to be more classifiable with the almost entirely forgotten balladeers of the time, such as his other friend John Trundell who published common-metered songs on broadsheets popular in the streets and taverns of the metropolis.

The Cavalier movement of poetry, exemplified by men like Robert Herrick, John Suckling, and Richard Lovelace, embodies the lusty world view of gentlemanly leisure. They celebrate copious drinking, aristocratic nobility, classical learning, and a love of the traditional way of life which was being swept aside by the new science and the new religion in equal measure. But where that "School of Ben" admitted the well-educated and the well-connected, Taylor was the equivalent of a New York City cab-driver (and would have been seen as such by his contemporaries). Though he was occasionally the head of the boatman's guild, the largest in the city, and he was not for want of privileged and powerful associates. As already mentioned, men like Jonson considered Taylor to be a friend, and encouraged his artistic ambitions. It's true that Taylor's verse can't possibly stand next to the true greats of English Renaissance literature. Unlike Barnfield, or even Greene, his reputation was not tarnished by implications of sundry behavior, but rather it rose and fell on the merits of its own quality. Yet if Taylor lacked the metaphysical conceit, the turn of phrase, or the sheer wit of men like George Herbert and Donne, then he still had charm. Indeed while Taylor doesn't match the technical virtuosity or the philosophical and technical acumen of more famous poets, he does in some ways have more of an accessibility.

Taylor had the consummate ability to turn a simple phrase, a skill that makes him more similar to a Madison Avenue advertising executive than to Donne. Indeed he was a master of marketing, as the gimmick of his trailing Jonson to Scotland demonstrated. In this way his working-class connections kept him grounded in the vernacular, to the pulse of the streets (or the river) where ballads and broadsheets were more popular that the erudite circulated manuscripts of the academic poets. As Taylor would have put it, "Better fed than taught." Indeed his work is replete with these sorts of aphorisms, as in, "A simple maiden in her flower is worth a thousand coat of arms," or, "For man is man, and master of his fate." Taylor's work extolled the simplicity of solid, conservative English values, and the aphorisms he penned reflected that. In some sense he reminds one of Benjamin Franklin, whose Puritan work ethic and plain style marked him as a particular type of writer, albeit one who was not above stating some of his adages with tongue planted firmly in cheek.

Indeed Franklin himself plagiarized Taylor directly, in the 1735 edition of *Poor Richard's Almanac* when he wrote, "God sends meat, and the devil sends cooks." It's consummate Taylor, simple, but with an eye towards classical rhetoric in its parallelism. But though he was not a Donne or Jonson, Taylor was at least an enthusiast for the joy in language, how it sounds in the ear, and feels in the mouth. He was in his own way a harsh critic of his own skills, yet he took a joy in playing with language, which is still apparent four centuries later. Witness his palindrome, "Lewd did I live & evil I did dwel," which despite its classic Calvinist message is an example of where form is more important than function. Taylor enjoys rhetoric and language, and the enthusiasm is obvious.

But Taylor, for his own self-image as a rustic entertainer who saw no shame in providing for the mass public what they wanted, was not averse to more serious messages. In his poem "The Description of Tyburn," he describes that cursed field in London that was wetted with the blood of martyrs both Protestant and Catholic. Site of so many executions under Henry, and then his Catholic daughter Mary, and then her Protestant sister Elizabeth; it was in many ways representative of the bloody sectarianism which marked the period. Though he was a solid conservative and advocate for the Church of England, it was the moderate via media of that denomination that in part attracted him. He writes, "I Have heard sundry men oft times dispute/Of trees, that in one year will twice bear fruit./But if a man note Tyburn, 'will appear,/That that's a tree that bears twelve times a year." The image of executed men being similar to a "Strange Fruit" reminds one of the jazz classic of that title by Abel Meeropol which took lynching as its subject. And for Taylor, despite this being the site of execution for ostensibly heretics, he allows that, "The dying fruit is well prepared for heaven,/And many times a man may gather thence/Remorse, devotion, and true penitence." He ends with "My pen from paper with this Prayer doth part,/ God bless all people from their sins depart."

In some ways it's anachronistic to label and categorize these poets by more modern categories.

Can we call Greene a bohemian, Barnfield homosexual, and Taylor working class? And though at the margins, is it fair to label them as transgressive? It's true that some of them did transgress the morals of their day (as in Barnfield) and others certainly did not (as in Taylor). And yet what they transgress are our own expectations of a world which often seems inaccessibly foreign. The past has been defined in particular ways, and who is mentioned and who we are silent about are all choices that construct that past in ways that can sometimes be arbitrary. Though in one way it's anachronistic to categorize these poets in particular ways, in others they came from a period not so unlike our own. If there is one thing they shared, it was access to the means of communication. England, indeed Europe, had undergone a media revolution after a century and a half of print, and in taverns and churchyards voices from the margins were able to reach a mass audience. Time has dulled those voices, but now we find ourselves in the midst of a new media revolution, with digital means of communication spreading information in ways that could revolutionize our culture as surely print did theirs. Debates have raged over who is allowed into a cannon and who is not, the potential of the digital is that it allows us to construct new cannons. In the Greek, "anthology" literally means a gathering of flowers. Greene, Barnfield, and Taylor are but three flowers that could be pressed into a collection. The period they represent was filled with more voices than those you have traditionally heard of, it was a mighty choir. Now that we have the means, it's time to listen to those voices as well.

Preachers from the Palace of Wisdom, or: Ranterism in the UK

"Thus saith the Lord, I inform you, that I overturn, overturn, overturn."
Abiezer Coppe (1649)

"I am an antichrist/I am an anarchist..."
Johnny Rotten (1977)

On June 7, 1977 the recently signed Sex Pistols chartered a boat to cruise down the Thames past the Houses of Parliament, planning to play their single "God Save the Queen." Cynics have long pointed out that the band was more media creation of producer Malcolm McClaren than they were a spontaneous outcry of disaffected youth. Yet the Debordian spectacle of Johnny Rotten snarling out "God save the Queen/She ain't no human being" across the placid summer Thames only two days before Elizabeth II's Silver Jubilee river procession would traverse the same waters was undeniably anarchic. Whether or not the Sex Pistols were more commercialism than revolutionary is of secondary importance to how shocking the planned (and failed) event was. It's been noted that the week the song hit number one the BBC left the title blank. Even if more media event than anything, one must admit that McClaren had absorbed whatever influences – performance art, American rock and roll, anti-establishment fashion and attitude – to generate a potent combination.

Readers who are familiar with Greil Marcus' magisterial rock music critique *Lipstick Traces: A Secret History of the 20th Century* may have heard of another group that were, if not an influence, at least a spiritual ancestor to the group. Always idiosyncratic and expansive in his interests, Marcus fingered an obscure seventeenth-century religious group with the descriptive name of the "Ranters" as being a type of early modern punk movement. Much as the punks refused to see anything as off limits – spewing obscenity, blasphemy, and political incorrectness all in the interest of challenging the mores of a suffocating and corrupt society – the Ranters paradoxically saw the road to salvation as being paved with the actions of sin. Much as Rotten and Sid Vicious would offend the middle-class sensibilities of a British public on the verge of Thatcherism, the Ranters addressed a public who had survived multiple civil wars and the execution of their King only to find themselves ruled under the increasingly conformist Commonwealth government of Puritan Oliver Cromwell.

Now lay-readers have a new resource for reading the Ranters directly in Nigel Smith's fascinating anthology *A Collection of Ranter Writings: Spiritual Liberty and Sexual Freedom in the English Revolution*. A Princeton professor of English, Smith has long elucidated the politics, culture, religion, and literature of the seventeenth century, writing foundational works on Andrew Marvell, John Milton, and the explosion of print at the end of the civil wars. This is Smith's second edition of this anthology, the first appearing in 1983 when he was, amazingly, still just a graduate student. Following the advice of the great Marxist historian Christopher Hill, Smith edited the works of Abiezer Coppe, Laurence Clarkson, and others into the first popular anthology of radical non-conformist religious writings from the English civil war. It is an important contribution not just for scholars, but for the general public as well. Smith has provided an invaluable service, a collection of fascinating religious writings that most people are scarcely familiar with, yet whose study can provide important elucidation not only on a particular time period, but also wider contemporary issues of religion and politics.

As Smith writes, "The literature that is still read today from the seventeenth century is incredibly rich in its originality and its enriching value: the later Shakespeare, Ben Jonson, Donne, Descartes, Thomas Hobbes, Milton, Marvell, Margaret Cavendish to name a few. The Ranter writings, in their outrageous way, are right up there with them." In reading through Smith's anthology, all of the authors are fascinating, but Coppe stands above the rest as the true prophetic genius of the group. In the tradition of all great prophets from Elijah and Ezekiel to Muhammad and Joseph Smith, Coppe found his initial theophanic experience to be terrifying. Journeying to hell, beset on all sides by demons, forced by the Godhead into painful bibliophagy, Coppe subverted and altered the expectations of the English language to convey an experience of the ineffable.

In his works we see an attempt to push English to its limits. If as Ludwig Wittgenstein says, "Whereof we cannot speak thereof one must be silent," Coppe attempted to bring voice to a quiet chamber. Coppe writes, "If I here speake in an unknown tongue, I pray that I may interpret when I may." He distinguished between the literal and the allegorical in scripture, the physically resurrected Christ is less important that the internally resurrected Christ of the human heart. He performed seemingly satirical and extreme pastiches of the scriptural idiom of the King James Bible, but like poet-prophets after him such as William Blake, Walt Whitman, and Allen Ginsberg he attempted to take mere language to its very limits, to apply signifiers to signifieds that exist in a transcendent realm. In his mimesis of scriptural language, we see chiasmus, tricolons, and repetitions. And always he writes with a relentless logorrhea. As an angel tells him, "Go up to London, to London, that great city, write, write, write." At some points Coppe alters the very structures of syntax and grammar, words run backwards, and sideways, English letters transform into Hebrew, a sentence alters into an Aleph and then the Latin letter "O," while Coppe provides gloss on his mystical etymology explaining it represents the divine.

At one point, Coppe gives us dueling concurrent panels of

passages, with paratextual glossing that challenges readers to construct their own official textual certainty. In brilliantly executed writings that would be easy to boringly dismiss as mere products of a diseased intelligence, we see experiments with language that we wouldn't see again till the avant-gardes of the twentieth century with the decadents, the symbolists, the surrealists, and the Dadaists.

The anarchism on the page reflects the anarchism of the era. This period saw a veritable Cambrian Explosion of unique religious sects and denominations, and I would argue that alongside the dozens of gnostic groups which flourished in the first centuries of Christianity as well as the American Second Great Awakening of the early nineteenth-century, this period is one of the most creative in Christianity. It's a matter of historical debate if the incredible flowering of unique religious groups with names like the Seekers, Brownists, Grindletonians, the Familists, the Muggletonians, the Levellers, the Diggers, the Fifth Monarchy Men, and of course the Ranters merely used the disorder of the English Revolution to emerge from the depths where they had already existed, if the chaos of the civil wars generated these movements, or as is most likely some combination of the two.

The two classic works of history that reinforce the idea that apocalypticism is merely the working-man's utopianism are Norman Cohn's 1957 *The Pursuit of the Millennium: Revolutionary Millenarians and Mystical Anarchists of the Middle Ages* and Christopher Hill's 1972 *The World Turned Upside Down: Radical Ideas During the English Revolution*. It is these two seminal academic works that reintroduced the Ranters, and though the Ranters' reputation was so notorious that some conservative historians argued that Hill was misreading the record to invent the group, an honest reading of the record shows the Ranters were very much real (if small). Cohn argued (as indeed Marcus did) that the Ranters were representative of a certain chthonic force that operates within the oppressed human soul and that must burst forth every so often to challenge the hegemonic structures that control and order our lives. The Russian formalist critic Mikhail Bakhtin called this phenomenon the "carnivalesque," and while identifying it in history and literature he was agnostic as to whether it represented a legitimate means of rebellion or whether it was simply a pressure valve utilized by the ruling classes and then appropriated into a means of oppression (as every Sex Pistols t-shirt sold at Hot Topic evidences). If the Ranters are part of a chain of the carnivalesque it is one that goes back to the medieval Brethern of the Free Spirit and which looks forward to the anarchists of the nineteenth and twentieth centuries. For them the central commandment is that which Rabelais carved above his antinomian abbey at Thelema (and which the Satanist Aleister Crowley coopted as his personal motto): "Do what thou wilt."

The Ranters taught, believed, preached, and supposedly lived an antinomian – that is, in complete rejection of the Law – gospel. As their greatest proponent Abiezer Coppe wrote in 1649, the year of regicide, "And all man's preachings, hearing, teachings, learnings, holinesses, righteousnesses religions, is as Theft, Murder, and Adultry." Their hermeneutic may have been one of rejecting literalism and embracing allegory, or casting off the chaff for the kernel as one of their favorite images had it, but if anything they took Christ's radical words not just literally but to their logical conclusion. Not only that, but they fully embraced Luther's doctrine of *sole Fide* and *sole Gratia* to the most radical possible understanding. Catholic polemicists had long accused Protestants inaccurately of antinomianism but Coppe, Laurence Clarkson, Joseph Salmon, Joseph Bauthumely, and other Ranters embraced the radical implications of faith alone. If we are to believe their critics like Thomas Edwards in his massive 1646 *Gangraena*, the Ranters' antinomianism was a type of sacred libertinism which embraced ranting (surely), blasphemy, fornication, perversion, drunkenness, and whoremongering as sacraments in a world where sacraments did not exist. Not only that, they were politically radical as well. If, as Christ taught, "the last shall be first" than the Ranters fully embraced a radically egalitarian if not communistic prophetic vision that warns the entrenched 1 percent of the mid-sixteenth-century that a reckoning shall soon be upon them. "Behold, behold, behold, I the eternall God, the Lord of Hosts, who am that mighty Leveller, am coming (yea even at the doors) to Levell in good earnest, to Levell to some purpose, to Levell with a witnesses, to Levell the Hills with the Valleyes, and to lay the Mountaines low" as Coppe writes in his prose masterpiece *A Fiery Flying Roll.*

Coppe's reference to that "mighty Leveller" would not have been lost on his audience. In 1649, the year of *A Fiery Flying Roll's* publication, a group calling itself the True Levellers (or Diggers) led by Gerard Winstanley occupied a plot of land outside London named St. George's Hill which would be used for collective farming, producing free produce to be shared by the common people. In a series of brilliant pamphlet's Winstanley argued a radical economic policy using the rhetoric of scripture – a theology that had at its core the idea that the Fall occurred with the invention of private property. Reacting to the enclosure of common lands which had been increasing at a rapid pace since the late fifteenth century, the Levellers took their name not just from the Coppeian image of God making all inequities level, but from literally leveling the hedges which separated private estates. And while the Levellers have not unjustly been compared to the Occupy movement of the modern day, they operated much closer to the sources of power with several prominent officers in Cromwell's New Model Army having Leveller sympathies and with their revolutionary politics playing a central role in the Putney Debates that tried to establish the parameters of an English Republic. The Ranters arguably emerged in reaction to the violent suppression of the Levellers; when seemingly possible political reform was eliminated Ranters like Coppe forged an even more radical ideology. While Ranters used the occasion of the collapse of licensing laws in the English Republic to embrace a type of free speech which had been unknown in the Western world, they still had to battle official censure and punishment from an unsympathetic Parliament.

Marcus' comparison to the punks of the 1970s is interesting, but perhaps not as revelatory as it seemed when *Lipstick Traces* was first published. Indeed reading Smith's anthology with its prophetic, incantatory, mystical language bolsters the arguments that the Ranters were far more radical than a few rock bands signed to a major record label more than thirty years ago. Rather the Ranters held a truly emancipatory theology and politics that were able to take biblical rhetoric and language (the "Great Code" of Western civilization as critic Northrop Frye had it) and to use these traditional tools of oppression in a subversive way.

The Ranters were not just political or social revolutionaries, they were religious ones as well, and they intuited a fundamental critique that radical politics has forgotten and traded in for an insipid materialism. This insight that the Ranters naturally understood was that the only means of resistance is at its heart religious, but the paradox is that the only systems ever worth resisting are in themselves also religious. That is to say that the mark of God and the mark of Cain are everywhere, even if they're secretly hidden behind a faux-secularism. For the Ranters the oppressive systems of government, the market, and organized religion weren't profane, they were their own types of sacred system, albeit one that is corrupt and that must be abolished – Mammon is a god after all.

And this is the same as it ever was – in a country and a world that sees the increasingly obscene concentration of fabulous wealth in the hands of fewer and fewer oligarchs, where the gulf between the mass number of people and these benighted few becomes more and more extreme, where woolly-minded

Libertarian utopians project their nightmares onto legislators' paper, the insight of the Ranters that the very thing we're resisting is somehow "religious" is more important than ever. Our system of oppression wants us to see it as rational, objective, material, scientific, but of course it is anything but. As Charles Baudelaire (that later "Ranter") said, "The greatest trick the devil ever pulled was convincing the world that he didn't exist," and so it is with the Cult of the Market. The Invisible Hand is a pagan idol as any other, and Coppe, Clarkson, and the rest would have understood that the means to resisting corrupt religion is through reformed ritual.

Much as some critics from a few years ago saw Winstanley in the Occupy movement, we should see Coppe in the possibilities of a new antinomian politics. There must be a call for a "Blakean Left," for if there is any true inheritor to the ethos of the Ranters it is not commercialized rock music but William Blake. Indeed in Coppe, Clarkson and Salmon's prose one sees the raw material that Blake would fashion into his own system (so as to avoid being enslaved by another man's) slightly more than a century later. Historical contingency has had Blake categorized along with the Romantic poets, but where they saw an aestheticized art for art's sake, Blake made no such distinctions between poetry, art, life, and religion. Blake more properly belongs to Coppe and the Ranters than he does to Wordsworth, Coleridge, and the Romantics. As an inheritor of the great non-conformist dissenting traditions of the seventeenth-century, Blake absorbed and encapsulated their teachings into his own heterodox bible. And like the Ranters he understood that the manipulation of religious language, texts, images, and ideas was the greatest means of resistance to Moloch's armies, against the "dark satanic mills" of today's modern-day all-encompassing pagan religion: capitalism.

But as Coppe and Blake understood, to rebel against these systems one must be honest enough to be a subversive. Like

Abraham in his father's workshop we must smash all idols of the mind. To rant, curse, swear, and blaspheme one declares independence from social tyrants and obedience to the higher God. It is to reject the Demiurge that is the Market, the Church, and the State and to return to a God who lives not within heaven but as allegory within every human's heart. It's a perilous and dangerous journey, especially for the individual. But as Blake said, "The road of excess leads to the palace of wisdom." Smith has assembled for us the minutes of some of those meetings in the many mansions of our Father's palace, it behooves us to read them and reapply their wisdom anew.

God in the Trash Fire: The Inflammable Thomas Traherne

"To burn a book is to bring light to the world."
Nachman of Bratislava (1772–1810)

"Every book burned enlightens the world."
Ralph Waldo Emerson (1803–1882)

Circumstances surrounding the occasional rediscovery of the poetry of the seventeenth-century divine Thomas Traherne are as something out of one of his strange lyrics. Intimations of the allegorical, when in the winter of 1896 – more than two centuries after he'd died – some of his manuscript poetry was discovered in a London book stall among a heap that was "about to be trashed." William Brooke, the man who rescued these singular first drafts, had originally attributed them to Traherne's contemporary, the similarly ecstatic Henry Vaughan, ensuring that at least until proper identification was made the actual author could remain as obscure in posterity as he had been in life. How eerily appropriate that among that refuse was Traherne's *Centuries of Meditation,* which included his observation that the "world is a mirror of infinite beauty, yet no man sees it." Not until he chances upon it in a London book stall.

Traherne's lyrics have re-emerged like chemicals in a poetic time-release capsule, with the majority uncovered only after that initial lucky find. As his poetry expresses sacred mysteries, holy experiences revealed, and the subtlety of what his contemporary George Herbert termed "something understood," how appropriate that Traherne's work should be revealed as if an unfolding prophecy? Traherne, after all, prophetically declares that he will "open my Mouth in Parables: I will utter Things that have been Kept Secret from the foundations of the

World," a poet of secrets whose poetry had been kept secret, a visionary of paradox whose work celebrates "Things Strange yet common; Incredible, yet Known; Most High, yet plain; Infinitely Profitable, but not Esteemed."

With prescience concerning his own reputation, Traherne wrote of that "Fellowship of the Mystery, which from the beginning of the World hath been hid in GOD, [and] lies concealed!" Like so many of his contemporaries, from Herbert to Vaughan, Traherne was of Welsh extraction, smuggling into English poetics the mystically-inflected Christianity of the Celtic fringe. Unlike them, he has remained largely unknown, with the Anglican priest born in either 1636 or 1637 to a Hertfordshire shoe maker and a mother whose name doesn't survive. Traherne published only a single book before his death in 1674, an anti-Catholic polemic entitled *Roman Forgeries*. Such didacticism obscured Traherne's significance, for in his other work uncovered during the twentieth century, Traherne has emerged as a luminous, ecstatic, transcendental advocate for direct unmediated experience of the divine, where he instructs in "many secrets to us show/Which afterwards we come to know."

Now an Anglican divine, honored by the Church of England on October 10 and Episcopalians on September 27, Traherne is venerated in votive candle and stain glass, exemplifying the High Church perspective he embodied – rituals of incense and bells, of Thomas Cranmer's *Book of Common Prayer* and the liturgy of hours. Traherne, it should be said, was a bit of a cracked saint, however. As Leah Marcus notes in her essay "Children of Light," reprinted in the Norton Anthology *Seventeenth-Century British Poetry: 1603-1660,* Traherne may have "loved Anglicanism" but "he built a large body of thought quite independent of it." Following the chaos of non-conformism which marked the years of civil war, Traherne's theology exceeded even the relative tolerance afforded by the developing policy of "latitudinarianism." Marcus explains that Traherne contradicted "many of the chief tenets of Anglicanism," possibly believing in a borderline pantheistic sense of God's immanence in the natural world. Traherne, Marcus writes, intuited that "Heaven, eternity, paradise...are not places. They are a state of mind."

Such a strange poetic saint has continued to pay academic dividends for scholars fortunate enough to come upon misplaced work, exemplifying Traherne's contention that "Some unknown joys there be/Laid up in store for me." Among several such discoveries of "unknown joys," there was the Traherne recovery by two scholars in 1996 at the Folger Shakespeare Library in Washington DC, when Julia Smith and Laetitia Yeandle found an epic poem that reworked the narratives of Genesis and Exodus. Only a year later, and Jeremy Maute working in Lambeth Palace, the London residence of the Archbishop of Canterbury, discovered Traherne's *The Kingdom of God;* unread for more than 300 years and regarded as a masterpiece, fulfilling the marginalia of an anonymous seventeenth-century annotator writing in that book's flyleaf, who rhetorically queried, "Why is this soe long detained in a dark manuscript, that if printed would be a Light to the World, & a Universal Blessing?"

For sheer miraculousness in the capricious contingency of the Lord, the most striking example of such a discovery is described by Kimberly Johnson in *Before the Door of God: An Anthology of Devotional Poetry,* where she writes that a "manuscript of visionary, rhapsodic work in mixed genre called *Commentaries of Heaven*...was rescued, half-burning and stinking, from a Lancashire trash heap in 1967." Singed and still smoking, these singular papers were chanced upon by a man scouring the trash yard for discarded car parts. If said scavenger had been tardy in his scrounging, those verses would have been sent heavenward like the images of luminescence which permeate Traherne's poetry. Helpful to remember the argument of Fernando Baez in *A Universal History of the Destruction of Books: From Ancient Sumer to Modern Iraq* who explained that when it comes to books, sometimes ironically, "Fire is salvation." Such power to "conserve life is also a destructive power," for fire allows us to play "God, master of the fire of life and death." After all, we often "destroy what we love," and if there is anything at the center of Traherne's poetry it is the ecstasies of God's obscured love, absconded away in lost books hidden at the center of fiery whirlwinds.

A parable worthy of Traherne: hidden scripture as a variety of burnt offering upon the pyre of the Lord, in the form of a smoldering Lancashire garbage heap. Browned paper blackening and curling at the edges, atoms of ink evaporated and stripped to their base elementals, literature reduced to an ash where poetry can no longer be read, but must rather be inhaled. Fortunate that *Commentaries of Heaven* was found, and yet there is a profundity in disappearing verse; the poem written, but not read; consideration of all which is beautiful that has been lost, penned for the audience of God alone. In that golden, glowing ember of such a profane place as a garbage dump, there is an approach to what literary historian Michael Schmidt references in his *Lives of the Poets* as Traherne's "Images of light – starlight, pure light" as belonging to the "fields of heaven and eternity."

As metaphysical conceit, the manuscript was not simply a burning tangle of paper, but it was as if finding God himself in the trash fire, where the words "Who cannot pleas far more the Worlds! & be/A Bliss to others like the Deitie" were rescued from an oblivion of fire. Baez writes that by "destroying, we ratify this ritual of permanence, purification, and consecration." After all, it was presumably only the heat and light that drew the scavenger's attention, a brief moment when the volume could announce its existence before it would be forever burnt up like a Roman candle, lest it rather forever mold and rot. Baez writes that "we bring to the surface" through flammability, there is a restitution of "equilibrium, power or transcendence." To burn sparks a light; to enflame such poetry is to set a purifying fire, and to find such an engulfed volume is to encounter a glowing divinity on the road from Lancashire. Traherne, the burning poet, who wrote "O fire of heaven! I sacred Light/How fair and bright,/How great am I,/Whom all the world doth magnify!"

Categorized as a "metaphysical poet," of which Dr. Johnson in his 1781 *Lives of the Most Eminent English Poets* described as being "men of learning" only interested "to show their learning." Dr. Johnson infamously defined the metaphysical poets, seventeenth-century figures including John Donne, Herbert, Vaughan, and (sometimes) Andrew Marvell, as trading in clever metaphorical conceits whereby "the most heterogenous ideas are yoked by violence together." In Donne's verse, for example, two lovers could be described as the arms of a compass, or as Herbert's devotional poetry took on the shape of objects he describes, as in "The Altar" from his 1633 *The Temple*. Often dismissed as more concerned with cleverness than depth, wit rather than rectitude, T.S. Eliot would refer to them as a "generation more often named then read." Defense of the metaphysical poets was a modernist endeavor, begun by criticism like Eliot's 1921 essay in the *Times Literary Supplement*, so that eventually the movement came to be regarded as the exemplar of the late English Renaissance.

Traherne's identification as a metaphysical, especially concerning his erudition and his religious enthusiasms, makes a certain sense. Yet he is less fleshy (and flashy) than Donne, less conventionally pious than Herbert, less political than Marvell, and nearest in tenor to Vaughan. It's true that they share mystical affinities, even while the enthusiasms of the former are far more optimistic than those of the latter. Yet Vaughan, associated with that philosophical circle the Cambridge Platonists, was privy to circulation – to being read and written about – to in short, *influence*. Traherne, by contrast, scribbled in obscurity. In designating him a member of such a group, we should remember that he had no influence on the rest of that school, for they hadn't read him. But as Schmidt writes, "Such obliquity doesn't obscure the material world; it illuminates what exists beyond it." Traherne may be a poet outside of history and a creature without canon, but his audience is in *eternity*.

Dr. Johnson wouldn't have read him a century later, either. For that matter, Eliot wouldn't have been able to read the majority of work attributed to Traherne, since the initial rediscoveries of the poet's work only saw print little more than a decade before "The Metaphysical Poets" was published in *TLS*. More apt to think of Traherne as being a poetic movement of one, for when reading his cracked verse, with its often-surreal content and its ecstatic declarations, it's just as easy to see Emily Dickinson as Donne, William Blake as Herbert. If anything, a blind analysis of Traherne's poetry could lead a reader to think that this was verse by an exuberant Romantic, a mystical Transcendentalist, a starry-headed Beat burning in the dynamo of the night.

Consider his startlingly modern lyric "The Person," where Traherne writes of "The naked things" that "Are most sublime, and brightest." Inheritor of a Christian tradition of our innate fallenness, Traherne focuses on the divine immanence that permeates creation, as well as that transcendence that nature points towards. Nature is precisely *not* fallen, as when Traherne writes that, "When they alone are seen:/Men's hands than Angel's wings/Are truer wealth even here below." An almost exact contemporary of the Dutch Sephardic Jewish philosopher Baruch Spinoza, Traherne evidences that pantheistic fervor which understands creator and creation to be synonymous, arguing for direct experience of the noumenal, for their "worth they then do best reveal,/When we all metaphors remove,/For metaphors conceal."

Traherne argues for divine language, a semiotics that approaches the thing-in-itself, poetry of experience that recognizes metaphor as idolatry, for the "best are blazon'd when we see/The anatomy,/Survey the skin, cut up the flesh, the veins/ Unfold, the glory there remains:/The muscles, fibers, arteries and bones/Are better far than crowns and precious stones." When Traherne wrote, Puritan typologists investigated scripture and nature alike for evidence of predestined fallenness; when Traherne wrote, Christian apologists charted irreconcilable differences between language and our world after Eden. But Traherne, rather, chose to write in that lost tongue of Paradise. His was an encomium to direct experience, an account of what the very marrow of life thus ingested did taste like. A language which in its immediacy seems both shockingly current and as ancient as gnostic parchment. Encapsulated in his poetry there is something not just of his era, but of all eras, occluded though that eternal message may be.

Demonstration of Stuart Kelley's description in *The Book of Lost Books* of "an alternative history of literature, an epitaph and a wake, a hypothetical library and an elegy to what might have been." Traherne's poetry was written during years of first Puritan Interregnum and then High Church Restoration, but for either authority the poet's views would be idiosyncratic. Detecting intimations of consciousness on the moon and in the sea, dreaming of both angels and aliens when he "saw new worlds beneath the water like,/New people; ye another sky." Marcus writes that Traherne couldn't "be entirely defended against charges of heresy," which might have been an issue had anyone read his poetry.

Arguments can be proffered that Traherne was a pantheist who believed that nature was equivalent with God, that he was a Pelagian who denied the existence of original sin, or that he was a universalist who anticipated eternal salvation for all. A poet for whom the human body is to be celebrated, who would opine that "Men are Images of GOD carefully put into a Beautiful Case," who with urgency would maintain that the souls of man are "Equal to the Angels" and that our bodies could be reserved for the "most Glorious Ends." With antinomian zeal, Traherne argues that "through many Obstacles full of gross and subterraneous Darkness, which seem to affright and stifle the Soul," the individual who transgresses will find themselves "at last to a new Light and Glory." He evokes Blake's *Proverbs of Heaven and Hell* a century before his fellow visionary would engrave his plates.

In *Eternity's Sunrise: The Imaginative World of William Blake*, Leo Damrosch accurately describes Blake's verse as presenting infinity "here and now in the real world we inhabit, not far away in unimaginable endlessness. Eternity, likewise, is present in each moment of lived experience," but so too is this a description of Traherne. Evocations of not just Blake, but Ralph Waldo Emerson's Transcendentalism, for when Traherne describes God as "a Sphere like Thee of Infinite Extent: an Ey without walls; All unlimited & Endless Sight," do we not hear the nineteenth century American philosopher's wish to "become a transparent eye-ball?" When Emily Dickinson sings of "Wild nights – Wild nights!" do we not hear Traherne chanting with declarative exclamation mark of "O ravishing and only pleasure!"

And when Walt Whitman wrote in his 1855 *Leaves of Grass* that, "I celebrate myself,/And what I assume you shall assume,/ For every atom belonging to me as good belongs to you," we are reminded of Traherne's conviction that "all we see is ours, and every One/Possessor of the While." Traherne anticipates Whitman's "conviction that all the world's loveliness belongs to him," as Marcus describes it, the two bards united in the faith that "although the world was made for him alone, it was made for every other single human being just as it was for him." Traherne derived his ethic from Psalm 139, an orthodoxy holding that we must "praise thee; for I am fearfully and wonderfully made." But from scripture Traherne finds a heterodoxy which plumbs the city that "seemed to stand in Eden, or to be Built in Heaven." In this New Jerusalem, Traherne would list with a catalog of Whitmanesque regularity that the "Streets were mine, the Temple was mine, the People were mine; their Clothes and

Gold and Silver were mine, as much as their Sparkling Eyes, Fair Skins and ruddy faces."

Such similarities could lead one to assume that Whitman had a copy of Traherne as he gripped notebook and looked out on the brackish waters of New York Harbor writing of those, "Crowds of men and women attired in usual costumes, how curious you are to me!", or that Emerson considered the poet in his Concord manse – save for the fact that it's impossible. Such are the vagaries of the lost man, the hidden poet who sings of "room and liberty, breathing place and fresh-air among the Antipodes," this gospel of "passing on still through those inferior Regions that are under...feet, but over the head." Traherne wrote in the seventeenth century, but he seemingly had memory of all those who came after. All those women and men who echo him even though they could never have heard him, who came to "another Skie...and leaving it behind...[sunk] down into the depths of all Immensity."

Writing poetry from a position of eternity, Traherne presents a fascinating anomaly of what Johnson describes as "poetic inspiration," for until 1896, or 1967, or 1996, or 1997 Traherne couldn't have inspired any of those poets who are so similar to him. Blake or Dickinson had never picked up a volume of his verse. Traherne's very life is oddly yet appropriately allegorical, his liturgy concerned with this "preeminent figure...[of] the Unknowable," as Johnson describes it. She writes that at the heart of devotional poetry is the "perceptual inaccessibility of the divine," defined by the "fundamental principle of mystery and unknowability." How perfect then is Traherne's verse, lost in libraries or singed in trash fires, hidden from view until revealed like some ecstatic epiphany? In the book of Acts, St. Paul speaks to a group of Athenians about their shrine to the "Unknown God." Traherne is our "Unknown Poet," overturning our ideas of influence and inspiration, whose work with a mysterious, thrumming electricity courses through the lines of oblivious

Whitman or the stanzas of unaware Dickinson, as powerful as magnetism and as invisible as gravity.

Prisoners of linear time that we are, hard to understand that the vagaries of influence don't simply flow from past to future. When Traherne celebrates "every Mote in the Air, every Grain of Dust, every Sand, every Spire of Grass" that is "wholly illuminated," do we not detect Whitman? When he sings of "O heavenly Joy!" do we not hear Dickinson? In Traherne's "On Leaping Over the Moon," one of his oddest and most beautiful lyrics, I like to imagine that when he writes, "I saw new worlds beneath the water lie,/New people; ye, another sky" and where in "travel see, and saw by night/A much more strange and wondrous sight" that what he espied were Blake and Whitman, Dickinson and Allen Ginsberg, you and me. Traherne is a poet who wrote for an audience that had not yet been born – perhaps still has yet to be born.

From his poem "Shadows in the Water," he writes of how, "Thus did I by the water's bring/Another world beneath me think:/And while the lofty spacious skies/Reversed there, abused mine eyes,/I fancied other feet/Came mine to touch or meet;/And by some puddle I did play/Another world within it lay," so that I imagine Traherne saw nothing less than that other world which is our own, looking onto the mirror of the water's surface as if it were a portal to this parallel dimension, these "spacious regions" of "bright and open space," where he sees people with, "Eyes, hands and feet they had like mine;/Another sun did with them shine." There is hopefully a future yet to come, where, "chanced another world to meet...A phantom, 'tis a world indeed,/Where skies beneath us shine,/And earth by art divine/Another face presents below,/Where people's feet against ours go," for in scribbling in secrecy what poet has addressed himself more perfectly to people yet to be imagined?

Proper understanding relies on imagination, not just the role played in his composition, but Traherne's strange status as imagined literature (for whatever manuscripts await to be plucked from burning trash heaps?). Alberto Manguel, writing with Borgesian elegance, argues in *The Library at Night* that "Every library conjures up its own dark ghost; every ordering sets up, in its wake, a shadow library of absences." What is most sublime and wondrous about Traherne are not just his literal words on a page, but how we can't disentangle him from what could have been lost, what perhaps still remains lost, and that which is lost forever. Perhaps in book stalls or trash fires there is more undiscovered Trahern; more rhapsodic, even more visionary than which we've been blessed enough to read. Traherne makes the comparison that an, "Empty Book is like an Infants Soul, in which any Thing may be Written. It is Capable of all Things" and so is the infinite multitude of not just Traherne's writings which we shall never read, but the full magnitude of all writings that we shall never see.

Traherne's magnum opus exists in the gaps, written in the lacunas, on a scroll kept inside the distance between that which is known and that which can never be found. Traherne describes this place as a, "Temple of Majesty, yet no man regards it. It is a region of Light and Peace, did not man disquiet it. It is the Paradise of God." Poetry of empty sepulchers and disembodied tombs, of empty rooms and cleared shelves; a liturgy of the Holy of Holies which contains no idol, but only a single, deafening, immaculate absence. At the Temple's center there is that ever tended, ever burning, ever consuming fire which gives off that sublime heat and light, where Traherne could imagine with prescient clarity that, "From God above/Being sent, the Heavens me enflame:/To praise his Name/The stars do move!/The burning sun doth shew His love." Power of such words written in light, heat, and flame. Such books can burn sacred holes in our soul, a holy immolation in our hearts, giving off that intense light, which diffuse though it may be awaits those eyes that have yet to be born generations hence.

The Science Fiction Before Science

An explorer builds a space ship and meets aliens on another world. They are a "people most strange," these extraterrestrials. They're twice as tall as humans; they wear clothes spun of a mysterious material, dyed in a color unseen by human eyes; they speak only in haunting musical tones. Then the explorer returns to Earth. This has been the plot of seemingly countless examples of pulp magazines and canonical science fiction in the past century. Similar themes have been explored by authors like Isaac Asimov, Ray Bradbury, and Arthur C. Clarke, classic television such as *The Twilight Zone* and *Star Trek*, and films like this month's *Arrival*. But this particular story isn't from the past century. Its explorer, Domingo Gonsales, is the fictional narrator of *The Man in the Moone*, a novel by Francis Godwin, a bishop in the Church of England. It was published in 1638.

Science fiction is sometimes understood as the result of modern science. According to this view, the genre emerged to make sense of the tremendous expanses in empirical knowledge and technological ability throughout the seventeenth and eighteenth centuries – the Copernican model of the solar system, discoveries in the New World, medical advances, microscopes. Critics like Brian Aldiss have argued that *Frankenstein*, Mary Shelley's 1818 masterpiece, is the first science-fiction novel because its fantastic events occur not because of magic or miracle, but purely through science. Yet many books written at the height of, or even before, the Scientific Revolution used the same narrative conceit. What makes these books fascinating is not just that they reflect the new science of the time, but that they demonstrate literature's influence on scientific inquiry. Like many contemporary scientists say that *Star Trek* inspired their love of discovery, or that modern technology is prefigured by stories from a half-century ago, *The Man in the Moone* disseminated ideas like heliocentricism and the possibility of extraterrestrial life.

Science fiction alone did not inspire the scientific revolution, but the literature of the era did allow people to imagine different realities – in some cases, long before those realities actually became real. A reading list of these early stories includes works of varying canonicity, such as Thomas More's *Utopia* (1516), Francis Bacon's *New Atlantis* (1627), Johannes Kepler's *Somnium* (1634), Margaret Cavendish's *The Blazing World* (1666), Henry Neville's *The Isle of Pines* (1688), and Jonathan Swift's *Gulliver's Travels* (1726). These texts all share the driving curiosity that defines so much classic science fiction. "There is no man this day living that can tell you of so many strange and unknown peoples and countries," writes More, describing the discoverer of the fictional island Utopia – a passage as evocative and stirring as "to boldly go where no man has gone before."

Though obscure today, Godwin's *The Man in the Moone* captivated seventeenth-century readers with its tale of a Spaniard who travels in a ship powered by geese. He flies through space, which, for the first time in literature is depicted as weightless, then spends time with the denizens of a lunar civilization, only to leave for an almost equally exotic and technologically marvelous land called China. The story's blend of natural philosophy, travel narrative, and the utopian and picaresque genres delighted English and European audiences. It also influenced literary stars for centuries. The French author Savinien de Cyrano de Bergerac poked fun at the book in his satirical 1657 novel, *The Other World*. Edgar Allen Poe referenced the novel in his 1835 story "The Unparalleled Adventures of One Hans Pfaall." And H.G. Wells' 1901 novel, *The First Men in the Moon*, was directly inspired by Godwin.

Godwin's influence was scientific as well. As the Oxford professor William Poole writes in his introduction to the latest edition of *The Man in the Moone*, "Literary or humanistic traditions and practical astronomy were not absolutely separate activities for early-modern astronomers." For Godwin, the humanities and sciences weren't just overlapping, they were often mutually reinforcing methodologies. John Wilkins, a fellow of the Royal Society and the inventor of the precursor to the metric system, argued in his book *Mercury* (1641) that Godwin's novel could "be used to unlock the secrets" of natural philosophy. Even more provocative when it was first published was *The Blazing World*, by the first woman in the Royal Society, Margaret Cavendish. The story is an account of travels to a parallel universe accessed through the North Pole and populated by sentient animal-man creatures: "Bear-men, some Worm-men...some Bird-men, Some fly-men, some Ant-men, some Geese-men," and others. There are flying vehicles and submarines, as well as discussions on scientific innovations, particularly the most recent discoveries afforded by the invention of the microscope. The novel is especially notable for its narrative complexity. The author herself appears as a character and reflects on writing, "making and dissolving several worlds in her own mind...a world of Ideas, a world of Atomes, a world of Lights."

The Blazing World was recovered as a subject of serious study by feminist critics in the last quarter of the twentieth century, and Cavendish has recently found herself in more popular discussions as well. Danielle Dutton, whose historical novel *Margaret the First* kicked off a renewed interest in Cavendish earlier this year, says that the first time she encountered *The Blazing World*, she found it, "totally bizarre, in the best possible way: the talking animals, the cities of amber and coral, the metafictional move wherein the soul of Margaret Cavendish travels to the Blazing World to befriend the Empress." The book conjures the clockpunk era of primitive microscopes and telescopes, of fleas made monstrously visible to the human eye, and magnetic lodestones pointing true North.

Godwin, Cavendish, and their contemporaries are important

for generating a freely speculative space of imagination – which is still science fiction's role today. In constructing worlds – or birthing "paper bodies," as Cavendish called them – the authors' acts of envisioning possible futures had a tangible impact on how reality took shape. Take this selection of technological marvels Bacon describes in *New Atlantis*: "Versions of bodies into other bodies" (organ transplants?), "Exhilaration of the spirits, and putting them in good disposition" (pharmaceuticals?), "Drawing of new foods out of substances not now in use" (genetically modified food?), "Making new threads for apparel" (synthetic fabrics?), "Deceptions of the senses" (television and film?).

And then there's this eerily prescient description of the Lunar technology in *The Man in the Moone:*

You shal then see men to flie from place to place in the ayre; you shall be able, (without moving or travailing of any creature,) to send messages in an instant many Miles off, and receive answer againe immediately you shall bee able to declare your minde presently unto your friend, being in some private and remote place of a populous Citie, with a number of such like things...you shall have notices of a new World... that all the Philosophers of former ages could never so much as dreame of.

Can one read that passage and not think of air travel, telecommunications, the internet, computers? This is prophesy, but not of scripture and myth; Godwin did not speak to angels, and had no scrying mirrors or tools of divination. Instead, he relied on empiricism and reason. And that gave him a rare quality as an oracle: He happened to be correct.

"What the scientific revolution did," writes the British historian Keith Thomas in *Religion and the Decline of Magic: Studies in Popular Belief in Sixteenth and Seventeenth-Century England*, "was to...buttress up the old rationalist attitude with a more stable intellectual foundation." That is, science fiction wasn't always derivative of scientific explanations themselves. Even before science had fully defined itself, literature offered a means for thinking about science. The capacity to envision alternative social arrangements, in particular, makes science fiction arguably the literary genre with the most revolutionary potential. Cavendish's "proto-feminist critique," Dutton says, was a "critique of dominate power structures." In seventeenth-century Britain, "these critiques...coming from a woman's pen, no less, must have seemed nearly as fantastical as [her] talking bears!"

Science fiction has since been the social laboratory of visionaries like Ursula K. LeGuin, Samuel Delaney, Margaret Atwood, Philip K. Dick, and Octavia Butler. The freedom of speculative fiction has allowed these authors to question real-life culture in radical ways. In the tradition of socially engaged science fiction, Cavendish is the first "Creatoress," as she called herself. In *The Blazing World*, Cavendish wrote that, "fictions are an issue of man's Fancy, framed in his own Mind, according as he please, without regard, whether the thing, he fancies, be really existent without his mind of not." Yet for her, Godwin, Bacon, and others, so many of the things they fancied later did become "really existent." Their imaginations didn't always require empirical discoveries to have happened first; their fancies were written in the poetry of delight and wonder, before being confirmed in the prose of experiment and logic.

John Milton, One of the Roughs, An American

Three hundred and fifty years ago, the poet John Milton wrote one of the greatest characters in all of British literature: Lucifer, the antagonist of the epic poem *Paradise Lost*. Feared by Puritans, fêted by Romantics, and reinvented by everybody else, Milton's fallen archangel has worn many different masks over the centuries, from *Moby-Dick*'s Captain Ahab to television's Tony Soprano and Walter White. Curiously, the deeply modern Lucifer could also be considered one of the greatest characters in American literature, even though he was created more than a century before the United States was founded.

That's in part because literary critics have decked Lucifer's creator himself in red, white, and blue bunting since the nineteenth century. In 1845, Rufus Griswold wrote that Milton was "more emphatically American than any author who has lived in the United States." More recently, the author Nigel Smith claimed in his cheekily titled 2008 book *Is Milton Better Than Shakespeare?* that "Milton is an author for all Americans... because his visionary writing is a literary embodiment of so many of the aspirations that have guided Americans." Indeed, America seemed prefigured in Milton's pamphlets, from *Eikonoklastes*, which celebrated regicide, to *Areopagitica*, which advocated for freedom of speech.

In light of this, it's little surprise Milton's Lucifer can be read as a kind of modern, American antihero, invented before such a concept really existed. Many of the values the archangel advocates in *Paradise Lost* – the self-reliance, the rugged individualism, and even manifest destiny – are regarded as quintessentially American in the cultural imagination. Milton may be a poet of individual liberty and conscience, but he was also one of the most brilliant theological explorers of the darker subjects of sin, depravity, and the inclination toward evil. Nothing demonstrates that inclination more than the long-standing appeal the charismatic Lucifer has had for audiences, an appeal mirrored by the flawed but alluring protagonists of some of TV's greatest American dramas. What Milton's *Paradise Lost*, the first version of which was published in 1667, also demonstrates is what can be so dangerous about mistaking an antihero for a hero.

But first, a reminder of the poem's narrative: Across some ten thousand lines, Milton writes "[t]hings unattempted yet in prose or rhyme," by retelling the Genesis story of "Man's disobedience, and the loss thereupon of Paradise." The poet recounts the aftermath of the war in Heaven, Lucifer's fall to Hell, and his ultimate tempting of Adam and Eve in the Garden of Eden. And though the epic's length may have inspired Samuel Johnson to quip, "None ever wished it longer," part of the maximalist brilliance of the poem is the universe it contains, which reflects Milton's immense erudition, ranging from the astronomy of Galileo to the subject of Lapland witches. *Paradise Lost* expands on the Bible's minimalist account, while altering received cultural representations of the devil. Milton's Lucifer is neither bestial, a reptilian Other, nor the goofy incompetent of a medieval morality play; rather, he's a conflicted, brooding, alienated, narcissistic self-mythologizer. In other words, he's a thoroughly modern man, and in a country as preoccupied with modernity as the United States is, he's arguably an honorary "American" as a result. Milton's fellow countryman, the novelist D.H. Lawrence, remarked in his under-read 1923 *Studies in Classic American Literature* that, "The essential American soul is hard, isolate, stoic, and a killer. It has never yet melted." The novelist had in mind not just the pioneer clearing lands that do not belong to him, but also the honey-worded con man who can justify his crimes in the sweetest language.

Lawrence's pessimistic appraisal of the American character

doubles as an apt description of *Paradise Lost's* central antagonist. Much as Lucifer invades Eden like the frontiersman who moved ever further west, he is also capable of justifying his actions with the most exalted of language. Milton writes, "But all was false and hollow; though his tongue/Dropp'd manna, and could make the worse appear/The better reason." Lucifer is a confidence man, rebel, and supposed advocate of liberty. He's also a self-made individualist setting out into the wilderness to make his own world anew. The spirit of the *Paradise Lost* author has persisted in the United States in large part because of Herman Melville, who once claimed that, "we want no American Miltons," while ultimately becoming an American Milton himself. Melville's 1851 opus *Moby-Dick* set the Miltonic template for subsequent US literary history, fully internalizing *Paradise Lost* and repackaging it as an American tale. The scholar William Spengemann wrote in 1994 that Melville "turned instinctively to Milton for one of his models; and there is no reason to suppose that Melville's Miltonism has played no part in the virtual identification of American literature with *Moby-Dick*." As Melville turned instinctively to Milton, many subsequent writers – whether of literature or television – turned to Melville, who helped establish the conception of the Luciferian antihero as an American type who invents his own rules.

The influence of *Paradise Lost*, by way of Melville, is apparent in many acclaimed TV dramas of the 2000s, most notably *The Sopranos*, *Mad Men*, and *Breaking Bad* – all shows that critics have identified as offering some grand statement on the American Dream. In *Mad Men's* very first episode, Don Draper memorably remarks, "What you call love was invented by guys like me... to sell nylons," which recalls Lucifer's famous assertion that, "The mind is its own place, and in itself/Can make a heav'n of hell, a hell of heav'n." Lucifer is not just a rebel, but also a character who has tricked himself (and many of his post-Romantic readers) into believing his very words can generate reality. Lucifer's line is a pithy and dark summation of the American credo of self-invention. His mercurial nature and his rhetorical chicanery recall the verbal dexterity of Draper, who, like Lucifer, shed his original name.

Or consider Walter White, who also adopts an alter ego, becoming the fearsome Heisenberg whose very name alludes to the devilry implicit in uncertainty. It's a renaming process similar to that which Milton's demons in *Paradise Lost* undergo; as the scholar Regina Schwartz observes in her 1988 study *Remembering and Repeating: On Milton's Theology and Poetics*, "Having lost their positive identity, they have lost their names." But as Lucifer discovered in his rebellion against heaven, extreme self-invention inevitably leads to the ultimate form of alienation: a radical distance from God and from fellow humans.

Think of the charismatic Tony Soprano, a Mafia Lucifer conspiring with his consigliere and his lieutenants just as the archangel does with the infernal parliament of Pandemonium in *Paradise Lost's* first book. Tony channels Lucifer's profound solitariness, telling his therapist, "All due respect, you got no fucking idea what it's like to be number one...And in the end you're completely alone with it all." Instead of Asmodeus, Moloch, and Belial, Tony's counselors have names like Big Pussy, Paulie Walnuts, and Silvio Dante, but the ultimate result of acquiring such impotent power, even when surrounded by ostensible compatriots, is the same – profound aloneness. The rage that results from such pride sums up both the Miltonic Lucifer and a version of the American tragic character.

Lucifer, the rebel who thought it, "Better to reign in Hell, than serve in Heaven," has an independent streak that appeals to the iconoclasm of some Americans. And not just Americans of course: It was the British Romantic poet William Blake who claimed Milton himself was "of the Devil's party without knowing it." Blake's assertion is the most famous example of one critical school that emerged around the so-called "Milton Controversy."

This question asks why Milton, a fervent (if unconventional) Protestant, would ultimately give the devil all the poem's best lines? Why make Lucifer the most attractive character in *Paradise Lost* if you're supposedly trying to "justify the ways of God to man?" Many in the Romantic tradition thus argued that Lucifer should be read as a revolutionary, a Promethean figure who tears at unfair strictures.

On the other side of the debate are the eighteenth-century essayist Joseph Addison and the modern Christian apologist C.S. Lewis, both of whom read *Paradise Lost* as an uncomplicatedly orthodox account of conventional belief. This central tension in the epic – why is such an ostensibly evil character so attractive? – wasn't reconciled until the scholar Stanley Fish's seminal 1968 book *Surprised by Sin*. Fish, known today for his pugilistic punditry, remains one of the greatest Miltonists of the past century for squaring the critical circle regarding the "Milton Controversy." Fish interpreted Milton's epic as "a poem about how its readers came to be the way they are...to provoke in its readers wayward fallen responses." In other words, Lucifer is *supposed* to be intriguing, because in forcing the reader of *Paradise Lost* to be drawn to evil, Milton demonstrates the original sin that he believed marked everyone's soul. That Lucifer gets the best lines isn't incidental to his evil, but central to it.

American prestige television dramas have also cleverly convinced audiences to empathize with charismatic-sinner types. Brett Martin in his 2013 book *Difficult Men: Behind the Scenes of a Creative Revolution* wrote that the "third golden age of TV" in the 2000s took as its central theme the anger felt by men who feel entitled to a respect and power that they are being denied, which then makes them dangerous. Think of how many viewers continued to love Tony Soprano, even after he strangled to death a Witness Protection Program informant in between taking his daughter on a tour of bucolic New England colleges. Or Walter White, the mild-mannered chemistry teacher turned meth kingpin executing a prisoner and dissolving his body in acid (and later dropping any pretense of misguided altruism when he tells his wife, "I did it for me. I liked it. I was good at it"). Or even the charming, handsome Don Draper with his serial adultery.

All these characters share a rage generated from feeling that they are owed something, which also describes Lucifer. If one has to identify a "difficult man," whom would be more fitting than the fallen archangel? Just as identifying with Lucifer's grand speeches can tell readers something ugly about their own state, so too does rooting for Walter White, a man who allowed his assistant's unconscious girlfriend to choke to death on her own vomit. These shows reveal to their audience not just what is debased about certain values, but indeed what is debased in the audience when they thrill to evil.

Milton, of course, believed that intrinsic depravity marked every soul. Sin may be universal, but there is something revealing in how the triumphalist values of American individualism are also the values held dear by Lucifer. Like Walter or Don, Milton's character is ruthless, innovative, creative, and dangerous – and also in many ways as American as apple pie. Envision Lucifer, "High on a throne of royal state," where he "exalted sat...To that bad eminence... insatiate to pursue/Vain war with heav'n." In his pettiness, decadence, narcissism, and privilege, Lucifer embodies the worst of a certain strain of American exceptionalism that celebrates power for power's sake. The best of prestige television has often done what Milton did, reminding audiences of what is pernicious and poisonous in their attraction to evil. Ultimately, Milton's genius isn't that he's "of the devil's party"; it's that he proved, deep down, so are his readers.

Cycle and Epicycle, Orb in Orb

Paradise Lost (1674) is a consummate example of scientific literature. In it, John Milton effectively mimics the debates that motivated the New Science of his era, and the result is a poem that is "scientific" not just because its content sometimes concerns nature, but also because its rhetoric imitates the emerging scientific method. And much of that, I argue, is due to Galileo, the man whom Milton described as "the Tuscan artist with optic glass." For readers who half-remember Milton from an undergraduate survey course, this might be a surprising contention. While the poet still generates reams of journal articles, dissertations, and academic books, when the general public thinks of him, it's often as a dour Puritan poet writing dour Puritan poetry (which assumes that "Puritan" is even an appropriate designation for him). But in fact his greatest work depicts, among other things, how scientific debate operates.

Far from seeing themselves in opposition to natural philosophy, many Puritans embraced empirical science as a practical application of their religious understanding, and while the simplistic reductionism that views the scientific revolution as a direct product of the Reformation has been made more nuanced by subsequent historiography, it remains true that many Puritans of Milton's era celebrated the burgeoning scientific method as an extension of their own theology.

Consider the scientist and philosopher Francis Bacon, writing a half-century before *Paradise Lost*. While not a Puritan per se, he was a steadfast Protestant who appropriated the language of the Reformation in his defense of the emerging science. Or examine the career of the American theologian Jonathan Edwards, writing a century after Milton, who is mostly remembered as the author of the hell-fire sermon "Sinners in the Hands of an Angry God" (1741). The historian George Marsden writes in *Jonathan Edwards:*

A Life (2003) that the preacher was "profoundly influenced by Isaac Newton" and that like "many men of his time, Edwards was determined to know everything and how it all fit together in God's universe." If Puritanism has an innate attraction towards a certain variety of scientific positivism, and if Milton is the most celebrated of Puritan poets, it would stand to reason that those scientific enthusiasms would be present in *Paradise Lost*.

The poem, a 10,000-line epic about the Fall of Man and the "ways of God," is the earliest and greatest example of a neglected literary genre – the scientific epic. What are the poetics of science, and what is a scientific epic? This is a poem that not only takes as its subject scientific topics but that also replicates a spirit of rational skepticism. There are surprisingly few texts that do this: that take the drama of scientific discovery, and of the worldview that makes that progress possible, as their subject.

The capable lyrics of the 1981 Nobel Prize-winning chemist Roald Hoffmann count as one example: "Essential amino acids, dexterously/synthesized, are a mix of mirror/image forms." In the early nineteenth century, Erasmus Darwin prefigured in scientific verse the theories of evolution through natural selection of his grandson Charles, writing:

Organic life beneath the shoreless waves
Was born and nurs'd in ocean's pearly caves;
First forms minute, unseen by spheric glass...
These, as successive generations bloom,
New powers acquire and larger limbs assume.

For a poet who arguably wrote within the mode of scientific epic, Walt Whitman's declaration "Hurrah for positive science!" should be taken literally, as I have argued elsewhere. Ancient poems, such as Ovid's *Metamorphoses* and Lucretius' atomistic *De Rerum Natura*, concern themselves with physical transformations and the working of the world, but were written in a cultural context without real science.

On the other hand, *Paradise Lost* was first printed seven years after the founding of the Royal Society and 20 years before the publication of Newton's *Principia*, in the midst of what the philosopher of science Thomas Kuhn in 1962 called a "paradigm shift," and what we know as the first scientific revolution. Evidence of that revolution permeates the poem, an influence that is attributable to Galileo.

Milton toured Italy in 1638, when he was 30, leaving his native Britain on the verge of civil war, claiming to have met the astronomer who was then under house arrest, though some historians question whether said event actually happened. Regardless, Galileo is the only contemporary figure mentioned in *Paradise Lost*, appearing in the divine vision of Raphael, an angel God sends to Adam and Eve to dissuade them from temptation:

...As when by night the Glass
Of Galileo, less assur'd, observes
Imagind Lands and Regions in the Moon

In *Paradise Lost*, Milton offered a retelling of that early account of natural forms: the Genesis myth. Milton's retelling explicated at length on an incredible diversity of subjects ranging from ancient history to New World geography. He presents the archangel Raphael in intellectual dialog with Adam among the perfumed groves of Eden. Raphael discusses the history of creation, from its origins to its future, while leaving some of the biggest questions of cosmology ambiguous. In Book 8, Milton writes of the motions of the heavens that:

Whether the Sun predominant in Heav'n
Rise on the Earth, or the Earth rise on the Sun...
Solicit not thy thoughts with matters hid,
Leave them to God above...

Milton's mastery was not limited to "things unattempted yet in Prose or Rhime," but debates about natural philosophy also concerned him. Scholars of the seventeenth century disagreed whether it was the geocentric Ptolemaic model of the solar system or the heliocentric Copernican model that was accurate. And though we have long since settled the question in favor of the latter, this was by no means a foregone conclusion when Milton was writing. The tension between those two models of the cosmos runs as one of the currents underneath *Paradise Lost*.

In general, Protestantism was no more amenable to Copernicus than was Catholicism, and at times *Paradise Lost* seems to evidence faith in Ptolemy. In Book 7, Milton writes of how

...Heav'n in all her Glorie shon, and rowld
Her motions, as the great first-Movers hand
First wheeld thir course;...

With his distinctly Aristotelian language concerning a "first mover," and the verb "wheeled," Milton calls to mind Ptolemy's complex cosmology with its epicycles upon epicycles. Or consider the line in Book 10, when Milton writes of how

...The Sun
Had first his precept so to move, so shine,
As might affect the Earth with cold and heat

explaining the seasons based not on the tilt of the planet's axis, but rather its distance from a sun that rotates around it. It would seem that Milton has firmly rejected new theories that placed the Sun at the center of the solar system. Yet in Book 8, Raphael says that God laughs at the "quaint opinions" of specialists, who:

...model Heav'n
And calculate the Starrs, how they will weild
The mightie frame, how build, unbuild, contrive
To save appeerances, how gird the Sphear
With Centric and Eccentric scribl'd o're,
Cycle and Epicycle, Orb in Orb.

Out of historical context, it would be easy to read this as a condemnation of natural philosophy, but what is being parodied is the increasingly baroque complexities of Ptolemaic cosmology. The defenders of the status quo had to long contend with empirical discrepancies that made Ptolemy's theories increasingly difficult to defend. Things such as the retrograde motion of Mars, whereby that planet seemed to move backwards and forwards across the sky over the course of the year, could be explained only if a complex system of orbital "epicycles" are hypothesized. Eventually, so as "to save appearances," the Ptolemaic model becomes a cumbersome mess, one that, to paraphrase Milton, had been built, unbuilt, and contrived. Copernicanism, on the other hand, more parsimoniously explained such phenomena. But why the contradiction in *Paradise Lost*, whose physics seem so resolutely conservative in one sense while mocking the very underpinning of that physics?

There is a reason for this astronomical equivocation. Milton wished to craft something that was eternal, and could survive changing understanding. Milton's concern was to glorify God as one for whom, "The swiftness of those Circles attribute,/Though numberless, to his Omnipotence." *Paradise Lost* might be a poem that uses those "circles" as an example, but the poem isn't about them, it's about God's grandeur. To venture an opinion as to whether Copernicus or Ptolemy was accurate was to write a poem that could potentially be wrong in the future, and Milton couldn't risk that. But in the process, he was able to depict how scientific debate operates in contrast to the absolute stricture of religious orthodoxy. In admitting that scientific knowledge is capable of change, Milton provides an accurate portrayal of the humble, dutiful method where one must always be aware of potential amendment to that knowledge. *Paradise Lost* revels in these ambiguities, and provides a representation of it.

A Bulwark Never Failing; or, How We Learned to Stop Killing Each Other

"But I suppose even God was born
too late to trust the old religion –
all those settings out
that never left the ground,
beginning in wisdom, dying in doubt."
Robert Lowell, Tenth Muse

"I could never divide myself from any man upon the difference of an
opinion, or be angry with his judgement for not agreeing with me in
that, from which perhaps within a few days I should dissent myself."
Sir Thomas Browne

Anne Dudley, in her father's Northampton library, had occasion to spend many happy hours as a girl engrossed in reading the hundreds of volumes which he had collected. She read about Sir Walter Raleigh's New World accounts of Ewaipanoma with their faces peering out from the center of their chests residing upon the banks of the Orinoco in Guyana, and that sweet hero-martyr of Dutch independence Sir Philip Sidney, felled by a papist bullet at Zutphen, and the immaculate verse of the Huguenot Guillaume de Saluste Du Bartas, with his accounts of the four ages of man and the four kingdoms before the coming Monarchy of Christ. She read historians such as William Camden and advocates for colonization like Richard Hakluyt. Like Miranda in Prospero's study, Anne had access to magical books which would prove useful upon enchanted isles. For most of all, she had the Bible.

Thomas Dudley was a staunch Calvinist who firmly believed that grace was revealed in the heart by the reading of God's word. He held that scripture was the only authority, and that the word of God was to be interpreted by the faithful heart of any true Christian. These beliefs were a Protestant given, an inevitable gift of Martin Luther's rebellion a century before. The Dudleys were Protestants of the "hot" variety, there was no via media for them, no halfway covenants, no room for tradition, no succor given to popish superstition.

If the Bible was the sole authority for the believer's interpretation of God's will, then it would hold that any competing claimants to power are usurpers, that they're anti-Christian – that they're antichrists. Peter's throne in Rome was the chief domain of antichrist, and young Anne and her non-conformist father would have firmly identified whoever occupied that throne and wore the Papal tiara as an emissary of Satan. A venerable Protestant tradition, as Luther's lieutenant Philip Melanchthon wrote in 1537 that, "the marks of Antichrist plainly agree with the kingdom of the Pope and his adherents." Luther, that same year, wrote, "the Pope is the very Antichrist, who has exalted himself above, and opposed himself against Christ."

Though the Catholic response to the accusation that the Pope was the antichrist was to in large part abandon belief in a literal antichrist in favor of an allegorical one (and thus to rehabilitate the slurred reputation of the Pope), some Counter-Reformation theologians were willing to give as good as they got. That strange old Calabrian utopian Thomas Campanella, writing in 1623, a century after Reformation (when Anne Dudley was an eleven-year-old girl in her father's study), claimed that Luther had been, "the last precursor of the Great and Most Savage Antichrist." Historian Bernard McGinn, writing of the years of Reformation and Counter-Reformation, claimed that, "Truly, this was the age of Antichrist divided."

Consider the great painter and engraver Lucas Cranach's multitude of images depicting the Pope as antichrist. Reformation scholar Eamonn Duffy has written that the German artist "more or less singlehandedly invented the visual vocabulary for

Luther's rebellion against the Catholic church," a code of images in the ironically iconoclastic movement (though Luther never gave us much credence to what the hotter Protestants would isolate out as the Second Commandment) which would firmly set in the collective consciousness of the reformed just what exactly the arch villain looked like. Cranach put woodcuts of Christ in contrast with his Papal enemy, the savior washing the feet of his disciples set against toadies kissing the pope's feet; he depicted the Pope as an ass-headed woman with reptilian legs; he presented us with the pope being birthed from the ulcerated sphincter of Satan. And, as shown below, Cranach depicted the Pope and his bishops kneeling in supplication before the Whore of Babylon, abreast the seven-headed dragon, a Europe laid to waste behind them.

Just as with Campanella's interpretation of Luther, Catholics were not to be outdone, with the renegade Augustinian monk himself depicted as that seven-headed beast of Revelation in pamphlets against Protestantism, as in an engraving by Hans Brosamer made in 1529. At the height of Cranach's career, the sincerest form of flattery was how universal his iconography of polemic had become, being fully absorbed by the very institution which had been its intended target, redirecting it back towards its source. This was the rhetoric across a harsh sectarian divide in the century between Luther nailing his 95 Theses to the door of the Castle Church in Wittenberg, to six-year-old Anne Dudley in her father's Northampton library. Christendom had wrenched itself apart at the very joists. The children of Paul, Martin, and John had divided Europe into an ever-malleable patchwork; Spain and Italy dyed the blue of the Virgin's robe, Scandinavia and occupied Holland a bright Orange, with the rest of the continent shifting back and forth between them. France, the Holy Roman Empire, eastern Europe, and of course those kingdoms in that small archipelago in the North Atlantic, ever malleable between those colors, a thousand rood screened curtains falling across the sectarian lines of Europe. A century which saw the Peasant's Rebellion, the Siege at Münster, hideous wars of religion in France, the St. Bartholomew's Day Massacre.

Anne's century wouldn't be less violent, the seventeenth would see almost a third of Germany's civilian population dead in the hideousness of the Thirty Years War, and her own Kingdom destroyed in the factionalism of her civil wars. I don't know whether that girl in the library in Northampton saw Cranach's engravings of the papal antichrist, but she surely saw images that were similar. I do know that Thomas and his daughter would have discussed papists like Queen Mary, and her black-bearded, cruel Spanish husband Philip, who had invited the Inquisition to English shores and watered the field at Tyburn with Christian blood.

From Puritan exegetes her father respected, dour, black-clad men like Joseph Mede and Thomas Brightman, she would firmly come to learn that they now lived in the end of days. Puritans like the Dudleys would have known that the recusants of England held allegiance not to the English throne (which after all they had once tried to blow up) but rather to the three-crowned pontiff in a foreign land. Non-conformists like her father worried that the new king with his rakish – if fussy – manner and his French Catholic wife had invited the antichrist into Westminster with the Queen's private Masses. People like the Dudleys became increasingly convinced that men like Archbishop William Laud were, bit by bit, fighting a secret war of attrition against the Protestant conscience of the nation, allowing Rome to gain a toehold among the English with the importation of terroristic Jesuits hid in priest holes across the kingdom. The machinations of the Gunpowder Plot weren't forgotten in any English home, least of all a Puritan one, and as the perfidy of the Catholics in their midst had led conspirators to once try and kill the monarch, it was ironically the case that Puritans would one day have to finish that job. Sometimes you have to kill a monarch to save him (or at least in preservations of that higher, celestial Kingdom). Such was the hatred of the antichrist, for as surely as Anne would have inherited the words of Genesis and Exodus, Jeremiah and Daniel, the Apostles and Paul, and most of all John at Patmos, she would have been raised with the hatred of Catholicism. As it also was for young Catholic girls Anne's age who considered Protestantism.

For Anne, reading the exegetical glosses supplied by those English exiles in Geneva which identified priests as emissaries of Satan and the Pope as antichrist, it would seem as if the font of all evil in the world was clear. She would describe what she saw as the degradations of her mother country years later, and living thousands of miles to the west, writing that in England the, "Gospel trodden down and hath no right...The Pope had hope to find Rome here again." She had the chance to write those words on the eve of civil war, for Charles and Laud were pushing an undesired uniformity with their suspiciously High Church prayer book, and their altars, and their kneelers. If legend is to be believed, the Bishop's War, prelude to the civil wars which would soon result in three nations ripped apart and the first regicide of modern European history, began when a tradeswoman named Jenny Geddes, loyal adherent to the Solemn Oath and Covenant and member of the Scottish Presbyterian Kirk, threw her kneeling stool at the Bishop as he read from the hated Book of Common Prayer in the coldly dark gothic environs of St. Giles Cathedral. The English Revolution was instigated over arguments about rood screens and statues, vestments and kneelers. Can you imagine such civil strife instigated over a question of when it is appropriate to kneel and who is expected to do so? But of course you can, such is the myopic substance of wars between relatives.

Surveying the aftermath in 1647, Thomas May writes in his The history of the parliament Of England, which began November the third, MDCXL that it was:

a war as cruel as unnatural; that has produced as much rage of sword, as much bitterness of pens, both public and private, as was ever known; and divide the understandings of men, as well as their affections, in so high a degree, that scarce could any virtue gain due applause, any reason give satisfaction, or any relation obtain credit, unless among men of the same side.

And so it was with the Reformation, of which the English civil wars were only a small conflagration when compared to the wider event, two centuries of warring between Catholic and various confessions of Protestantism, a terrible and divine fire which burnt across Europe, and eventually that New World which Anne read about as a child in her father's study, imagining fantastic beasts and men on the paradisiacal shores of the Orinoco.

As it would come to be, Anne would spend the vast majority of her life in that New World, but rather than Ewaipanoma peeking out behind tropical trees she would find rocky shoals and snow squalls, festering summers and winter nor'easters, Pequod and Abenaki. From the decks of the Arbela, which had traversed the Atlantic in 1630, she first espied the Massachusetts coast, writing that she, "found a new world and new manners, at which my heart rose. But after I was convinced it was the way of God, I submitted to it and joined to the church at Boston," here at the western most terminus of the Reformation. As her fellow poetic genius Edward Taylor would describe it, Anne had arrived in America with "Plymouth on the left, and Salem on the right," which as literal as the geographic description might be is also an apt explanation of every American's figurative inheritance as well. For if the poetess, this tenth muse sprung up in a New World, was to be the grandmother of all American literature, than she was also a consummate daughter of the Reformation as well. On the frontier, it at first seemed as if Anne and her new husband Simon Bradstreet were far from the apocalyptic urgency of England on the verge of civil war. Across the Atlantic, as historian Diarmaid MacCulloch describes it, the Puritans longed "to establish a truly godly state in England, which would indeed by a New Jerusalem," yet as the fortunes of that cause rose and fell, Anne would begin to see that religion had indeed moved westward, as in keeping with the prophecy of the divine George Herbert when he wrote, "Religion stands on tiptoe in our land, Ready to pass to the American strand."

In her poetry, arguably the first in English written on the American continent, she emphasized this fortress on a hill as a bulwark never failing against the imposition of popery from Rome. Her poetry is sometime the verse equivalent of Cranach's engravings, writing about "bloody Popish, hellish miscreants," "dark Popery," and agents of Catholicism who are "Rome's whores." A Church whose sins were, "the breach of sacred laws./Idolatry, supplanter of a nation,/With foolish superstitious adoration." With little ambiguity, she exclaims that, "These are the days the Church's foes to crush,/To root out Popelings head, tail, branch, and rush;/Let's bring Baal's vestments forth to make a fire,/Their mitres, surplices, and all their tire,/Copes, rochets, crosiers, and such empty trash,/And let their names consume, but let the flash/Light Christendom, and all the world to see/We hate Rome's whore with all her trumpery." When it comes to the Roman Catholic Church, Anne Bradstreet leaves little ambiguity as to what her opinions are.

Except either in that wood-timbered house, the kind with dimple glass windows after the old English manner, located on the site of a Starbucks and MBTA Station at the center of what was once called New Towne and is now named after an English university famed for its Puritan students, or in her thatched cabin in Ipswich which famously burnt down in that apocalyptic year of 1666, she kept a separate diary with thoughts which never made it into her published verse. A journal intended for her children, to explain the vortices and eddies of a mind in the process of thinking about itself, a testament to that most enduring Protestant invention of interiority. Suffering a period of doubt and uncertainty, instigated by the very practice of obsessive self-scrupulosity which Calvinist theology dictates for us so that the individual Christian can search the contours of their own soul for evidence of their election, Anne informs her children that she had begun to ask herself some non-orthodox questions. There, in her neat hand and sitting in an archive box of the North Andover Massachusetts library, you can see where Anne Bradstreet wrote that though she may, "admit this be the true God whom we worship, and that be his word, yet why may not the Popish religion be the right? They have the same God, the same Christ, the same word: they only interpret it one way, we another."

This is not the story of a conversion, Bradstreet's or anyone else's. This is not a story of ecumenism. This is not a tale of rapprochement, reconciliation, or reconstitution. Watchwords of this narrative do not include the following – tolerance, pluralism, religious freedom. All of that would come later. Nor is this the story of Evangelicals overcoming centuries of Romish superstition, as it is also not the narrative of noble defenders of the Holy Roman Catholic Church winning back hearts from the machinations of heretical schismatics. Rather, what Anne's story embodies is a small volley in a war against war, a faint whisper of how we began to not murder one another.

What the Protestant Reformation signaled was the division of "heresy" as separate from the Church itself. Luther and company allowed for the creation of Christians whose very views made them separate from the Church, not simply in error within the Church, as those previous "heresies" would have been understood. The direct result was the French wars of religion, the Ninety Years War, the Thirty Years War, the English civil wars, and so on, and so on, and so on. Enmity and unspeakable violence were the result of such fractures, and yet the old, dull, aching, glowing throb of that body of the mystical Church militant could endure, because the Reformation(s) – the Catholic one included – scrambled any idea of unity.

Yet some human bond of fraternal affection was able to still tend its wisps across those seemingly unsurmountable divisions which resulted from the fracturing of Christendom. Any coherent language of ecumenical rapprochement, and even more importantly secular latitudinarianism, would wait until the eighteenth century and after. But for all of the deep scars and fissures of the Reformation – that ever mercurial patchwork map, the blood-soaked ground of the Holy Roman Empire and the streets of Paris, the executions at Tyburn and the accounts of Protestant and Jesuit martyrs, the horrific scenes of immolation accounted for by John Foxe in Acts and Monuments – for all of the true scale of horrors which erupted in religious violence in a manner never seen before or since, there was always the possibility of connection and affection between those who were now theological foes. Again, Europe awaited a theory of ecumenicism, but the means for constructing it simply existed in the innate goodness which sometimes surprisingly exists somewhere in the black souls of men. We awaited the prose to write a possible theology of reconciliation, but the poetry was already in our hearts.

Even with the divisions of those early years of the Reformation, the record is replete with instances of mutual tenderness between Catholic and Protestant, instances as surprising as Bradstreet's declared skepticism. Scholar Benjamin J. Kaplan writes that, "tolerance was an issue not just for intellectuals and ruling elites, but for all people who lived in religiously mixed communities." A chronological chain of instances of this tolerance can be traced, a metempsychosis of sympathy for enemies across the divide, from the Reformation's infancy through its maturity. It would include examples such as Catholic Philip II mourning the martyrdom of his namesake and godson, the Protestant Philip Sidney, who was felled by a bullet fighting in a war against the King himself. Or the Huguenot convert to Catholicism Henry IV, he for whom a Mass was a small issue if Paris would come along with it, and yet who after his baptism still financially supported Theodore Beza, Calvin's successor at Geneva. Or the steadfastly Puritan preacher and pamphleteer Thomas Crashaw, as fulminous an anti-Catholic as ever set print block, who still drew succor from the spiritual exercises of Ignatius Loyola, and whose reading of that Jesuit's books perhaps led his son Richard to convert to Catholicism and become the caretaker at the shrine of Laredo, ascending to be the greatest English baroque poet along the way.

Of those same Jesuits, that poet John Milton wrote against and yet whom he stayed as their valued guest when his European tour reached Rome. Or Bradstreet's poetic successor Edward Taylor, as Calvinist as her and Thomas Crashaw, reading the same Ignatian books as the latter and drawing the same strength from those words written by one on the other side of that sectarian divide. Ecumenicism is hammered out by theologians and councils, but that which is infinitely more valuable, tolerance, finds its origin in the simple interaction of people, in their tenderness and kindness, their mutual affection and their sympathies. Tolerance is what allows the Protestant poet George Herbert and his friend Nicholas Ferrar to live monastically at Little Gidding, in imitation of that which they found valuable within Catholicism; and it's what allowed Catholic congregants to sing their songs to the melodies of Methodist hymns.

For since Luther's rebellion there has never been a Protestant who isn't sometimes Catholic and a Catholic who isn't sometimes Protestant. There is neither Catholic nor Protestant, there is neither bond nor free, there is neither male nor female: for we are all one in our contradictory natures, before each of our beautifully confused consciousnesses. Easy to see those divisions between celestial blue and nominalist orange as inviolate, as if those who created and tended the Reformation sprung from European soil as fully formed Protestants, and yet their religious upbringing was one of pilgrimages and icons, indulgences and sacraments. Luther's religious anxieties were Catholic, Calvin's theology was scholastic in origin, and even that hot Protestant Ulrich Zwingli adored the Virgin. Eras of religious discord and rupture, where even the possibility of secularity remained an intellectual impossibility, didn't quite have the vocabulary by which to speak of ecumenicism, but they certainly were capable of the empathetic emotions which would ultimately allow for tolerance (or something that looked like it).

In that regard, the cure for the disease was within its very cause, for the careful accounting of the soul which Bradstreet and her coreligionists made their watchword was that which allowed for a skepticism which would in turn bring all theological postulates into question. And that chink of doubt within the wall of faith, as uncomfortable as it must have personally been, was also that which allowed for a space to contain a noble tolerance, a space into which a true Christian effect of mutual understanding could grow. But the first thing you must understand about this process is that it is the inevitable, common sense result of humans being humans. And common sense, far from being the metaphysics of morons, as philosopher Bertrand Russell had it, is a system of a priori conclusions drawn from the observation of men and women and how they behave. And as common sense would tell us, nobody is so simple as to be all one thing or all the other. Luther's priesthood of all believers was appropriately but also ironically that which perhaps made that truism theological axiom, but in no priesthood which admits all believers can there ever be one Church. Luther was not the founder of this concept, he merely inadvertently identified it, for the common sense reality is such that individual humans, in all of their glorious complexity and sacred contradictions, have never been entirely reducible to any one belief or system. There has never been a theist so pious that she does not doubt God's existence, and an atheist so irreverent that he doesn't sometimes wonder if He is real.

We draw the distinctions too tight, we divide too starkly, not just today but especially then, and though we academically know this we sometimes still function as if the border between Catholicism and Protestantism within the individual soul were as firmly drawn as the line on the map. But as Europe's actual geography ever shifted between that blue and orange, so too does the individual soul turn between Rome and Wittenberg. We've always been as a house divided, each of us individually and collectively, but the beauty of that can be that a house divided ultimately results in a room for everybody. The soul split against itself provides a model for a polity which can contain everybody, for as no mind can be consistent – we should not expect a civilization to be either. These were human lives and the soul is ever malleable in its uncertainty, hence the irony in building any theology on the mercurial basis of faith, for we always must shift between faiths. A quality perhaps as fleeting as enlightenment, for sometimes we are Protestant and sometimes Catholic, sometimes nothing at all, sometimes all in the period of a Mass. That we ever killed one another over faith is an unimaginable tragedy, that we mostly stopped is an unbelievable miracle, and that we could ever possibly begin again an incomparable horror.

The Thinking Reed Tries God's Luck

On the evening of November 23, 1654, the brilliant, prodigious French mathematician, physicist, inventor, and all-around polymath Blaise Pascal was thrown from his horse, the creature having been frightened by a thunderstorm. Pascal was left dazed in the road; the horse fell off the bridge they had been crossing into the turbulent river below. That night, toward the midnight hour, a frightened yet grateful Pascal (who was still recovering from the death of his beloved father three years before) had an intense vision: light flooded his room, blinding the 31-year-old philosopher for close to two hours. Following the vision, Pascal wrote on a piece of parchment, "Fire. God of Abraham, God of Isaac, God of Jacob, not of the philosophers and the scholars... Joy, joy, joy, tears of joy...This is life eternal that they might know you, the only true God." He sewed the parchment into the lining of the coat, and seemed to have carefully moved it to new garments every time he changed his clothes. He told no one – a servant found it in the last jacket he wore, years after he died.

And so, the theorist of projective geometry, the inventor of a system that allowed for tabular presentation of binomial coefficients, the originator of the field of probability theory, an early researcher into the disciplines of hydrodynamics and hydraulic fluids (which included the invention of the syringe), and the engineer of an improved barometer had found religion. Pascal, who was such a prodigy that Rene Descartes was flabbergasted that a man of his youth could have written the masterful mathematical proofs, had turned his life over to that which he believed superseded mere reason. Pascal, explorer of the nascent Enlightenment, rejected the god of Anselm, Aquinas, and Aristotle with their perfect logical proofs in favor of the wild and ecstatic God of the intoxicated patriarchs and prophets. Pascal was not simply rejecting secularism (as the possibility of a genuine secularism did not yet quite exist) but he was rejecting a particular view of God which held that knowledge of the divine could be circumscribed by syllogism. Rather Pascal was embracing a new God, one of paradox, irrationality, and pure faith, a God for whom the old logical proofs of His existence (so similar in format to something like Pascal's own proof for Faulhaber's formula) would no longer do.

Pascal may have almost died that day, and he was supremely lucky to have not. The mathematician believed that he was lucky in another way as well, for this singular event so focused his mind that all of the spiritual writing he had been drawn to during years of his father's illness was crystallized. He believed the incident had saved his soul as surely as blind chance had saved his physical body on that bridge over stormy waters. That the means of Pascal's conversion (actually sort of a second conversion, though the mathematician had previously backslid) should take such an equine manifestation is perhaps not surprising; after all, Saul was transformed to Paul on the road to Damascus when he was shrugged off a horse. Though, what do the rest of us do; those of us who don't have lucky horses that almost kill us and trigger ecstatic visions of the Lord? How do we find the grace which Pascal believed he was lucky enough to have been imparted with? The young mathematician (and future theologian) was lucky to have survived that accident, and indeed he would place luck at the center of his Christian apologetics. Fortune's wheel may be a medieval conception, but it turned through Pascal's early modern era, and for Pascal it in turn becomes a handy symbol for the probabilities and chances which define all of our lives – for an appeal to the probabilities of luck would be precisely how he would convince the rest of us to embrace that same "God of Abraham, God of Isaac, God of Jacob" whom he had embraced.

Pascal's theological masterpiece *Pensees* (or *"Thoughts"*) was where he elaborated on perhaps his most famous concept, more widely known than his work on hydraulics, his treatises on the philosophy of mathematics, or his design for a primitive mechanical calculator. Some of his most important work in mathematics was in probability, born out of an obsession with gambling inculcated during his libertine years in the wilderness between his father's death and his conversion (Pascal was the inventor of a type of early roulette), and indeed probability lay at the heart of his Christian apologetics as well. From this strange union of luck and theology Pascal conceived of his infamous and celebrated wager, the still-controversial (and for many still unconvincing) argument not for the rationality of God, but for the rationality of *belief* in God.

Reflecting the skepticism of the age, Pascal affirms that when concerning divinity, "We are then incapable of knowing either what He is or if He is." Assuming the law of non-contradiction, Pascal assents that, "God is, or He who is not," but, he asks, which preposition should we believe? He argues that reason tells us nothing as to the reality of God's existence; the patristic churchmen and medieval scholastics used gallons of ink and yards of vellum to rationally prove the existence of God, but reflecting the fideism of rival Protestants and prefiguring Immanuel Kant's critique of pure reason a century hence, Pascal claims that such proofs are for naught. Between man's apprehension and the true nature of reality there is, "an infinite chaos which separated us." The mathematician argues that all of the celebrated proofs of God's existence – Anselm's ontological argument, Aquinas' five proofs in the *Summa Theologica*, and so on – are meaningless, for God himself cannot be constrained by mere meaning. But while God may be beyond meaning, the mechanism for one's own personal faith can be supremely rational, and to make his case, Pascal returns us to the smoky gambling dens of his youthful dereliction and indiscretions.

Pascal famously reasons that life is a sort of "game," and that our faith in God, or lack-there-of, is our wager as to the ultimate nature of reality – and what we stand to win (or lose) is nothing less than eternal life. Because we cannot find any full-proof reasoning for our faith in God, we have to decide to arrive at our faith using different means. Imagine that all of reality is as if a coin-toss with one side of the coin affixed with the phrase "God Exists" and the other "God Does Not Exist." The question that Pascal asks is, "What will you wager?" The essence of his thought experiment is that if one wagers that God does exist, and he does not, the gambler loses comparatively little (perhaps a bit of wine, women, and song, as Pascal may have enjoyed during his wild years). As he writes, "If you gain, you gain all; if you lose, you lose nothing. Wager, then, without hesitation that He is." However, if one makes the bet that God does exist, and that coin lands heads-up, then the gambler is rewarded with an eternity in paradise. If, however, the gambler bets that God does not exist, and he is confirmed in that bet, they've gained very little (again, a life of finite pleasures). But if the gambler betting against God finds that their tossed-up coin comes up with the Lord's face looking upward at them, then they are punished with eternal damnation. Pascal has nothing to say about whether God actually is real or not, rather he provides a cost-benefit analysis of whether belief in God is rational, and he comes up in the affirmative. Pascal writes, "there is here an infinity of an infinitely happy life to gain, a chance of gain against a finite number of chances of loss, and what you stake is finite." According to the philosopher it would be irrational not to place your bet on God.

This essay is too short to enumerate the problems with Pascal's reasoning, or to engage with whether it is particularly convincing or not. I largely defer to religion writer Nathan Schneider, who reflecting on proofs of God's existence and arguments for utility in belief that such arguments are "taught, argued about, and forgotten, sometimes saving a person's particular faith, sometimes eroding it, and usually neither."

Certainly in presenting the risks and rewards of belief and unbelief Pascal greatly reduced the potential complexity of the universe into a simple binary. Perhaps God rewards skeptics and doubters? Perhaps there is a terrifyingly malicious God who punishes the faithful and rewards the apostates? Perhaps willed faith engaged for simple self-regard is no faith at all? And crucially, perhaps faith is not the ultimate arbiter of salvation (certainly a contentious argument, especially during those years of Reformation)? There are a plethora of metaphysical possibilities which Pascal's relatively simple wager does not account for.

So, I do not argue for the efficacy of the wager itself – I assume that as a work of sterile and cold apologetics it has been generally less effective at moving people towards belief than the normal emotional and personal reasons that actually lay at the heart of conversion narratives. Rather, what I argue is that we need to dispel the interpretation of history and biography which reads the famous wager as somehow in contradiction with the mathematician's earlier work. Furthermore, I argue against reading the wager as some sort of medieval throwback, an embrace of an antiquated scholasticism that was stereotypically obsessed with enumerating the capacity of an angel dance party held at a head-of-a-pin discotheque. No, rather, whether we are convinced by Pascal's reasoning or not, the wager itself is not a product of some irrational pre-modern past, but rather it is consummately modern, and could only be a product of a world that was undergoing rapid intellectual changes.

My reasoning that sees Pascal's wager as supremely modern is born out of two related reasons – Pascal's justification in conceiving of the proof, and the presence of doubt in the burgeoning modern world. The famous medieval proofs of God's existence written by scholastic theologians were not penned to convince anyone of God's existence, for during that era nobody seriously doubted the existence of God. Rather those proofs were written as rational expressions meant to demonstrate God's elegance and beauty. Though written in the language of reason they were not works meant to defend, but rather to glorify. But Pascal's wager is not meant to glorify the parsimonious perfection of God as apprehended through pure reason, there are no appeals to God as unmoved mover, first cause, by contingency, degree, or teleology (as Aquinas' five proofs were structured). Instead Pascal offers a rhetorical or psychological argument, but the argument that it is more reasonable to believe implies that disbelief is always a potential option. Those earlier proofs don't imply the possibility of disbelief in the same way, for the simple (if surprising) reason that disbelief, at least in the same manner, wasn't really a possibility during the era in which those earlier proofs were composed. Historian Peter Laslett writes that, "All our ancestors were literal...believers, all of the time."

In fairness I must point out that many contemporary intellectual historians would dispute the claim that pre-modern men and women were somehow incapable of unbelief in any serious or sustained way. Italian historiographer Carlo Ginzberg has enumerated the properties of Renaissance skepticism for a generation, more recently Tim Whitmarsh has claimed that the classical world of Greece and Rome was home to a dynamic atheistic possibility. But I am not arguing that people were psychologically incapable of doubting religious affirmations or that there aren't particular individual examples of the phenomenon, but rather that the complex philosophical language for fully expressing disbelief in any sustained way simply didn't exist until the era that Pascal lived in.

The great French historian Lucien Febvre explained in detail how "atheism" wasn't a conceptual possibility until relatively recently in his classic *The Problem of Unbelief in the Sixteenth Century*. Words like "atheist" don't appear until 1502 in Latin, 1549 in French, and 1561 in English. "Materialist" did not appear until 1668, and "freethinker" not until 1692. The word "agnostic" wouldn't appear until the nineteenth-century. And while it's fair to argue that concepts can exist before the terminology to describe those concepts does, it's notable that even when the word "atheist" was used in the sixteenth century it was to describe a type of religious straw-man. With the possibility of the lost, and most likely apocryphal, anonymous pamphlet entitled *The Three Imposters*, there is no first-person declaration of atheism until well into the early modern period. In earlier cultures Pascal's wager would serve no purpose, pre-modern men and woman would have taken belief as a matter of course.

Scholar David Wooten explains that the early modern period saw "an epistemological break, a conceptual caesura" which allowed for the possibility of unbelief. And where there is the possibility of unbelief, there is the need for arguments to shore up faith, there is the need for something like Pascal's wager. In a culture where the question wasn't whether God existed or not (since everyone assumed that He did), but rather what were the contours of proper belief about God, Pascal's wager would make no sense. And in a society where doubt becomes a possibility, that is to say in a modern society, Pascal's wager becomes much more pertinent.

Doubt wasn't the only concept undergoing a profound shift in meaning during the years from the fifteenth century Renaissance through the eighteenth-century Enlightenment. Concepts like "truth," "faith," and "reason" were also altering in connotation and definition. A correspondence theory of truth which argued that "truth" was simply defined according to whether prepositions matched to an objective and empirical reality became dominant as more archaic contextual and mythic understandings of truth declined; faith increasingly was understood as involving assent for prepositions for which there was no empirical verification; and contrary to expectation, reason's authority actually diminished with the advent of modernity. Christianity, after all, has at its center an understanding of the Word, or "logos," made flesh. Theology obliged this preoccupation with rationality, firmly believing in the possibility of logically demonstrating God's existence – that is until the Reformation and then Enlightenment knocked King Reason from his throne. Forget not that Kant's great work was a "critique" of pure reason; raised as a faithful Lutheran, Kant believed that prepositions about God could only be approached through faith, and not reason. Pascal's wager is the product of the early modern period, where Martin Luther and other reformers saw faith as paramount but where knowledge was increasingly open to doubt. This was the same world that birthed philosophical positivism, and which increasingly saw the scientific methods as the most definite means of approaching knowledge. Pascal's wager is neither scientific nor anti-scientific, yet the wager and science are both products of the same modernizing impulse.

One contemporary humanist website, with Pascal's wager clearly in mind, unfairly describes Pascal as a "classic example of a great intellect perverted by conversion." *The Pensees* were the height of seventeenth-century French literature, where Pascal prefigured contemporary philosophical movements like existentialism. We lose much if we denigrate the humility and poignancy of the soul who declared, "Man is but a reed, but a thinking reed." His sentiment marries the humility of science with the humility of faith; understanding that nothing is ever known definitely by reason, for reason can always be overturned as surely as one's luck can deplete itself. That Pascal should turn his life so fully over to faith (and in the process become one of the great theologians of seventeenth-century Catholicism) may seem aberrant or inconsistent – but it is not. Pascal's religious belief may have had long antecedents such as the austere Augustinianism of Jansenism (the "puritanical" Catholic movement he associated with), the writings of Luther and other reformers, and the Church Fathers of early Christianity. But in another sense Pascal's faith was strikingly modern, paradoxically all the more so for its abandonment of pure reason in favor of complete faith. Pascal's rejection of reason was not a rejection of modernity, or even of science, in fact his faith and his scientific work were twins born of the same modernizing mindset (whether you share in Pascal's faith or not).

Fuckadillia's Man at Court

With characters like "Buggeranthos," "Cuntigratia," "Cunticula," "Clytoris," and of course "Fuckadillia," the late seventeenth-century play *Sodom, or the Quintessence of Debauchery* would seem to simply be pornography, and yet I'd argue that it embodied the Restoration. The slender manuscript would be anonymously penned in 1672, only twelve years after King Charles II's return from exile during the Commonwealth's rule over his executed father's kingdom, and in its prurient themes of sodomy, incest, and prostitution it would seem that the English were very much ready to sluff off the stern-faced Puritans. A closet drama – a play written not to be staged but simply read – *Sodom* would wait another twelve years until it would be available in smudgy print from the book-sellers on Fleet Street, but it was arguably so congruent with the spirit of the era that it was already the literary work exemplar of the king's reign the moment its author dipped his quill into the inkwell.

Sodom's likely author, John Wilmot, the Second Earl of Rochester, deployed his ample wit and his exceeding genius to plumb the depths of the sewer, to triangulate the vagaries of anonymous fucking in public parks, to wax rhapsodic on "pricks" and "cunts," and to sing a song praising buggery, sodomy, and all other manner of inserting certain body parts into other body parts. If Charles' grandfather's rule was marked by literary works of a particular philosophical profundity like Shakespeare's *Hamlet,* than *Sodom* would seem to cover an exceedingly different set of concerns, a harsh, hilarious, scurrilous, and scatological satire where "nowhere else has Charles II stood so utterly naked of royal majesty," as Richard Elias writes in *Studies in English Literature, 1500-1900.*

It's not that writing blue was novel – there are abundant examples of sexual and scatological themes, sometimes extreme, in Elizabethan and Jacobean literature. And anyone who's read Geoffrey Chaucer's "The Wife of Bath's Tale" knows that ribaldry has a venerable tradition in English letters. But, as Austen Saunders makes clear at the *American Spectator*, Rochester was "original in being so explicit." A poet like John Donne's verse may be erotic, but his meaning is ingeniously encoded in metaphorical conceit; Rochester, on the other hand, was the first English poet to fully reject euphemism, with Saunders pointedly declaring that the Earl was "always more than happy to call a dildo a dildo."

Figure that such bluntness was a function of his era, for writing of Restoration the poet drolly observes "Oh! what a damn'd Age do we live in!" A damned age perhaps, but also the germinating embryo of our own era, for it was during Restoration that the rough shape of the contemporary formed; a society broadly recognizable to us, London becoming a massive city where one could purchase a newspaper and read of scientific discoveries or about emerging political parties, while getting your caffeine fix in a coffeehouse. But this was also a world in the shadow of regicide and the subsequent draconian theocracy, where hopeful Restoration ultimately delivered its own oppressions as well. Charles' 1660 London arrival on Oak Apple Day may have been a liberation from all that was dreary about Oliver Cromwell's Protectorate, but such newfound optimism was twinned with deeper anxieties. David Vieth writes in "Rochester and the Restoration: An Introductory Note and Bibliography" that the "decade and a half following the restoration…probably marks the most traumatically rapid set of cultural changes the English-speaking peoples have ever experienced." Such a traumatized world, where all inherited beliefs and moralities were questioned, calls for a poet Laurette, and that debauched dilettante Wilmot answered that call.

Well hung between Italy's Aretino in the sixteenth-century, and France's infamous Marquis de Sade in the eighteenth,

Rochester is the single greatest pornographer produced in the English language, with Carol Fabricant writing in "Rochester's World of Imperfect Enjoyment" published in the *The Journal of English and Germanic Philology* that the "poems focus to such an extent upon genitalia of various sizes and capacities that these, by their sheer quantity, emerge as the central objects of Rochester's world." Wilmot's verse was so scandalous that he awaited the early twentieth century to see his complete works compiled, and even then many of his lyrics were deleted, lest academic publishers find themselves charged with obscenity. As Peter Smith explains in *Between Two Stools: Scatology and its Representations in English Literature, Chaucer to Swift* it wouldn't be until 1953 when Routledge released Rochester's full work that the poet could join "Sir Thomas Wyatt, Sir Walter Raleigh, Ben Jonson, and Andrew Marvell in their list of impeccable sixteenth- and seventeenth-century poets."

Canonicity may have come, but it was of a cracked type. Examine the official portrait of Rochester which hangs in the British National Portrait Gallery off Trafalgar Square. That imposing, gray Victorian museum is a secular temple to kings and queens, poets and playwrights, but there also hangs a portrait of the man who wrote, "My prick no more to bald cunt shall resort –/Merkins rub off, and often spoil the sport." In a building with paintings of serious, sober-minded men like Milton and Dryden, there is Rochester the rakish son of Cavaliers, as painted by the Flemish artist Jacob Huysmans. As is the French style brought back with Charles from his exile at the court of the Sun King, Wilmot effects a delicate androgyny, more pretty than handsome. Curled ringlets of his gray wig fall about sumptuous orange and purple clothes which hang like drapes upon his slender frame. On an Italianate marble table there is a small pile of books, for Rochester is a scholar after all, and atop that sits a diabolical, mischievous little monkey, a smile that is red like a gash upon his furry head, the simian clutching one of the volumes in his paw. And above him is Rochester's delicate, pale hand, so effeminate that it might as well have been modeled by the actress and friend of the poet Nell Gwynne, Charles' mistress and his infamous "Protestant whore." In that hand the lyricist holds a crown of laurel branches, to be brought down upon the little monkey head, crowning the beast as a Laurette in his stead.

"Simian" is the word that critics might find appropriate for Wilmot, a creature enthralled to his baser desires, for as Jonathan Brody Kramnick makes clear in "Rochester and the History of Sexuality" from *ELH,* the libertine understood that "desire [is] our presiding faculty, the cause behind our actions;" and as a monkey would no sooner wonder about the nuanced propriety of fornication, so too would Rochester not be concerned with bourgeoisie morality. As he wrote in his infamous *A Satyr against Reason and Mankind,* if he were a, "Spirit free, to choose for my own Share,/What sort of Flesh and Blood I pleas'd to wear,/I'd be a Dog, a Monkey, or a Bear,/Or anything, but that vain Animal,/ Who is so proud of being Rational." While Milton explained the ways of God to man, his royalist colleague explicated the ways of Priapus, a predilection towards filth the primary basis of his worldview. Poet Thom Gunn reflects in "Saint John the Rake: Rochester's Poetry" from the collection *Green Thoughts, Green Shades* that the Earl was "of course defiant, and the defiance is connected with one of the most frequent effects of all pornography, which is not only to excite but also to shock." Restoration was marked by explicitness, from the double entendre of dramatist William Wycherley to the saucy meditations of Samuel Pepys, but Rochester stood as the dirtiest, and shock was the currency he traded in.

Creature of the court, a royalist and a fop, dandy and dilettante, Rochester scandalized with verses like "A Ramble in St. James' Park" with its depiction of orgiastic public sex and with his extended metaphysical meditation, *A Satyr Against Reason and Mankind.* A volley cast against the logocentric impulses of

Anglicanism as well as a preemptive attack on the fetishizing of rationality that would dominate the coming century. Sarah Ellenzweig in her *Journal of British Studies* article "The Faith of Unbelief: Rochester's 'Satyre,' Deism, and Religion Freethinking in Seventeenth-Century England" argues that Rochester's *Satyr* reflects a type of ecstatic, iconoclastic, antinomian counter-faith which bares similarity to the esotericisms of religious non-conformists like the Ranters and Seekers who occupied the other side of the political divide during the poet's lifetime.

Rochester's life and philosophy were figured as a cautionary tale, which Karel Vanhaesebrouck and Pol Dehert make clear in *The Journal of Early Modern Cultural Studies;* propagandists for piety configured that the reason for Rochester's death at the age of 33 (the age of Christ...) was "more than clear," brought about by "alcohol, abuse, and syphilis." Whether or not Rochester's death-bed rejection of atheism and conversion to Catholicism happened, his work merits consideration as more than cautionary tale or titillating filth, for Gunn suggests that the libertine was a "kind of existential saint in his life," because for "Rochester, as later for Blake, the devils were angels and the angels were devils" becoming a "dedicated libertine and a saint of debauchery." Easy to see him as simply a pornographer, but an actual reading of his verse reveals a coherent, albeit nihilistic and transgressive philosophy; the culmination of not just his own debauched behavior, but arguably a strain of emerging, dark modernity as well. Like those antinomian mystics who reject the law so as to be closer to God, Rochester's "defiance was full-time."

One can see Rochester's fusion of concerns in his "Regime de Vivre," still often not anthologized, and which maintains the power to shock in the twenty-first century. Calling forth rock-and-roll wantonness as much as the Restoration court, the poem's narrator recounts a soulless, addicted, mechanical life of empty excess. Wilmot writes: "I rise at eleven, I dine about two,/I get drunk before seven, and the next thing I do,/I send for my whore, when for fear of the clap,/I spend in her hand, and I spew in her lap." After a fight and the filching of his money, the narrator passes out, but, "If by chance then I wake, hot-headed and drunk,/What a coil do I make for the loss of my punk!/I storm and I roar, and I fall in a rage./And missing my whore, I bugger my page./Then crop-sick all morning I rail at my men,/ And in bed I lie yawning till eleven again."

A cursory reading of the poem might interpret it simply as smut rendered technically proficient, but Rochester's purposes are never cynical, only nihilistic. For "Regime de Vivre" is both an expression and explanation of the conclusion that a certain type of emerging modernity posed. The issue isn't (and never was) that the language is ribald, there are countless examples of puckishness in literature. But Wilmot has traded the carnivalesque joy of those earlier poets for the mechanistic joylessness of commodified, contemporary prurience. Smith writes that the, "diurnal round of eating, drinking, molestation, quarrelling, theft, and exploitation seems, at first sight, to be brazenly and aggressively self-determined." Easy to read this Anacreontic as an expression of complete liberty, especially for those who've focused in on the confession of homosexual sex (while ignoring that what Wilmot depicts is also a rape). Rather, what Smith argues is that this reiteration of "daily activities in a banal inventory...intimates ennui rather than gratification."

There is a profound egocentricity in the poem, an anaphora of the first-person pronoun begins the first four lines, with Smith elaborating that "every line contains at least one use of the first-person pronoun and in no fewer than nine lines it appears twice or more." But what Wilmot expresses is neither confidence nor genuine self-love, but rather "bleak solipsism in the alembic of despair." Divorced from the question of whether or not Rochester celebrates this behavior (for there is nothing in the actual poem itself which merits that reading), we can consider if the sonnet isn't an expression of a particular type of alienated, detached, distanced, dead-eyed contemporaneity; the poet presenting a "vicious circle of addiction...[where] the Cavalier eats, drinks, spews and fucks his way to oblivion." Indeed the *volta* of the poem finds the narrator precisely where he was at the beginning of the sonnet, nothing gained, nothing lost, other than the agency of those whom "exist only to satisfy his pleasure, whether they be his servants against whom he rails, his whore with whom he quarrels, or the pageboy."

Paradoxically Rochester is a consummate moralizer. Not because he provides prescriptions for behavior (of course not), but rather because he diagnoses the malignancy itself: indulgent, narcissistic egocentricity. Saunders writes that, "One of the qualities that keeps bringing us back to the same works is that they let each age find what they're looking for in them," and this seems undoubtedly true, but where his contemporaries read him as a profligate atheist, and others as an advocate for complete freedom, today we can see him as the poet of the porn addict, the compulsive gambler, the phone junky, and the internet slave. His was a picture of mechanistic joylessness, distant from the Falstaffian happiness of medieval and Renaissance literature, prefiguring where the ethos of man being the measure of all things can sometimes end. A perspective where all individuals are means unto an end, commodified and turned into products for consumption, and where sexual revolutions can often result in the valorization of the individual's desires at the expense of all others' consent. As regards the poet's subjects, judge if you must; but Wilmot instructs in a crucial lesson – that in libertinage there is often scant liberty.

Praying for the Awful Grace of God

No portrait exists of the seventeenth-century prophetess Anna Trapnell because she was not of the station for whom people made portraits. Poor daughters of Stepney shipwrights don't have paintings made; women whose parents didn't baptize them are not fixed in stained glass. But God, or whatever you call Her, doesn't always just visit those whom icons are made of, for when Trapnell was in her twenties (the exact year of her birth being unknown) she traveled to the palace of Bridewell and sat in ecstatic vigil against the increasingly tyrannical theocracy of Lord Protector Oliver Cromwell.

In 1654 she spent twelve days in trance, speaking paradox and poetry, prophecy and prayer, predicting the collapse of the government which so many had initially welcomed after monarchical absolutism. Attended by non-conformists, dictating to an amanuensis, Trapnell repeated prayers like, "The Voice and Spirit have made a league/Against *Cromwel* and his men,/Never to leave its witness till/It hath broken all of them." Cromwell was less than enthused by the prophecy or the prophetess.

Having preached a gospel of resistance to tyrants and equality of the sexes, it was upon going into Cornwall that Trapnell was apprehended and put on trial for witchcraft. Against all our presumptions of her era, Trapnell beat the charge. She was simply too popular, too brilliant, and too powerful for the state to end her ministry.

Strange to consider the political power of prayer, especially leveraged against a State that also enshrined its efficacy. Some on the left assume that whenever anyone talks too much about prayer they've got an agenda, normally a reactionary one. After all, there are plenty of contemporary Cromwells legislating and dictating their religious beliefs. With men like that (and they're normally men) it's easy to forget the radical, awesome, subversive power of prayer, even while those whom we're resisting also claim prayer as their own. After being offered perennial "thoughts and prayers" in the never-ending season of American blood-letting it's easy to grow cynical, but what if we took prayer seriously? What if we embraced prayer in all its awful grace? What if we answered the Cromwells of America with the vast legion of Trapnells bursting with prophecy? Then we'd have a real revival. Then we'd have a revolution.

Central to any appraisal of our current situation is an inviolate truth: any system worth resisting is at its core religious, but any effective means of resistance must also be religious. "Religion" need not mean what we're normally told it means, a limited definition focusing on beliefs and rituals. All sorts of things are religions – capitalism is a religion. Fascism is a worse one. Democracy a better one. Religion has not only to do with sanctuaries and scripture, but has to do with *meaning,* and how we orient ourselves to things of ultimate significance. And the language which facilitates this is sometimes called prayer.

Empty "thoughts and prayers" are really anti-prayer, a negating speech act which mocks the actual function of divine language. Part of their nihilistic power is that they engender a cynicism. Those Cromwells, who see prayer as only their provenance, fear the divine resistance of genuine prayer. We must not forget the profound subversivness in speaking prophecy, in opposing tyrants while genuflecting before the infinite. Sitting Bull watching the Sioux Ghost Dance across the western prairies understood that. Dietrich Bonhoeffer martyred at Flossenbürg understood it too. And so, of course, did Anna Trapnell.

I proffer a defense of prayer not by recourse to the magical logic of those who pray for rain (though I suspect that those who mock such intercessions have never experienced drought). No illusions should be peddled that shouting to the Lord will convince Her to alter our lot, for ours is not the prayer of the fundamentalist trying to worm their words into the mouths of schoolchildren and court house monuments. Fundamentally, our prayers are not offered because of those that oppress, but despite them. Paradoxically, as a result, these prayers are even more incendiary in their charged power.

Every Spanish *Ave Maria* repeated by the detained immigrant child, even after their rosaries have been confiscated by an ICE agent; every *Salah* prostrated by the Syrian refugee; every funeral prayer for a black son murdered by the police or recited by a friend mourning a shot classmate; all the Serenity Prayers duly mouthed by junkies and drunks; every ecstatic hymn of praise uttered by a drag queen are an act of opposition against authoritarianism, they enact revolutionary love by their simple existence.

In *Prayer: A History,* Carol and Philip Zaleski identify categories of prayer like "petition, confession, adoration, sacrifice, intercession, contemplation, thanksgiving, [and] vows." Prayer's radical, glorious, enchanted, beauty is implicit in all of those functions, and there is a pragmatic and moral utility in its use by the progressive religious revival our nation is undergoing as embodied by movements like the Poor Peoples' Campaign, which the mainstream media has been slow to understand.

But prayer's radicalism goes deeper; its full measure is not in objective effects, nor whether it can convince a deity (or your fellow citizens). Prayer doesn't even have that much to do with God, or if you believe in God (I've always been dodgy on this issue myself). Prayer is rather the temporary establishment of your own little republic, your own garden, utopia, paradise. In prayer we see intimations of a better world. A glimpse of perfection not in a place, but for a period. A psychic balm for this world; for in that awful grace we remove ourselves from life's transitoriness. Prayer displaces us from this fallen world of Twitter screeds, newsfeeds, and push notifications. In such true privacy there is an anarchic freedom.

Seminarian Lauren Grubaugh prayed at a memorial following

the hideous events in Charlottesville, "Do not let our spirits be colonized by the depressing fear of our oppressors. Transform our minds that do not think of you existing without these heavy chains we have placed on ourselves and on each other." True prayer has always been about that one thing – the removing of chains.

CULTURE, SOCIETY & POLITICS

The modern world is at an impasse. Disasters scroll across our smartphone screens and we're invited to like, follow or upvote, but critical thinking is harder and harder to find. Rather than connecting us in common struggle and debate, the internet has sped up and deepened a long-standing process of alienation and atomization. Zer0 Books wants to work against this trend. With critical theory as our jumping off point, we aim to publish books that make our readers uncomfortable. We want to move beyond received opinions.

Zer0 Books is on the left and wants to reinvent the left. We are sick of the injustice, the suffering, and the stupidity that defines both our political and cultural world, and we aim to find a new foundation for a new struggle.

If this book has helped you to clarify an idea, solve a problem or extend your knowledge, you may want to check out our online content as well. Look for Zer0 Books: Advancing Conversations in the iTunes directory and for our Zer0 Books YouTube channel.

Popular videos include:

Žižek and the Double Blackmain

The Intellectual Dark Web is a Bad Sign

Can there be an Anti-SJW Left?

Answering Jordan Peterson on Marxism

Follow us on Facebook
at https://www.facebook.com/ZeroBooks and Twitter at https://twitter.com/Zer0Books

Bestsellers from Zer0 Books include:

Give Them An Argument
Logic for the Left
Ben Burgis
Many serious leftists have learned to distrust talk of logic. This is a serious mistake.
Paperback: 978-1-78904-210-8 ebook: 978-1-78904-211-5

Poor but Sexy
Culture Clashes in Europe East and West
Agata Pyzik
How the East stayed East and the West stayed West.
Paperback: 978-1-78099-394-2 ebook: 978-1-78099-395-9

An Anthropology of Nothing in Particular
Martin Demant Frederiksen
A journey into the social lives of meaninglessness.
Paperback: 978-1-78535-699-5 ebook: 978-1-78535-700-8

In the Dust of This Planet
Horror of Philosophy vol. 1
Eugene Thacker
In the first of a series of three books on the Horror of Philosophy,
In the Dust of This Planet offers the genre of horror as a way of
thinking about the unthinkable.
Paperback: 978-1-84694-676-9 ebook: 978-1-78099-010-1

The End of Oulipo?
An Attempt to Exhaust a Movement
Lauren Elkin, Veronica Esposito
Paperback: 978-1-78099-655-4 ebook: 978-1-78099-656-1

Capitalist Realism
Is There no Alternative?
Mark Fisher
An analysis of the ways in which capitalism has presented itself
as the only realistic political-economic system.
Paperback: 978-1-84694-317-1 ebook: 978-1-78099-734-6

Rebel Rebel
Chris O'Leary
David Bowie: every single song. Everything you want to know,
everything you didn't know.
Paperback: 978-1-78099-244-0 ebook: 978-1-78099-713-1

Kill All Normies
Angela Nagle
Online culture wars from 4chan and Tumblr to Trump.
Paperback: 978-1- 78535-543-1 ebook: 978-1-78535-544-8

Cartographies of the Absolute
Alberto Toscano, Jeff Kinkle
An aesthetics of the economy for the twenty-first century.
Paperback: 978-1-78099-275-4 ebook: 978-1-78279-973-3

Malign Velocities
Accelerationism and Capitalism
Benjamin Noys
Long listed for the Bread and Roses Prize 2015, *Malign Velocities*
argues against the need for speed, tracking acceleration
as the symptom of the ongoing crises of capitalism.
Paperback: 978-1-78279-300-7 ebook: 978-1-78279-299-4

Meat Market
Female Flesh under Capitalism
Laurie Penny
A feminist dissection of women's bodies as the fleshy fulcrum of
capitalist cannibalism, whereby women are both consumers and
consumed.
Paperback: 978-1-84694-521-2 ebook: 978-1-84694-782-7

Babbling Corpse
Vaporwave and the Commodification of Ghosts
Grafton Tanner
Paperback: 978-1-78279-759-3 ebook: 978-1-78279-760-9

New Work New Culture
Work we want and a culture that strengthens us
Frithjoff Bergmann
A serious alternative for mankind and the planet.
Paperback: 978-1-78904-064-7 ebook: 978-1-78904-065-4

Romeo and Juliet in Palestine
Teaching Under Occupation
Tom Sperlinger
Life in the West Bank, the nature of pedagogy and the role of a
university under occupation.
Paperback: 978-1-78279-637-4 ebook: 978-1-78279-636-7

Ghosts of My Life
Writings on Depression, Hauntology and Lost Futures
Mark Fisher
Paperback: 978-1-78099-226-6 ebook: 978-1-78279-624-4

Sweetening the Pill
or How We Got Hooked on Hormonal Birth Control
Holly Grigg-Spall
Has contraception liberated or oppressed women?
Sweetening the Pill breaks the silence on the dark side of hormonal
contraception.
Paperback: 978-1-78099-607-3 ebook: 978-1-78099-608-0

Why Are We The Good Guys?
Reclaiming your Mind from the Delusions of Propaganda
David Cromwell
A provocative challenge to the standard ideology that Western
power is a benevolent force in the world.
Paperback: 978-1-78099-365-2 ebook: 978-1-78099-366-9

The Writing on the Wall
On the Decomposition of Capitalism and its Critics
Anselm Jappe, Alastair Hemmens
A new approach to the meaning of social emancipation.
Paperback: 978-1-78535-581-3 ebook: 978-1-78535-582-0

Enjoying It
Candy Crush and Capitalism
Alfie Bown
A study of enjoyment and of the enjoyment of studying. Bown
asks what enjoyment says about us and what we say about
enjoyment, and why.
Paperback: 978-1-78535-155-6 ebook: 978-1-78535-156-3

Color, Facture, Art and Design
Iona Singh
This materialist definition of fine-art develops guidelines for
architecture, design, cultural-studies and ultimately social
change.
Paperback: 978-1-78099-629-5 ebook: 978-1-78099-630-1

Neglected or Misunderstood
The Radical Feminism of Shulamith Firestone
Victoria Margree
An interrogation of issues surrounding gender, biology,
sexuality, work and technology, and the ways in which our
imaginations continue to be in thrall to ideologies of maternity
and the nuclear family.
Paperback: 978-1-78535-539-4 ebook: 978-1-78535-540-0

How to Dismantle the NHS in 10 Easy Steps (Second Edition)
Youssef El-Gingihy
The story of how your NHS was sold off and why you will have
to buy private health insurance soon. A new expanded second
edition with chapters on junior doctors' strikes and government
blueprints for US-style healthcare.
Paperback: 978-1-78904-178-1 ebook: 978-1-78904-179-8

Digesting Recipes
The Art of Culinary Notation
Susannah Worth
A recipe is an instruction, the imperative tone of the expert, but
this constraint can offer its own kind of potential. A recipe need
not be a domestic trap but might instead offer escape – something
to fantasise about or aspire to.
Paperback: 978-1-78279-860-6 ebook: 978-1-78279-859-0

Most titles are published in paperback and as an ebook.
Paperbacks are available in traditional bookshops. Both print and
ebook formats are available online.
Follow us on Facebook
at https://www.facebook.com/ZeroBooks
and Twitter at https://twitter.com/Zer0Books